BE MY GUEST

CONRAD N. HILTON

PRENTICE HALL PRESS
New York   London   Toronto   Sydney   Tokyo

Published in 1987 by Prentice Hall Press
A Division of Simon & Schuster, Inc.
15 Columbus Circle
New York, NY 10023

Originally published by Prentice-Hall, Inc.

PRENTICE HALL PRESS is a trademark of Simon & Schuster, Inc.

ISBN 0-13-071598-0

Manufactured in the United States of America

15   14   13

ACKNOWLEDGMENTS

Within the covers of this book I have tried to show the gratitude I feel for many individuals—among them a bellboy in Dallas who once loaned me eating money—a Chicago entrepreneur who made possible two of the biggest deals of my business career—a blacksmith-dentist in San Antonio, New Mexico—a pioneer woman named Mary Laufersweiler—each of whom has contributed to the pattern of my life.

I would like, too, to make certain acknowledgments in connection with writing this book. No job in my life has ever been accomplished without help and this one has been no exception. First, I am indebted to John Joseph, an associate who believed most persuasively that it would be worth while for me to set down my personal recollections and philosophy even in view of two excellent existing biographies. Together with the publisher, John worked out such a neat trap of reasons and arguments in favor of this autobiography that when it was sprung on me in a surprise attack I was not nimble enough to find an excuse. Nevertheless, today I am glad. It has been a remarkable experience for me to sort out my past, to re-live the high points, the valleys, the laughs, the sorrows that have woven themselves into many years of eventful living. It has been worth while for me personally to evaluate where I stand now, how I got there, how many loyalties and graces have been granted me, and where I hope to go from here.

In digging into the past my administrative assistant, Olive Wakeman, and my executive secretary, Ruth Hinman, have assisted me in going through box after box of material, old letters, papers, pictures, and have shown an enthusiasm for the project beyond the call of duty and loyalty. Arthur Foristall, a valued counsellor, has been my patient sounding-board, giving me the full benefit of a Harvard education which enabled him to hold my split infinitives to a minimum, and of his invaluable ability to say "no" in matters where he felt that certain of my reminiscences would not interest the general reader.

ACKNOWLEDGMENTS

I am grateful to my old friend, William Keleher, of Albuquerque, New Mexico, to my brother Carl and my sisters Felice, Eva, Rosemary and Helen for their interest and help in refreshing my memory, and to Elaine St. Johns for her assistance in organizing and presenting the material.

And to Rosalie Montgomery who typed, and typed, and typed!

My greatest debt, however, is to each individual who has ever been my guest in any hotel—whether in Cisco, Texas, New York or Istanbul—and to all those who will be my guests in the future. Without each and every one of them there would be no story to write.

Conrad N. Hilton

Casa Encantada
Bel Air, Los Angeles, California.

CONTENTS

CONTENTS

Dedication:
to the memory of
MY MOTHER and FATHER

1. YOU'VE GOT TO DREAM

I was not born in Texas.

This unalterable fact caused a brief moment of embarrassment for Beauford H. Jester, one-time Governor of the Lone Star State. Governor Jester had kindly offered to make me a "Texan of Distinction." I had accepted the honor. The press was alerted; the guests bidden to the traditional banquet.

At the eleventh hour a specter rose over the feast. There were many men to swear personally that I had bought my first hotel in Cisco, Texas—built my first hotel in Dallas, Texas. But would anyone swear that I was actually born in that state? This condition, unbeknownst to me, was the prime requisite for the pending honor. Texans, it would seem, whether distinct or otherwise, are born and not made.

I got a frantic phone call from the Governor at my California home. "Connie," he said, "you were born in San Antonio, weren't you?"

"I was," I replied proudly. "San Antonio, Socorro County, Territory of New Mexico."

There was a silence. Then Governor Jester bounced back. "You will," he said, "become the only *honorary* Texan of Distinction in the world." At the banquet he added that, in Texas, they "recognized only one San Antonio." I replied mildly, as became an honorary Texan of Distinction, that where I was born we knew there were two. But the last time I revisited my native state a few months ago I couldn't help wondering whether the Governor was more a prophet than a wit that night.

For it appeared that perhaps there was only one San Antonio after all.

I had not planned to check into it. One does not assume that the town where one was born will vanish from the face of the earth. I had gone to New Mexico because the city of Albuquerque, with full knowledge of my background, including my birthplace, had honored me by declaring a Conrad Hilton Day.

Nor did I expect to find everything unchanged. From the

moment my plane landed I was congratulating both Albuquerque and myself that we had changed a good deal—for
the better, of course.

Albuquerque had been my first "big town." I arrived there
initially on a train of rattling old-fashioned cars to attend a
small military school. I was met at the station by an older
boy all too obviously pained at having to ride herd on such
an insignificant young student as myself.

This last time I arrived in a giant silver plane, sweeping
down on Kirkland Field with that feeling of power, of man
reducing space, shrinking time, that never fails to move me.
I remembered seeing Kirkland Field first as mesa land, feeding ground for jackrabbits, gophers, prairie dogs. Now it
was the scene of vast installations pertaining to Atomic
Energy—that herald of a new age for mankind, or the restraining threat of the Last Trumpet if we slip into war.

When my reluctant fellow student shepherded me through
Albuquerque for my first schoolboy view, we trudged over
rutted dirt roads through a sprawling mud-brown collection
of dwellings, an adolescent railroad town housing some six
thousand hardy pioneers, railroad men, adventurers, shady
ladies, and gunmen.

On this last trip I was met by a police escort, whizzed
through a hustling modern city of one hundred eighty thousand, and deposited at the door of the Hilton Hotel.

I explained all about these changes and my great pleasure
in them to my sister Felice, to Will Keleher, perhaps my
oldest friend, and to Monsignor Peter Joseph Pelzer, who
had been a missionary priest in Socorro County when I was
a boy.

"It's a great thing," I said. "Progress!"

And each of them asked if I planned to go down and see
San Antonio.

It was my oldest sister Felice who suggested that the trip
might do me good—Felice, who has always taken pains to
help me keep my sense of values. I remember when we
opened the luxurious Beverly Hilton in Beverly Hills in 1955
with a spectacular burst of silver trumpets, a gala show
studded with screen stars, in short a maximum of fanfare
and elegance, I begged Felice to come to California and attend the celebration with me.

"My dear Connie," she replied by post card. "It was nice

of you to ask me to your party, but you have probably over-looked the fact that it is time to can peaches."

Now, with Conrad Hilton Day about to become a fact, with me in a mood of high satisfaction, my sails billowing, Felice was right there to apply her deft hand and spill some of the wind.

"I never dreamed then," I told her, referring to the prog-ress made by Albuquerque and me since we first saw each other, "that one day the Albuquerque Hilton would stand right in the middle of it all, tall enough to cast a shadow on the railroad station and even outshine the old Alvarado, pride of the Fred Harvey system."

"Let's see," said Felice thoughtfully. "You were eleven-going-on-twelve when you first came to town. No, you weren't dreaming of hotels. You were dreading boarding school, wishing you were home, and hoping maybe some day you'd grow up to your feet."

For an instant I tasted the slight bitterness that comes with a touchy memory. A skinny, shy kid being hauled through town by a superior stranger, overwhelmingly aware that his feet, like those of a St. Bernard puppy, had reached full growth well ahead of his body, and very often entangled in them.

Felice dragged me back to the present. "Well, you may have put your mark on Albuquerque. The town of Socorro still has family fingerprints all over it. But there's no monu-ment to you in San Antonio. In fact you should go down and see your birthplace."

Will Keleher wasn't worried about any monuments to me when he suggested I go down. He was thinking about my father. "Your father built that town almost single-handed, Connie," he said. "And when he died the town started to die, too. There just isn't any business to support it any more."

The fact that the railroad had ceased to stop in San An-tonio was almost a personal blow to Monsignor Pelzer. I understood his feeling well, for when he was the missionary priest at San Marcial he had covered his parish on foot or horseback until the railroad men of the Atchison, Topeka, & Santa Fe took pity on him and he was able to reach such churches as touched the Santa Fe line, including ours, riding in the caboose. "I cannot imagine the trains not stopping at San Antonio," he said, shaking his head sadly.

No more could I. But on my day of days it was confirmed by an old schoolmate. Jose Antonio Gonzalez had made the long trip up the Rio Grande in his ancient Ford to shake my hand and when I asked, "How are things in San Antonio?" his lined brown face wrinkled as though he would weep and he replied softly in his native Spanish, *"Muy triste,"* (very sad). And he, in his turn, advised me to see for myself.

The following morning I did. It was a trip in space of course, but, for me, it was a trip in time as well.

Thirteen miles down the highway from Albuquerque I stopped at the Isleta Indian pueblo, rising moundlike on a plain of gray sand. This had been one of my mother's favorite outing places and inside the old church still hung a painting that had fascinated me when we first saw it together. It was a holy picture pierced by an arrow when these Pueblo Indians sought safety there during an attack by marauders.

These Indians, Mother had explained, even before they fully understood the way of the one God whose religion they had adopted, had sensed the strength and refuge within those walls and had sought and been granted protection there.

This comforting thought had stayed in my consciousness, and later when I, too, did not fully understand His way, I knew I could still seek His protection.

Outside the church the pueblo slept in the sun with a kind of timeless dignity. It was just, I thought, for while the nomads, the Apaches and Navajos, roved and plundered and were eventually subdued and lashed to reservations, the Pueblo Indians had walked serenely in the individual cultures, the disciplined community living and self-government which had been theirs long before the first Spaniard set foot in their land hunting gold.

Old-timers viewed them with affection because they had, for the most part, been quiet and peace-loving, ready to share their expert knowledge of farming and irrigation and to live in amity with their conquerors.

Slowly, now, they were dying out. But I felt great respect that, although they might disappear, they would faithfully follow their own way of life until there were no more of them to carry on the traditions.

But there, too, I found changes.

My sentimental reverie was penetrated by the sight of two

jaunty television antennas perched rakishly on the rounded dome of a tiny dwelling. I moved hastily on, pursued by the quite unsentimental thought that the well-behaved little Indian lad who had demanded and received "just one nickel" from me at the church door was probably spending his evenings absorbed in some far-off Hollywood producer's garbled interpretation of his heritage.

Below Isleta, when I had crossed to the west bank of the Rio Grande, I followed the green-gold thread of cottonwood trees that traces the river's course southward toward El Paso and Old Mexico. The golden green along the banks shaded off into olive and silver as the cottonwoods shrank to juniper, rabbit brush, and wild pumpkin on a carpet of tawny sand. Occasionally there were flat-topped adobe farmhouses, bravely wearing their strings of drying red chili peppers, surrounded by neat fields.

Then suddenly, as I left the life-giving river, there was nothing. No sign of habitation or life. Now I was on the high desert, an ever-changing land where drought and overgrazing have left nothing but shifting sand dunes, where vicious sand storms move mountains in a day. I could remember when, before the land was exhausted, the rains would transform it into pasture. Today there seemed to be mile upon mile of waste.

Once again, from the high desert, the highway swept down on that finger of green tracing the Rio Grande and there, seventy-five miles south of Albuquerque, was the town of Socorro, next-door neighbor to San Antonio.

Years seemed to roll away and I was home . . . home where I had spent the first twenty-five years of my life. In this land five thousand feet above the sea, a land of winds and storms, of dazzling sunshine, blue mountains, startling cloud formations forever drawing shadow pictures across the sand, I could feel the romance, poetry, and stark reality which I knew as a very young man. For the moment the poetry had the upper hand.

There was a vastness here, more air, more sun, more space, and I thought that here a man drew some of that vastness into his soul. He could dream big dreams, think big thoughts because there was nothing to hem him in.

Reality attacked through my stomach.

I suddenly realized that a man could also develop a vast appetite in this country. Fancy dishes were all very well in the civilized confines of New York or Hollywood. What I wanted now was beefsteak, one that had been carved with no thought but that of plain hunger, a beefsteak such as I had known at the hotel in Socorro when I was a student at the New Mexico School of Mines.

The young hotel manager greeted me hopefully but when I said, "I hope I'm not too late for lunch," he shrugged.

"I'm afraid you are, sir," he said. "About ten years too late." Trade had fallen off so much it had been that long since they served luncheon.

Socorro was like that. Everywhere I looked I was ten, or maybe forty, years too late to fit back into the living picture.

As Felice had said, there were Hilton fingerprints all over town. On the old Plaza was the Hilton Drugstore, established by Mrs. Emily K. Hilton, a distant relative still living there. Beside San Miguel, the twin-towered white church which has stood for over a century, where the Sisters of Loretto had built their humble adobe convent a hundred years ago, there was now a modern, glistening school and convent, the Hilton Mount Carmel School. The school was a memorial to my mother, buried beside my father in the old cemetery on the hill behind the town.

The School of Mines, which had been a simple affair of three brick buildings when I attended, had spread over a huge campus and was now, as the New Mexico Institute of Technology, the main support of the town.

The mines themselves were abandoned.

On a shaded street the two-story house which Father had built for Mother after the last of her children was born, had somehow shrunken from the palace I thought it then to an ordinary gray house of cement blocks with a wooden verandah. Strangers lived there. I did not stop.

I took flowers to the old cemetery and stood looking over the twin headstones where my father and mother lay side by side, up to the deep blue of the Magdalena Mountains. Somewhere, just around the bend of the biggest mountain, there was a wind-sculptured figure that appeared to be a kneeling nun, from which the mountains got their name. Once I had ridden there on my sorrel mare, Chiquita, when my dreams could travel no farther than my eyes.

Looking back over the town, I knew that, although the fingerprints were there, the living hands that made them had moved on.

Eleven miles farther down the river I found what was left of San Antonio. Felice had said I should see it, but there was little to see.

The town, as I had known it, seemed to have been reclaimed by the tawny hills, swallowed up in space.

True, there was still a huddle of mud houses hugging the river's edge, surrounded by untidy fences, fronting on dirt roads where the chickens, the dogs, and the children scavenged happily in the sun. But of the tidy little empire my father had built—the store, the warehouses, the corral and barns—fire and time and souvenir hunters had devoured all but some foundations and one crumbling wall.

The railroad station, once the main artery that fed life into San Antonio, had been sold.

Trains no longer stopped twice daily.

The coal mines at Carthage had been closed for years.

The Governor of Texas had been right. It was hard to recognize more than one San Antonio.

And my old schoolmate was right. It was *"muy triste,"* very sad.

There remained, however, two links with my old life. The tiny schoolhouse that still stood on the hill was not one of them. It was not the schoolhouse I attended and I do not recall that one or any other having a strong effect on my life.

My so-called formal education was pretty informal from the beginning. Between the one-room adobe building which served as our grammar school, the now famous New Mexico Military Institute at Roswell, New Mexico, and the School of Mines at Socorro, I entered briefly a number of other institutions offering to teach me something. I do not remember graduating very often nor, with such exceptions as a freak gift for higher mathematics and an early and enduring love for the Spanish tongue, learning very much.

It was the other two buildings still standing, far apart along the dusty road, that reminded me of how much I had been given here when this ghost town still lived and breathed.

One was the church, San Antonio Du Padua, kept in white-washed repair by the faithful while the town disintegrated.

The other was a small, empty, box-like building that had once housed a bank—*my* bank.

They represented the two lessons I did learn in San Antonio. One from my mother. One from my father.

My mother, Mary Laufersweiler Hilton, was the loveliest lady I have ever known and the most gallant. As a young bride, with her hazel eyes wide open, she made the journey from the then highly civilized town of Fort Dodge, Iowa, where her German-born father was a successful merchant, to what her friends called "that Godforsaken Territory outside the States." She did not know much about Apache Indians, although she was aware they had once almost murdered her bridegroom. She knew less of the Spanish language, almost universally spoken in the Territory of New Mexico in the 1880s. And absolutely nothing of frontier hardships.

One thing she did know. No spot on earth could be "Godforsaken."

Mary Hilton was a woman of deep and abiding faith and this faith she passed on to the eight children she was to bear. Most of us were born in a primitive adobe dwelling which also housed my father's general store, set down in the midst of vastness, high deserts, stark mountains, in the town of San Antonio about midway between Albuquerque and El Paso on a muddy trickle of water known ironically as the Great River—the Rio Grande.

By the time I remember her clearly my mother still had a very straight nose, a lovely mouth, but her black hair was almost gray though she was still a very young woman. Those early recollections encase her slight figure in a huge cotton apron and she always seemed to be carrying a baby on one hip. I think my father had money then, but there were few luxuries to be bought in the Territory and Mary Hilton's hours remained long and hard. Although plenty of Mexican help was available, there were certain things they would not or could not do. Gregorio, a handyman who was with us off and on until he died, would wash the dishes and do the cleaning. But he would not wait on table and, so far as we were concerned, he could not cook. He, on the other hand, did not care for our food. He lived in a room off the barn and there slept and cooked his own frijoles. But even with Gregorio and other untrained help there was a great deal for Mary Hilton to do, cooking, baking, washing, bearing children and tending them, yet never did Mother lose her courteous soft-spoken ways nor depart from a quiet reserve except when she bubbled over with laughter at her growing brood.

Nor did she depart one iota from her faith. To this there were no exceptions.

My mother had one answer, one cure, for everything. Prayer!

For her it was a normal part of life, every day, precisely as necessary and life-giving as food or air. She not only believed in it on Sunday, when we would ride miles to the nearest church where Father Pelzer was to celebrate Mass, but morning and evening she gathered her children around her for family worship.

In an emergency, when we were troubled or dismayed, it was her ever-present remedy and help. I was nine when my cherished sorrel mare, Chiquita, died from old age and faithful service to my adventurous spirit. I could ride almost as soon as I could walk and Chiquita had been a lifelong companion.

Mother and I stood on the dusty road outside the store looking over at the corral where Chiquita lay while I demanded an explanation. I wanted Chiquita back. Mother did her best with words, but when words ran out and tears were close she turned me firmly in the direction of our small white missionary church.

"Go and pray, Connie," she said. "Take all your problems to Him. He has answers when we don't."

Because I trusted her I went, praying at first with a kind of convulsive hurt and fury. Then, as the peace of the old church settled on me, as I was reassured by a sense of His timelessness and goodness, I made a gentler prayer. When I came out half an hour later, I was quite satisfied about my mare and, with the heartlessness of boyhood, planning to replace her with a pinto pony the next time a friendly Apache band pitched camp in our corral as they did from time to time on a peaceful journey to hunt deer in the Gila River country.

Later, when my father's financial sun was eclipsed by the panic of 1907 and with it my hopes for a formal education at Dartmouth, that elegant eastern college where they would magically turn me into a fine gentleman, Mother's advice was the same. "He knows what's best for you, son. Go and pray."

Then I was a grown man and the Great Depression of the '30s tossed my own life's work from a tidy little mound of success into a bottomless pit of debts, humiliations, and mortgages. Men were jumping from hotel windows, *my* hotel windows, but Mother was perfectly calm. "Some men jump out of windows," she said. "Some go to church. Pray, Connie. It's the best investment you'll ever make."

My father had other ideas about investments. I don't know how he stood on the matter of prayer for he never discussed it with me. I suspect he himself prayed occasionally, especially when he had the blues. But his churchgoing was mostly social, weddings and the like, for Sunday was a busy day for my father.

He was always busy.

His own family had given him the name of Augustus Holver Hilton before they left Norway but he was known throughout the Territory and beyond as the Colonel or *El Coronel*. My mother called him Gus. Gus was just as sure he held the magic key to success and happiness as Mother. Precisely as necessary to him as food and air, an ever-present refuge in trouble, was Work. I feel sure my father spelled it with a capital "W."

Gus Hilton was a big man physically—a robust six-footer with big hands, big feet, handlebar mustaches, and a big voice. He pioneered in a community in which he was obliged to be resourceful, a village with a Spanish-American background, which had been isolated and remote from modern civilization for many years and which had been given new life in a new era—that of railroad transportation—with the coming of the Santa Fe Railroad.

He had vision which few men of his day possessed, and he made good in a time and place in New Mexico when most other man would have failed. Above all he was a Viking of a man with energy to burn.

In those days the whole town turned out their coal oil lamps early and rose with the chickens, the cows, and the dogs. Father was always up just a little earlier. In his book, six-thirty or seven o'clock was the middle of the day.

He *was* a worker.

A. H. Hilton was one of those fortunate men born to his time, having found his rightful place, whose work and play were one and the same thing. He was in his glory haggling in the store, or riding into the mountains to acquire wool and furs and at the same time disposing of his own wares among the miners, ranchers, and trappers, or having an occasional drink at the long bar in San Antonio with the hardy drummers who traveled the far west for the manufacturers of civilization. This lot had little in common with the Fuller brush man of today. The time was just over their shoulder when an agent for the Singer Sewing Machine Company in New Mexico had to undertake collection or repossession of machines sold on the installment plan, at the point of a gun.

When doing business, any sort of legitimate business, with lusty men, Gus Hilton was in his element. He loved work.

Father would have been as shocked at the thought of a four-day week as his wife would have been if they threatened to close all the churches on Sunday. The juvenile delinquents of the world, the Teddy boys and zoot suiters, would have posed no problem for Mary and Gus Hilton.

"Teach them to pray," Mother would have insisted.

"Give 'em something to *do*," Gus would have boomed.

He gave his own family plenty to *do*, and that starting as soon as they could walk. As time went by Father and I didn't see eye to eye on every issue, but here we remained in complete accord. There was no slave driving about it, no enforced child labor. He was all for our swimming in the irrigation ditch or adventuring down the river, *if* we had done a day's work.

Possibly because of our mutliple shared tasks we were a very close family. Each newcomer was greeted enthusiastically as an added hand. Father also believed in incentive and the Bible law that a workman is worthy of his hire. But he never overpaid us. We earned every penny we got. When I had been working in the store for two summers at $5.00 per month he gave me what we would now call a merit raise. At thirteen I jumped to $30.00 for the summer vacation and rarely since have I been so downright pleased.

With Gus, as with Mary, he was offering us the best he knew and it never occurred to him that we would resent it or fail to appreciate his efforts. And we never did.

Business praise from my father was hard won and much cherished by his children. And the reverse cast us into the depths. Only once do I ever remember his openly despairing of me. I had been up late meeting the night train on store business and overslept. Mother, I suppose, hadn't the heart to awaken me. At seven o'clock I opened one eye and both ears just in time to hear my father say forcefully, "Mary, I do *not* know what will become of Connie. I'm afraid he'll never amount to anything. He'll sleep his *life* away."

This was a pronouncement of doom. It made an indelible picture on my mind of a kind of living death. If Mary's son had the hope of heaven hereafter through prayer, no boy raised by Gus could expect a decent life here and now unless he got out of bed early. I got up at once. I have seldom overslept since.

Of course, by Work my father did not mean putting your nose to a single grindstone and letting that grindstone wear your life away. He never connected it with the sweat of the brow nor the punishment of the sons of Adam. He was all for the joy of the thing, for imagination and versatility.

Before I was eighteen I had been a clerk, a roving trader, a minor speculator, and had my first experience in the hotel business at approximately the bellboy level. I had owned my own produce business and as my own sole employee had hoed the corn, watered the vegetables, and then toured the town selling my harvest from door to door, or on order to my mother. I got ten cents for twelve ears of corn, I recall, and thought I was doing very well.

I had also been a student and several times was hired as pianist at local weddings. Mother played the piano like an artist, and a piano was the first luxury she managed to import from Fort Dodge. Whereupon Father, who loved music, insisted that each child learn to play something—and I selected the piano and later the cornet. My piano playing for hire came to an abrupt end when I was told to choose my own selections for a wedding and, quite innocently, led off with "I Picked a Lemon in the Garden of Love."

By the time I was twenty-five I had added to this variety of activities politics, banking, partner in a mercantile business, a flier at grubstaking, and a quite disastrous adventure into managing a musical trio, a scheme evolved by my father to bring culture to the southwest.

To this day I enjoy variety in my work. Recently I made my debut as a television actor playing the only part for which I am qualified, Conrad Hilton, in "Eloise." My "rate," established I suppose by A.F.T.R.A., for I am sure I had nothing to do with it, was $241.50, and for this I appeared at three rehearsals and spent the whole of Thanksgiving Day, from ten A.M. to eight P.M., at the Columbia Broadcasting Studios. I also signed a loyalty oath, a withholding card, a social security slip and enough papers to close a deal on a major hotel.

These two things I learned from Mary and Gus Hilton—the necessity of prayer and work—seemed so valuable to me that I tried valiantly to pass them on to my own sons as the "open sesame of life."

Theoretically, at least, they always agreed. But as they got older they began to insist that something was missing from my formula. "There just has to be something more, Dad," Nick, the oldest, insisted.

"Sure," I said. "There's enthusiasm, and finding your talent, and a lot of other things that go to make up successful living. But these two are the basic ones. Without *them* you can't even start."

"Look," my second son, Barron, chimed in, "I know plenty of fellows who work hard and pray faithfully. And nothing happens. There must be some other ingredient that goes in but I can't put my finger on it."

Nor, at that moment, could I. Was there anything I had to add, after almost three score and ten years of living, to the basic wisdom handed me by my mother and father?

I got an idea when I made a flying trip to New York. Sitting in the Grand Ballroom of the Waldorf-Astoria I thought maybe I had the answer. Looking at what remained of San Antonio, New Mexico, months later, my theory seemed to be confirmed. This was the missing piece.

You had to dream!

I'll admit this is the last suggestion most people would expect to be thrown into the pot by a businessman. I'll also admit no one ever called me a dreamer and that you can't succeed without the other two parts, but it's where you start. At least, I realized, it's where I started.

When I sat in the Waldorf on Park Avenue a few days after my talk with my boys, unofficial host at a dinner dance which was part of that great hotel's twenty-fifth birthday celebration, I was more deeply impressed than anyone there. I suddenly realized that I was seeing a dream, a wild, all but impossible dream, fulfilled—and that can't help but fill a man with awe.

Here I was, Connie Hilton, from San Antonio, Territory of New Mexico, at the Waldorf's Silver Anniversary, president of the company which operated this most costly, most luxurious, most famous, of all hotels. Sometime during the evening I would hand to the United Nations Children's Fund a check for $65,000 made possible by our providing food, drink, and entertainment at an absolute minimum. It was a sparkling event in the social season and the eight hundred guests, according to the society columns, were "prominent in diplomacy, government, business, the armed forces, society, and the arts."

Why, when I saw my first photograph of the recently built "new" Waldorf in 1931, read of such luxuries as a private railroad siding in the basement, a private hospital for guests, a golden rivet in her innards where her construction had started, six kitchens, two hundred cooks, five hundred waiters, one hundred dishwashers, not to mention two thousand rooms, I was beating my way around Texas half hidden under a ten-gallon hat, existing on a voluntary loan from a bellboy. My laundry was in hock and a gun-toting constable was trying to find places to hang up the court judgments against me.

It was a presumptuous, an outrageous, time to dream. Still I cut out that picture of the Waldorf and wrote across it "The Greatest of Them All." As soon as I had won back a desk of my own I slipped the dog-eared clipping under the glass top. From then on it was always in front of me.

Fifteen years later, in October, 1949, "The Greatest of Them All" became a Hilton Hotel.

It had taken a lot of work, four years of delicate negotiation and even before that, careful planning.

It had taken a lot of prayer. During the final crucial days I had attended church at six-thirty each morning. No matter how late we worked into the night, I started the day on my knees.

The week-end of the Waldorf's Silver Anniversary I went again to kneel in St. Patrick's Cathedral. I was giving thanks, not for the Waldorf, but for the All-American right to dream with the actual possibility of seeing that dream come true.

Right there I think I saw the reason why so many successful men keep an almost boyish love of America and democracy. It isn't because she doesn't ask sacrifices. We all know better than that. It isn't because she offers an easy route. I guess nobody ever had it harder than Abraham Lincoln. It isn't because we are always getting "Pie in the Sky," or are automatically entitled to two chickens in every pot. I myself had looked up from the bottom of the heap with thirty-eight cents in my pocket and seen only a mountain of debt.

But even then I had the complete confidence that our way of life offered me the freedom to crawl back up and eventually push out my horizons as far as my vision and strength would carry me.

Going even further back, what could have seemed more impossible than that the gangling youngster who rode Chiquita, swam in an irrigation ditch, worked fourteen hours a day in a general store in an isolated, sunbaked town, doing business with Spaniards, Mexicans, Indians, rough trappers and miners, would one day whirl around a dance floor in white tie and tails with some of the loveliest and most distinguished ladies of the world? Or be host two days later to thirty-five hundred guests at a reception in the Waldorf's Grand Ballroom? Or, on the Official Birthday, greet 350 of New York's most prominent men at luncheon and follow that with a dinner in the Sert Room where we wined and dined one hundred or more employees who had been with the "new" Waldorf since it opened its doors, long before I ever ventured out of the southwest except in dreams.

Yet, there I was, amongst the gourmets, being served Fumet of Gumbo Chervil with Lucullus Crusts, loving every minute of it, and as nimble among the vast array of knives, forks, and spoons as a Chinaman born to his chopsticks. I could not help chuckling inside, remembering how my mother always refused to be impressed by the trimmings. Under her breath she would have been saying, "It's only fancy fish soup, Connie. And don't you forget it."

I don't. I wouldn't want to. It would spoil my private fun if I were to forget the original dreamer and get lost in the dream.

The type of dreaming that appeals to me has nothing to do with a reverie, an idle daydream. It isn't wishful thinking. Nor is it the type of revelation reserved for the great ones and rightly called vision. What I speak of is a brand of imaginative thinking backed by enthusiasm, vitality, expectation, to which all men may aspire.

To accomplish big things I am convinced you must first dream big dreams. True, it must be in line with progress, human and divine, or you are wasting your prayer. It has to be backed by work and faith, or it has no hands and feet. Maybe there's even an element of luck mixed in. But I am sure now that, without this master plan, you have nothing.

My own dreams were smaller than some—bigger than others. Some had flaws in them and fell apart before they could take form. Others were misguided; the energy behind them had to be redirected according to a sounder plan, and all that is part of this story.

Six months after the Waldorf anniversary, however, when I looked at what remained of San Antonio, my father's town, at what had once been my bank, I knew for sure that the beginning was always the same.

It always started with a dream.

It was hard to believe that this small, this very small, square building with the barred windows, the dusty interior, so recently vacated when the United States Post Office moved out, had once been my greatest pride, the New Mexico State Bank of San Antonio.

Yet this had been my first "big" dream and I worked harder making it a reality, suffered more heartbreak, struggled against bigger odds over this infinitesimal building in the middle of nowhere than at any other time in my career, barring the Depression. And that, of course, is another story.

Standing there in the hot sun, I wondered who had had the biggest—and bravest—dream. Connie, daring to dream a bank into existence in this, desolation and parlaying that dream into a chain of hotels, or Gus, who had had the audacity to envision building a life raising a family, making his fortune, in this isolated spot?

For Gus, too, started with a dream.

San Antonio could not have looked much more inviting on the day in 1882 when my father first saw it than it did on this day in 1957.

To Gus Hilton, San Antonio was the end of a search, and the trail which led him there was devious.

When he was ten his family, emigrating from Norway, settled in Iowa. It looked to them like a land of unlimited opportunities. By the time he was twenty-six, Gus was finding Fort Dodge all too limited. Real opportunity was beckoning farther west.

Gus was in love with Mary Laufersweiler even then.

As early as 1878, when Mary was seventeen and had been chosen May Queen by her senior class and had her coronation ceremonies at Sacred Heart Church, Gus was writing her stiff, formal, little letters. He was also calling her by her middle name. There is one in Mary's memory chest written on the typewriter with mysteriously typed purple ink.

Fort Dodge, Iowa,
March 29th, 1878

Miss Genevive:
All the young gentlemen belonging to the club dances last winter will attend a masquerade at the parlors of Mrs. Jas. Swain, on Friday eve next.

If you have no previous engagements and would like to attend, I would be glad to have the pleasure of your company at that time.

Answr at your convenience and oblige
A. H. Hilton
P. S. If you accept and wish to mask, I will come up Tuesday evening and we will talk over what we will wear.

A.H.H.

To which my mother replied in an elegant script on lined notepaper:

City, March 30, 78

Mr. A. H. Hilton:
Certainly it is with greatest pleasure that I accept your kind invitation, and many thanks for it,
Yours etc.
Mary G. Laufersweiler

Gus was clerking then in Fort Dodge, and saving what he could. But he felt sure there was a bigger, better life out west for the hardy spirit who was willing to go out and find it.

Two years after the masquerade at the parlors of Mrs. Jas. Swain, Gus went.

First to Leadville, Colorado, where reports filtering back held out the lure of a carbonate ore strike and a gold-filled town that had mushroomed from it. This much was true, but the town was wild, carousing, and as unsubstantial as a

movie set. It was no place for Mary. Mary was a lady. It was
no place for Gus. He moved on. In the wake of the Santa Fe
Railroad, he broached the newest New Frontier, the Territory of New Mexico.

New Mexico had been technically open for business since
1846 when General Stephen Watts Kearny and his Missouri-
ans rode over Raton Mountain and bloodlessly wrestled the
Territory from old Mexico. But actually, until the Santa Fe
Railroad pushed over that same mountain in 1880, with Gus
right behind, the Territory had been isolated and almost
completely undeveloped. Without a railroad or a navigable
river, it depended for communications on freighter caravans,
emigrant trains, lumbering stagecoaches, or a rare, if spectacular, dash by fast horse and rider to the nearest center of
civilization, St. Louis, over one thousand miles away.

Thus the coming of the railroad truly opened this vast
country, and Gus rode into Santa Fe on "the cars." He found
the old capital all he could wish in beauty and solidity but it
had been well settled already and the existing merchants had
most of the opportunities sewed up. The wild beauty of
Santa Fe's appearance masked the soul of Fort Dodge. Gus
moved on.

He went south to Albuquerque, a growing railroad center, then rivaling Socorro as the busiest town in New Mexico. But, though it was growing apace, Albuquerque was
railroading clear through and too far from the coal and
copper mines. So Gus headed into the thick of the excitement, the town of Socorro.

Socorro was a town to stir a man's blood as well as his
imagination. At that time there was no branch line from the
railroad at Socorro to the Magdalena mines and the town
was the center for brisk freighting with horses and mules.
Westbound supplies went out of Socorro to the mines and returned with copper ore. Socorro had the smelter for the district.

The town supported one bank, six saloons, a generous
number of sporting houses, a storied Plaza and an opera
house. The bank got 18 per cent on the best securities, the
bars never closed, and the opera house offered culture "with
the original New York cast."

Yes, Socorro had possibilities, and Gus paused there to
ponder them, turning his hand to the first work that offered.
It happened to be a subcontract to quarry rock for the new

smelter being built three miles off in Blue Canyon. Had it been something different it might have changed the course of all our lives.

As it was, early one morning Gus and six other men were attacked in the canyon by a band of Apache Indians. Only Gus and one other man lived.

Gus liked excitement, but this was not his chosen variety. There was Mary to think of, and the value of his own scalp. He began to eye the less spectacular, quiet little town of San Antonio, farther down the Rio Grande.

San Antonio had less to offer. But there was a bridge across the river which connected it to the coal mines at Carthage, nine miles away. Across this bridge would come the traffic and trade from the entire southeastern country seeking access to the new railroad. It could be a trading center for trappers, miners, ranchers. Since the Piro Indians, irrigation had been used in the valley and the farms produced grain, vegetables, wine grapes. Farther back in the hills was grazing land for cattle, sheep, Merino goats. A man who would work could make something of it.

Gus bought what supplies he could afford, hardware, groceries, dry goods, a coffin or two, moved his few belongings with him, and went into business.

He had staked his claim in San Antonio.

Gus was, from the first, what was affectionately called a "trafficker and trader." These men were the backbone of the frontier and dealt in any legitimate business that came to hand.

Gus had courage and initiative, a willingness to embark on new enterprises. He sought out opportunities. Instead of waiting for business to come to his store he went out into the wilderness country, along the Gila and Mimbres rivers, in the wilds of the Black Range; bought or traded for beaver pelts and deerskins, all kinds of furs, from trappers in those areas, then turned them into money when he shipped them to St. Louis, an early day center for the fur trade. The trappers, long out of touch with civilization, were hungry for salt, flour, tobacco, conversation, anything Gus had to offer.

He also carted supplies to Carthage and brought back coal. He circled the far-flung ranches, sold his wares, and took in produce, wool, hides, beef.

When he wasn't pursuing trade, he was writing to Mary.

This long-distance courtship challenged his ingenuity. In reading the faded letters that went by the cars from San Antonio to Fort Dodge, a faint suspicion arises that, en route to America, the Hilton family hesitated long enough in Ireland for one son, at least, to kiss the Blarney Stone.

My mother must have been well known in her native city, for the envelopes were addressed simply—Miss Mary Laufersweiler, Fort Dodge, Iowa. And while the contents were strictly the products of Gus' heart, the hand employed was that of a graphic Cyrano, the local stationmaster, Mr. Buell, whose penmanship boasted the elaborate sweeps and curls and flowing elegance so much admired by ladies in those days. Mr. Buell also had the talent of being able to spell, an art which my father, although an educated man, never mastered.

Two years after Gus had last seen Mary he wrote her from San Antonio, scarcely mentioning the Apaches, but dwelling at some length on the naked beauty of the country. He specialized, however, in the little nonsenses we are led to believe girls like to hear. She keeps him awake at night, he insists. Through the stationmaster's artistic pen, he writes, "There is nothing more strange than the human heart. I laid awake all night from twelve until five and I'll try to tell you the wanderings of my heart."

To follow those wanderings too closely seems a little prying, even at this late date, but they certainly appealed to Mother, for she kept them all. But I can tell you now I wish I had seen those letters when my father was alive. I never regarded him as a romantic man.

A year later his heart and thoughts are still wandering to Mary while his feet plod weary miles to secure their future. The stationmaster is now scheduled by Gus for an even more active role in their courtship. Gus has hit upon the idea that Mary will be happier in this outpost of civilization if she can bring a girl friend with her, and to this purpose he has turned Cupid. Pointing out that the stationmaster, who must have blushed to pen the words, "is worthy of the best girl that ever breathed," he suggests Emma Rank, a friend of Mary's, as the lucky girl and directs Mary to "fix it up." He elaborates the theme that both young men are music lovers and both girls accomplished musicians, and that the stationmaster is already smitten. "I told him that Em has a $25,000 inheritance coming up and he is quite gone on her."

Father did not get so lost in matchmaking that he forgot the sugar frosting for his beloved. He reports showing the stationmaster a group picture in his album with both girls in it, "but he didn't stop to look at her but picked *you* out, at which I gently demurred."

Ironically enough, Gus was a success as Cupid, for Em did come west and marry the stationmaster—exactly thirty years after Mary burned her bridges in Fort Dodge.

Gus, the romantic, never let Gus the businessman get out of hand. If his poetic words were designed to appeal to Mary, he knew full well his financial security would weigh heavily with her father whose consent, in those days of chivalry, was necessary.

Two years after his meager beginnings in San Antonio, he had built an adobe store with two living rooms in the rear, and sent to Iowa for his sister's son, Holm Olaf Bursum, to join him. Olaf tended the store while Gus made even more vigorous and lengthy forages into the surrounding territory.

At last, in the early spring of 1884, and with Mother's glad conniving, he wrote that all-important letter to Conrad Laufersweiler. Then he waited—two interminable months. The answer came late in May.

C. LAUFERSWEILER,

**Manufacturer, Wholesale and Retail Dealer in all kinds of
FURNITURE, UPHOLSTERY GOODS, MIRRORS, PICTURE FRAMES,
MATTRESSES, WOOD AND METALLIC BURIAL CASES.**

Fort Dodge, Iowa, May 20th, 1884

Mr. A. H. Hilton
Dear Sir

Yours of 10th April rec'd. Should have answered before but have been very busy of late, and been trying to get some information as to the Country where you are living now, but have not yet been favorably impressed by anyone that has been there. We never had anything against you personally while living here but some scruples against your connections, I never care or ask for any ones wealth as long as he is good moral character which is the main feature for a suitor in my estimation also the Society and Surroundings is another matter of consideration where anyone should place his lot, and lastly would the matter of Religion have to be considered very seriously on our side as to avoid further mis-

understandings in which I had some experience myself.
I can therefore give no definite consent for the present.

Very respectfully yours,
C. Laufersweiler

In a word, Father Laufersweiler said "No." But he left the
door open.

Gus waited a reasonable length of time, then wrote again.
On the matter of religion he tried to give Mary's father full
assurance. Conrad Laufersweiler, as Gus knew, was a Roman
Catholic. His wife was not. Mary's father hinted at misun-
derstandings. My father promised there never would be.
And there never were.

His respect for my mother, as he wrote, took cognizance
of the fact that her faith was responsible to a large degree
for what she was. He liked what Mary was, then and ever
afterward. And he admired and respected her faith, both in
her and her children.

He sent off the letter and then plunged into the mountains
on a trading trip. He could not sit and wait for the answer.
He had to work. When he returned, the stationmaster was
holding a letter for him.

Mr. A. H. Hilton

Fort Dodge, Iowa, Sept. 15th, 1884
San Antonio, N. M.

Dear Sir

Yours of 1st inst received and in reply must say that
I am still under the same impression of your Country, notwithstanding the inviting description you give of it.
W had considerable talk with Mary on the subject and
find, the same as you say, that she is quite willing to go,
and finally told her if this was the case and she had her
mind fairly made up to that fact we had nothing more
to say, and she would have to stand the consequences let
come what it will, although we would much rather prefer if you would settle here or somewhere in the States,
or at least give us the promise if she should not like it
there in course of time that you would sell out and move
back here, I know quite well the disposition of her as
well as most others of her age, to go to travel or take a
big excursion trip the farther the better and if it was to
Europe is her delight, but to go and live in a half civ-

ilized Country amongst strangers may not be so delightful, but as long as she is willing we say all right.

> Respectfully yours,
> C. Laufersweiler

Mary and Gus set the date, Lincoln's Birthday, 1885. In February Gus set off by train to claim his bride. He had worked hard for her—and won. From Fort Dodge they went by train to New Orleans and, after a two-week honeymoon, Mary arrived in "that half civilized country amongst strangers," prepared to "stand the consequences, come what it will."

The first consequence of any note was Felice, who arrived about a year later. And then, on Christmas Day, 1887, I came along. I don't know exactly what Grandfather had in mind, but if this was what was to come, Mary Hilton seemed delighted.

At any rate, there I was, ready to begin my childhood.

2. GROWING PAINS

When I was two my sister Eva arrived and when I was four, my brother Carl. I do not remember either event specifically, but I do remember that by the time I was fully awake to my surroundings, there was quite a flock of little Hiltons to gather round Mother morning and evening and lisp their prayers.

With each new arrival two exciting things happened.

Mother took the baby to be baptized, which entailed a beautiful ceremony, a long dress which she kept secreted in a sweet-smelling box (the same dress, still fresh after half a century, which my son Barron and his wife have used for the christening of their six children), and a lot of howling from the newcomer.

And Father built a new room onto the house.

I had been christened Conrad (for Grandfather Laufersweiler) Nicholson (for the family doctor in Fort Dodge), but I was Connie from the start, except when somebody was angry.

The room Father built to celebrate my arrival was not large, but it had a glass window imported from St. Louis, a great luxury.

By the time I was eight and my brother Julian came along, there were five additions to our house and we were definitely living in elegance. When we knelt for prayer now there were warm wooden floors covered with carpets. That helped our concentration a good deal.

I was seven-going-on-eight (that Christmas birthday always put me in the "going-on" class) when I first trudged off to school with Felice as my custodian. Felice, who was already eight and going-on-nine, was very firm with me. Each morning she crept quietly into the store and returned with a large white handkerchief fresh from the box, which I invariably lost before sundown.

"Now," she'd say, "keep your nose *well* blowed, Connie."

She's been saying it one way or another ever since, bless her!

Since there were only about half a dozen "Anglo" families in town, the school was conducted in Spanish and English and there was keen competition to see whether Felice and I could completely master Spanish before the others mastered English.

I do not remember who won—but we children spoke Spanish as easily as English for many years.

I don't remember much about that school either, except that it had four grades and I somehow passed through all of them.

It is quite clear in my mind that when Carl was old enough to march to school under my wing, I more than once led him off to play hooky. With a young Spanish-American pal, Louis Miera, we would carefully circle the sand hill behind the school building, cut through an orchard and arrive, breathless and triumphant, at the irrigation ditch.

On one very hot day Father rode by within thirty feet of us, but he carefully looked the other way. It was Mother who believed in education. Father believed in work.

We never played hooky from work.

Not only had our house grown but the business had expanded. Our warehouses stretched up and down the road across from the railroad station with the store and attached house in the center. A. H. Hilton still took orders and delivered merchandise, traded for every known commodity across half the Territory. He also grubstaked prospectors. Old-timers like the one-eyed Italian, Jim Lovera, who was to play an important part in Gus Hilton's future fortunes, hung over the store counter to down three fingers of "Nelly's Death" with Father and spin ever-hopeful yarns of the treasures in "them thar hills." Besides this Gus wrote, for the sheer fun of it, articles about his travels, one of which, "Five Hundred Miles above the Clouds," appeared in the Albuquerque paper and described his journeys into the mountains. He read it in a loud, pleased voice at dinner one night and promptly started writing another about the Blue Canyon attack by the Apaches. He had also opened another stage line to White Oaks, a gold mining camp in Lincoln County, some fifty miles from San Antonio, which Billy the Kid at one time used as a rendezvous.

The stages meant corrals and stables and my work, even before I was in school, took me there often. Until we were half-grown, Mother and Father were Mamma and Pappa to us, and one morning Pappa simply arrived at the door of my little room about sun-up with a shiny new pitchfork in his hand. The fork was about twice my size and I inspected it gingerly.

"You can start in the corral," said Father with gusto. "Just follow your nose."

"*After* prayers," said a firm, gentle voice behind him.

And that was the way it was.

The Rio Grande, as a river, was of little or no use to the children of San Antonio. True, in the spring it could flood with majesty and vengeance, and we would teeter along the edge and frighten our mothers. But during its normal seasons there was not enough water for swimming and very few fish.

Still, there was an abundance of things to do and see and Gus, who played with as much energy as he worked, encouraged us to do them—after our jobs were finished. It was he who provided Chiquita and taught me to hurl myself on her bareback from a corral fence when I was certainly too small to mount in any normal way.

"Now, go out and taste the countryside," he'd advise, giving Chiquita an encouraging whack on the rump. And off we would go into the greasewood and mesquite, smelling and tasting and dreaming, and sometimes adventuring so far that we forgot to be home before dark.

Then Felice reproved me. "Mamma," she'd say severely, "has said two extra rosaries and burned the pies, and I'm sure I do not know what will become of you, Connie, you're that thoughtless."

I would be very contrite, for I loved my mother enormously, and I'd ride close to town, and be extra affectionate to her—until the next time. I think it must be very hard to be a mother—but my own never complained.

If I sometimes worried Mother, I almost drove our music teacher mad.

This good and genteel lady, who journeyed down from Socorro in a wagon once each week at my father's behest to bring culture to the little Hiltons, had the sterling virtue of honesty.

At the piano, under Mother's patient direction, Felice and I had at least mastered a basic technique. But Eva, who already showed signs of the striking beauty she was later to develop, didn't wish to play the piano. She wished to play the violin.

Father was delighted and decreed that we were all to expand our musical knowledge by one instrument. From a catalogue I selected the cornet, which duly arrived from St. Louis along with Eva's violin.

Eva's talent was instantly apparent. Had I had any way of foreseeing how that talent would eventually involve me, Chiquita and I would have ridden off with the beloved instrument into the Magdalenas and buried it at the foot of the kneeling nun, the wind-sculptured figure from which the mountains drew their name. She had looked, the time Chiquita and I sneaked off to visit her, as if she would like such an offering. Fortunately or unfortunately, I had no talent whatsoever for the cornet. After the first month the genteel musical lady, her aesthetic senses no doubt strained beyond the urgency of her purse, spoke to Gus.

"Conrad," she said rather breathlessly, her thin fingers waving one of the many strands of jet beads she affected, which swung in time to her beating hand and hypnotized me, "Conrad will never learn to play the cornet."

"Nonsense," bellowed my father.

"Never, never, never," she cried faintly, swinging the beads to emphasize each word.

"All he needs to do is work harder," my parent declared.

But for once Gus was wrong. I blew faithfully for years while the jet beads swung the rhythm. But I never learned to play.

Probably the most exciting regular event in our lives was Sunday church.

Mother was twenty-three when Gus brought her to the Territory and never, in those twenty-three years, had she been over a mile from daily Mass. If there was anything else that surprised or disappointed her in San Antonio she never mentioned it, but occasionally she did wish we had a resident priest.

Father Pelzer, our missionary, was miles down the river at San Marcial. Socorro had a resident priest but that was an eleven-mile drive in a wagon or buggy and not to be undertaken lightly. One didn't "run over" to Socorro in those days.

One Sunday a month Father Pelzer arrived in San Antonio. He was a small, spare, young Belgian with humorous, bright-blue eyes and a marked accent. He came directly to us from his ordination in France to wrestle with our two languages, our customs, and a fairly poor parish.

For a while, so Father said, he trudged on foot, and then rode an old horse from San Marcial to Carthage, to Monticello, and San Antonio, bringing the sacraments to his scattered flock. Eventually he acquired a buggy and by the time I remember him, the railroad men, who came to hold him in great respect, offered him free passage and he always arrived on the caboose.

There was great excitement in San Antonio when he was due to come on the Saturday train. His parishioners went to the station to vie for the honor of entertaining him that night, and to admire the way he swung agilely down the steps of the bright red caboose. The church was freshly decorated and shiny, and Mother quite frequently brought him home in triumph to spend the night in our home behind the store.

Mother's victory in carrying him off caused no real ill feeling, for she played a very special part in the church life. Sometime, somehow, in the past St. Anthony's had acquired an organ, but it had been silent for quite a spell before Gus brought home a bride. Now on the Sundays when Mass was celebrated there, it was Mother who coaxed music from the panting old instrument.

Father was as pleased as Mother when Father Pelzer was our guest. The Belgian had a wry, dry wit which Father appreciated and the Padre in turn appreciated Father's stories of the days before he came to the Territory.

In Gus Hilton's eyes the Belgian priest had wrought a service to the whole community when he taught the village ladies to play whist, a game Father considered a cultural triumph. While he didn't insist on education, Gus was strong on culture, desiring San Antonio to keep abreast of the outside world.

And, while never adopting the faith, as a frontiersman he greatly admired the versatility and resourcefulness of the early Catholic missionaries who had done so much, so valiantly, to establish the character of New Mexico.

Gus considered it a privilege, as he often told Father Pelzer, to know such men as Father Robert Garrassu, who had once saved the beautiful cathedral at Santa Fe for Archbishop John B. Lamy.

"Now *there* are the kind of pioneers who built this Territory," Gus would boom.

Then he would tell the story of how the Archbishop, with his cathedral half completed, ran out of money, was behind on wages and material, and on the verge of having to abandon the project most dear to his heart after a lifetime of service to the people of New Mexico.

On a last and rather forlorn quest for a loan, for which the Archbishop was willing to pay high rates of interest, he traveled to Mora County, the parish of Father Garrassu.

"I don't seek a donation, but a loan with interest," the weary Archbishop told the Padre. "But I must have $2,000 or abandon the whole cathedral."

Father Garrassu thought long and hard. He knew what the cathedral meant to his superior. He knew, too, what it meant as a symbol to the faithful throughout the archdiocese. Yet his was not a rich parish and a continued drought had brought the cattle and sheep close to starvation. He was deeply distressed by seeing this life dream fail, yet—what could he do?

"How much money have you at this moment?" Father Garrassu suddenly asked his Archbishop.

"Only a few dollars," was the reply.

"Let me have them, then, and take care of my parish for a few days," said Father Garrassu.

On his return he handed the Archbishop a bag of gold. "Here is your $2,000," he said.

"And to whom do I make the notes payable?" asked Archbishop Lamy, deeply moved.

After a moment's hesitation he got a reply. "The donors prefer to remain nameless. They do not require notes," said Father Garrassu firmly.

It was not until some years later when the Archbishop, his cathedral finished, had retired, that the Padre revealed the source of the money to his superior, on the promise that he would not be scolded.

"I won the $2,000 playing poker with the army officers at Fort Union," he confessed.

Repeatedly the officers had insisted that he should play with them, but never before and never since had the good Father joined their game or any other gambling game. Only

in his Archbishop's extremity had he dusted off a talent he
had known he possessed since his early days in the French
army, what the Americans called "card sense." In this isolated instance it had turned his Excellency's few dollars into
wages and materials to get on with the cathedral.

"And knowing the gang at Fort Union," my father was
wont to conclude, "that makes it a minor miracle. It was a
miracle that an officers' poker game ever produced such
stakes."

I was never sure my mother really appreciated this story.
She always did a mite of fussing when it began. Myself, I
loved it. However many times Father told it, I always listened spellbound. But Mother was glad that Gus and the
gentle Father Pelzer remained fast friends although our
priest never played cards for money in his life.

Another story which Father told about Archbishop
Lamy and his cathedral never failed to fascinate us children.
This, too, was a "business" story, and it made a deep impres-
sion on me.

After paying wages and pressing obligations on his building, the old Archbishop, the ranking Roman Catholic prelate in the Southwest, went to Abraham Staab, merchant
prince of Santa Fe and leading member of the Jewish faith in
New Mexico, to ask for an extension of promissory notes he
had given in exchange for funds Staab loaned for building
the cathedral. They were friends of long standing, and besides becoming banker for the undertaking, Staab had made
substantial gifts to the Archbishop's project.

"Times have been bad," the Archbishop said simply. "I
have come to ask for an extension on my notes."

Staab took all the notes from a large iron safe and held
them up. "Let me have some say in the building of the cathedral," he challenged, "and I will tear them all up."

"To what extent, Mr. Staab?" asked the Archbishop.

"Let me put only one word above the entrance, chiseled
in stone."

"And what is that word?"

"You must trust me, Archbishop," said Abraham Staab.

For a moment the two faced each other, looked into each
other's eyes, these two pioneers. One had brought the word
of God as he knew it to a wild country. The other had
brought money and trade. So often in later life I have been

told that these two things were opposed. But the Jewish merchant and the Catholic Archbishop saw it differently.

"I do so trust you," said Archbishop Lamy.

Abraham Staab tore up the notes.

Later I went to the cathedral at Santa Fe and was moved by its beauty. I was equally moved to see over the arch the part Abraham Staab had played in its building. There were the Hebraic initials, JVH, symbolic of the word "God" of the Christian faith, "Jehovah" of the faith of the Jews.

This story Mother must have liked better than the one about the poker game, for she never tried to shush Father when he started it, and it delighted Father Pelzer. But the occasions on which we had Father Pelzer were all too rare.

When Father didn't come to our town on Sunday, we went to him.

This, for us children, was high adventure. Off we would go in the wagon, sometimes to San Marcial or Carthage, wherever he happened to be saying Mass that Sunday. Mother sat in front by the driver, looking very pretty in a feathered hat, with her youngest clutched on her lap, and the rest of us hung on as best we could.

Mother could do without a lot of things in her life, never without her church.

Almost as much as going to church or playing hooky, I liked going down the road to talk with Charles Hislie, the carpenter, or Carl Jenks, the village blacksmith and dentist. Mr. Jenks shoed horses or pulled teeth, whichever service was required at the moment. My brother Carl, after an extraction, claimed that he used the same instruments for both operations, but I have no first-hand knowledge of that.

As I seldom had a toothache I loved to hang around Mr. Jenks' emporium and smell the pungent hot smell and listen to the hammer ringing on the anvil. I also liked to hear Mr. Jenks cuss. He was very talented in that direction and to this day I believe he had as extensive a vocabulary as any man I ever met.

This hero worship was rudely interrupted when an unsuitable word escaped my lips at dinner table. Mother was shocked. Gus paused in carving the roast only long enough to glare at me and say, "You stay away from the smithy." From that time I did, except on dental business when I was accompanied by my lady mother.

Next to Carl Jenks I most admired a surly Texan who must remain nameless. The name he used wasn't his own anyway. He kept an apiary on the outskirts of town and supplied honey to the housewives. It must be a fallacy that beekeepers have to rub themselves with flowers or other good smelling things to encourage the bee's affection. My beekeeper stooped to none of this. Nor did his bees sense in him, I feel sure, any purity of mind and soul. Perhaps we just had gentle bees or he was so tough they couldn't penetrate his hide.

At any rate, they never stung him although they climbed all over him. And for this talent I had a wild childish admiration. I also considered him wise beyond most of my adult acquaintances. No matter how long I talked at him, or what wild dreams I propounded, he never interrupted me. In fact, he never said anything much at all.

This remarkable fellow, so I later learned, had come hurrying over from Texas with the smell of gunsmoke clinging to him and never expressed any desire to go back. I only wonder how he had imagination enough to wind up keeping bees in San Antonio.

Every other summer Mother took her children back to Fort Dodge, and since the intervening year usually produced a new baby, and the weather was always hot, these trips on the Pullman were outstanding.

In Fort Dodge we were supposed to be starched, mannerly and subdued. Grandfather Laufersweiler was a very subduing sort of man. But since Grandmother was very jolly and spoiled us satisfactorily, we had a pleasant time.

There was a fine crop of uncles and aunts to lend a hand in the spoiling for Mother was one of ten children, eight of whom were living. Aunt Bertha was a particular favorite of ours and Aunts Edith and Elsie, being twins, an interesting novelty.

Felice was somewhat overworked on these excursions, partially trying to secure my behavior, but I did elude her long enough to fall off Grandfather's roof and break my arm.

Fortunately old Dr. Nicholson, from whom I got my second name, lived next door and I almost lit in his front yard; so I was set, splinted, and swaggering with a sling before my mother knew what had happened.

On these trips Gus was left behind.

Mother, as she told him firmly, had her hands full already.

Since Father was often overcome with what he called an "urge" when a train pulled out, Mother sometimes had to be quite brisk. She would remind him of deals pending, or the Business. Once, on the plea of "Business" he accompanied us part way.

Traveling with Father was like traveling with the barker for a full-fledged circus. Mother's idea of "proper travel" was to cross her feet tidily at the ankles, see that we did the same, and above all warn us "not to talk to strangers."

Father talked to everyone. He was back-slapping, jovial, gay. He introduced Mother to these "strangers" as though he had known them all his life. He carted us children up and down the aisles to show us to traveling grandparents. When he finally got off, Mother smoothed her skirts, settled her brood, warned us not to talk to strangers, and heaved a great sigh of relief.

"I feel," she remarked to Felice who, as the eldest, was entitled to confidence, "like I'd been traveling with a presidential candidate out to win a majority vote when I travel with your father."

But I knew what she meant. Father was exhausting, gay, stimulating, and I could see why Mother loved him devotedly for the rest of her life. But he *was* exhausting. When my children today accuse me of the same thing, I only wish they could have spent a day following Gus.

For one thing, Gus could not resist a parade, and at least I do that. If there was a Booster's convention anywhere within miles, Father would hear of it. And there he would be, in an outlandish hat, with his pockets bulging, not with gold but with *papers* (he never believed in a desk, preferring to carry his business with him).

Being Father, he was never content to carry the banner or bring up the rear. Gus was always right out front leading the parade.

Mother, too, could be very gay, but hers was a reserved gaiety and socially she liked best a proper party. She was completely at home in the old world customs and ceremony that surrounded the social life of San Antonio.

For San Antonio did have a social life.

Our Four Hundred was made up of five or six families who came to old Mexico with the Emperor Maximilian, the puppet planted on the Mexican throne by the French in 1864. Defeated in battle Maximilian was executed by the Mexicans in 1867 and his conquistadores scattered. Some of them strayed as far as New Mexico and lived now on their large ranchos, self-contained little kingdoms which they acquired as Spanish land grants.

Weddings, christenings, religious festivals were excuses for the Montoyas, the Pinos, the Gonzalezes, the Apodacas, to throw open their magnificent haciendas and greet guests from miles around. Our whole family would pile into the buckboard all dressed in our best, and drive long distances to attend. Sometimes the party would last three days.

Mother's apron disappeared at such times and we would gape to see her all decked out in her role of fashion plate, for the wife of the owner of San Antonio's leading emporium was the local fashion leader.

Generally speaking, Mother took little interest in the store, but when a drummer stepped off the train with five or six trunks full of ladies' things from the civilized world, Mother appeared as if by magic to inspect the latest styles and make her selections.

Mother's favorite event was a wedding and she always got a little soft and sentimental when she heard of a betrothal. To Father, however, it meant business. Our store would be called on for all the furnishings and, if it was to be very elegant, he might have to order the bridal gown and trimmings from St. Louis.

To us children weddings meant a lot of rich food and a thimbleful of the native sweet wine. To me personally it was a chance to watch the dancing. As the lovely daughters of the dons with their ivory skins and sweeping mantillas moved gracefully across the polished floors, I would dream about the gallant way in which I would some day bow low over their hands to claim the next dance. I was approaching the romantic age.

Then something happened which took all the romance out of life for a while.

Real sorrow first touched our family when baby Julian died. He was just two years old.

Mother spent long hours on her knees in her beloved church.

Father plunged off into the wildest mountains on a trading trip.

Our house was, for the first time in my memory, subdued and cheerless. There were no baby noises, no unsteady feet trailing at Mother's heels. I had a feeling that each afternoon I must come home from school and stay near Mother. One day I found an old Mexican woman in a black shawl trying to comfort her. She, too, had lost a son. "You have lost a little boy," she said in halting English. "I have lost a grown man. To you it will be a memory. To me always a *dolor*."

Mother could not know then that an unborn son would one day grow to manhood only to one day be her *dolor*, but there was sorrow and pain enough for us all just after Julian went.

For the first time I tasted the compulsion to turn from distress and plunge into work.

Faith sustained us but time hangs heavily in a house bereft.

Besides my usual duties I dusted the stock in the entire store and occasionally my grown-up cousin Olaf let me make a simple sale. When Father returned from the mountains, I begged a bit of land from him on the outskirts of town and began my produce business. Those heavy hours now were given to hoeing, weeding, irrigating my plot. I did not make my fortune but I did well enough, for although I never displayed an all-round green thumb, I had quite a way with corn and beans.

When harvest time came I walked from house to house like a mailman, my wares in a paper sack under my arm, and if at the end of my route I had failed to dispose of them, Mother would appear at her door and decide she needed exactly what I had left for dinner that night. We ate a great deal of corn and beans while I was in the produce business.

Little by little after Julian's death life resumed its usual pattern. Time did take care of that much. But somehow the house wasn't the same. It was not until the following spring when a baby girl, Rosemary, arrived, and Mother had the cradle filled again, that it really sounded like home.

I was not to enjoy it for long, however. The all-important decision had been made that now I was ready to "go away to school."

When I went to Goss Military Institute in Albuquerque, the newspapers reported me as "not yet in his teens." Nor was I. In the fall of 1899 I was almost twelve and very little aware of the world outside of San Antonio. I knew that William McKinley was President. That Jim Jeffries had knocked out Bob Fitzsimmons to become heavyweight champion of the world. And that, according to a magazine Father read aloud one night, the "horseless carriage"—a vehicle which we had never seen—"will never, of course, come into as common use as the bicycle." Since Gus was a great man for "firsts," I believe this prediction was most welcome to Mother.

The fact that the Gay Nineties were ending and a new century rolling round meant nothing to me except that Felice had acquired the sheet music of the latest song, "She Was Only a Bird in a Gilded Cage," and played it constantly on our piano. So constantly, in fact, that, except for a small cold lump that attacked my innards at the thought of leaving home, I almost welcomed the idea of boarding school.

Goss Military Institute was a small, rather homey affair on a sand hill on the outskirts of town where we got a drilling in the three Rs—and a uniform of gray with black braid down the trousers. Although I found it very uncomfortable at first, I preferred the uniform to the instruction. Outside of arithmetic, I was never to be a sparkling student.

It was while I was at Goss that I had my first adventure into night life.

With another boy, who was also feeling the confines of a not so "gilded" cage, I slipped out a window after taps had sounded, for the purpose of taking in a traveling show with, we hoped, the "Original New York Cast."

The main street of Albuquerque was muddy and rutted but for us glamour oozed out of its brightly lighted saloons as we marched along to the tinny music spilling from each swinging door. We had to pick our way carefully among the unsteady patrons, the horses and wagons, to Grant's Opera

House. Much to our chagrin it had burned down at some previous time and we retraced our steps to Colombo Hall where Hoyt's "A Midnight Bell" was playing in a makeshift theater.

The seats were all on one level and we couldn't see very much after we got there. What little we could see, crouching and weaving between some loud, whiskered gentlemen obviously just escaped from a saloon, was disappointing.

"Do you suppose there'll be dancing girls later?" my pal whispered as a large, not-quite-young woman in an opera cape went into a tragic speech.

If there were we never got to see them, for at that moment a strong hand grasped each of us by the collar and a firm voice said, "All right, you two. Come along with us." It was City Marshal MacMillan, complete with flashy badge and guns, and the eyes of the whole theater watched as he lifted us bodily and carried us dangling and limp, as a woman carries wet fish, out of Colombo Hall.

We never found out whether the school had reported us missing or some motherly lady had noticed two small lads in uniform, frightened but thrilled, adventuring through the wilds of western night life. We never even asked. It was a very touchy subject.

Colonel Goss said not a word but the confinement became more rigid than ever. Shortly afterward the school burned down, an event which, although I took no active hand in it, pleased me very much. I figured I could go home at once. I figured wrong. The Colonel simply rented another house, smaller and farther out, and continued his efforts to educate us as before.

That summer most of the boys went home for vacations. I went home to work.

There had been a few major changes in San Antonio during my absence. El Coronel, for Gus was now a Colonel, had shaved his mustache. The wooden porch and crisscrossed laths which had decorated the entrance to our house since the birth of Carl, were freshly painted. And the coal mines at Carthage, and with them the coke ovens in our town, had finally ground to a full stop. This coal vein, which as far back as 1861 had fed coal to the United States forts in the territory, was presumed exhausted and the Santa Fe Railroad, which had been working them, closed down the operation and gave up.

But the Hilton store was doing business as usual. Gus had things humming. It now housed the post office, and the telegraph, the key handled by a cynical middle-aged man whom I much admired, and Father had become the Studebaker dealer for wagons and buggies. A new warehouse now stood south of the livery stable filled with lumber and other building materials.

The coal mines might collapse, but the A. H. Hilton mercantile business expanded.

My place was behind the counter in the store as assistant clerk. I had gotten $5.00 a month the summer before and Father saw no justifiable reason for raising me from my apprenticeship. However, I was learning. Business in a general store in those parts, a good store, meant that you had to supply all the communities' wants, and I learned to sell a side of bacon, a plow, a feathered hat, a coffin, or a postage stamp with equal facility. Our slogan was—YOU NAME IT, WE'VE GOT IT!

I learned another thing that summer.

Gus had always refused to carry a gun. In my young eyes this was exceedingly silly. Besides the Apaches, I knew my father had been in a lot of rough spots, faced drunks, tough characters, desperadoes. And always unarmed. I couldn't understand it.

"Listen, Connie," he had once tried to explain. "You have to decide one way or the other and then stick with it. Either you *never* carry a gun, or you *always* do. One way you depend on your wits. The other on your draw. But if you carry a gun, the time to draw will inevitably come, and I've seen a lot of men stone dead from drawing too late."

I still thought I'd carry a gun.

One night after I'd closed the store, Mother sent me down to the saloon for Gus. It was not a question of "Father, dear Father, come home with me now." Dinner was ready and Gus, down at Bianchi's with a couple of drummers, would wish to know.

As I stepped inside the swinging doors of the false front building which housed Bianchi's drinking emporium, I did not have to look around for Father. He was on stage, front and center.

In a perfect hush, with all action frozen, like a movie still, Gus stood in front of the bar looking into the business end of a gun trained on him by a very drunken rancher. The rancher, fired with whiskey, was profanely offering him time to say his prayers before he pulled the trigger. I had the feeling that every man there, and surely myself, was holding his breath. Then Gus began to talk, softly, calmly, reasonably. I couldn't hear what he said, but I saw the gun waver, finally fall, and the rancher weep drunkenly on Father's shoulder, swearing he loved him like a brother.

"And he does, too," Gus told me as we walked home in the dusk. "But you see, Connie, if I'd had a gun, *one* of us would be dead."

Years later, when I had to make a similar decision, I was to remember what I had seen in Bianchi's that night, and what Father said.

In the fall I was sent to Roswell to the growing New Mexico Military Institute. It seemed to me a great waste of time since, as I told Mother, "All the things I want to know, I am learning at home." But she insisted I would have plenty of time to learn those later and what was indicated now was a solid foundation.

The trip to Roswell presented a fine problem in transportation. Cross country the distance was about 115 miles. By train, however, I would have embarked on the Atchison, Topeka & Santa Fe for El Paso, Texas. At El Paso I would have boarded the Texas & Pacific for Pecos, Texas, and thence ridden 180 miles on the Pecos Valley Railroad from Pecos to Roswell. After some conversation my father solved all this by sending me overland in the buckboard with a hired man. We camped out for two nights, cooking over a campfire and it was a boy's idea of the way to travel.

I returned the same way at the close of school. All that had apparently been added to my life was a very fancy uniform covered with gold, which I had acquired by exchanging the cornet for the bugle. This uniform had been a romantic asset with the young ladies of Roswell but no one at home seemed impressed. Its romantic attractions, however, had an immediate effect on my life.

One morning, when I had been home several weeks, I was finishing breakfast while Mother straightened my room, completely unprepared for the gales of laughter that suddenly floated out to me. Standing at the door with napkin in hand, I demanded to know what was so funny.

Then I saw. In her hand Mother held a daintily scented pink envelope. "You've been reading my mail," I gasped, not knowing then that this is a way mothers have, and my own was simply caught out by her sense of humor.

She didn't reply directly. Instead she read aloud, "I have never loved another boy in my life like I love you!" When her laughter subsided again, I said, with dignity, "I don't think that's so funny."

"How long has she lived?" asked my mother.

I was offended. "She is going on fourteen," I said, "and her skirts are down and her hair is up." I had a picture to prove it. I have it still. Maggie Hinson, my first girl, a laughing, pretty face with shiny white teeth, and lovely hair on which is perched a smart white sailor hat.

Mother was duly impressed and assumed a serious air. If her eyes twinkled, I didn't notice, and I thought that was the end of the matter—until the wedding, of course. But almost immediately Mother began to talk of a change of schools for the following fall. There was, she said, a "fourth R"—Religion—in which I should be well grounded before I got married.

I didn't pay much attention. My summer was very busy for I was out of the apprentice class, making $10.00 a month, and my father expected twice as much work for twice as much money. And he saw to it that he got it. My cousin Olaf, now a man of property with a ranch of his own, came in as a buyer and would subject me to a skirmish at bargaining which amused him and sharpened me. I had a whirl at learning telegraphy at the beginning of summer when Maggie was still fresh in my mind, thinking it might have a future in it. While I had to give up, having no distinct talent, I knew enough to follow with fascinated attention in September when President McKinley was shot and the telegrapher kept in touch with the news and the rest of the country by his magic dots and dashes.

Outside of working hours I was beginning to lose my interest in boyish "play." Instead, I conceived a very deep and lasting affection for the newest arrival in our household, another brother, August Harold Hilton. It was a ridiculously long name for such a small fellow, and the family called him "Boy." Thinking, no doubt, of Maggie and dreaming of sons of my own some day, I spent a good deal of time with my youngest brother and found it very rewarding. I walked him, pushed him, pulled him, and "bubbled" him, drawing the line at changing him, and found that the ability to bring actual happiness to another being's face, even such a small red one, simply by walking into the room, made me feel ten feet tall. I had never had it before, and possibly never shall again, but it established a bond between Boy and myself that, when it had to break, took a bit of me in the breaking.

Between Boy and the store I had a very full summer and was somewhat surprised when it ended to find myself on a train en route, not to Roswell, but to Santa Fe and St. Michael's College. I can't say I was unhappy about it. Maggie was not nearly as clear in my mind as the price tags on a new line of plows we had just received, and my mother was once again the leading lady in my life. Mother was pleased. Besides, on the seat next to me, as the train pulled out, was a good friend, one Jack Bruton, whose rancher father was sending him off to St. Michael's as well.

"I don't hold much with this religion stuff," Mr. Bruton told Jack at the station. "But I want you to get some book larnin'."

My mother placed the values the other way round. She was all for "book larnin'," of course, but she wanted me to have "one year of sound religious training." She felt the Christian Brothers at Santa Fe would give it to me. And they did.

I made my First Communion at St. Michael's. It was a big event in my life. Afterward Mother wrote in her fine, clear hand: "Stay close to the sacraments, Connie, always, and you will be able to draw the strength and courage you need for anything that comes to you."

This I found to be true. During the lowest ebb I was to know, I turned to them daily and later when, through an act of my own, I was cut off from them for a while, I realized that this intangible sustenance had become more necessary to me than the tangible things in my life.

At St. Michael's I also found a patron into whose hands I was to commit with complete confidence all the projects which lay in my future. Father Jules Derasches, my first confessor, introduced me to St. Joseph. Of course I had always known him as the foster father of the Holy Family, but the good priest now widened my knowledge to include him as the patron saint of workers—of builders. Here was one who had, with humility, industry, love, working as a carpenter, patiently provided for the needs of his family. He could understand the problems of the workingman. He could understand me.

I gave little thought to him as a builder then, but when my first hotel was going up and I was beset by problems, I found that builders do indeed need a friend in Heaven—and I was grateful that Father Derasches had already introduced us.

"Connie," he promised, "if daily you will say a 'Hail Mary' and then 'St. Joseph, Pray for Us,' three times, he will always take care of you."

Since that day my prayers have altered to suit my needs, most of them coming spontaneously, conversationally, but that particular prayer I have said in exactly the form I learned it every day for fifty-three years.

From St. Michael's I came home with holy pictures instead of girls' pictures and Mother relaxed. Having carried her point she was willing that I should spend the next two years at New Mexico Military Institute with, of course, summers in the store.

In San Antonio things were booming for A. H. Hilton. Gus had grubstaked Jim Lovera when the one-eyed prospector insisted that there was more coal in the Carthage mines, and little by little Father acquired ownership. The coke ovens were again active and now the coal that fed them was *our* coal.

El Coronel had indeed achieved his empire and the consequences bleakly hinted by Grandfather Laufersweiler turned out to be that Mary had become frontier royalty, albeit still clothed in a cotton apron. Gus had even subsidized a San Antonio band which met him at the station when he had been on buying trips to St. Louis and gave him a truly royal welcome.

Mother, with only two babies at her heels, had occupied herself with a correspondence course in photography and, using her brood as subjects for her camera, spent a good portion of her time shut up in an evil-smelling little closet from which she emerged with dark sepia prints inclined to fade with disheartening speed.

For myself, I, too, was doing very well. I had been raised to $15 a month on the strength of my first serious bargaining bout. It involved a rich old Spanish widow and a pair of shoes.

Father saw her coming. "She's a tough customer," he said, "and she's all yours. Just make sure she doesn't get her coffin for the price of a postage stamp." With which stern admonition he disappeared behind some rolls of baling wire.

The situation was delicate. We traded heavily with the Señora in wool and hides. I had to keep that trade with some concessions and at the same time keep her respect by getting a fair price.

Now bargaining was—and is—a very personal thing with a great deal of tradition behind it. You have to know the rules. But if you do, and have a zest for it, a good bargaining bout between well-matched opponents can be as exciting as a major league ball game.

The trick is to know the value of an article, to learn to regard a price tag so that it is flexible—not, of course, on staples like salt or coffee, but on such items as feathered hats or coffins. The buyer is entitled to a bargain. The seller is entitled to a profit. So there is a fine margin in between where the "price is right." I have found this to be true to this day whether dealing in paper hats, winter underwear or hotels.

The Señora and I commenced our skirmish with a careful inspection of the pair of shoes she required. The merchandise was without blemish. The game could begin. In Spanish she asked the price. I quoted the price tag. She sailed into action.

"Ladrón!" (Unvarnished thief!) she shrieked and clutched her black lace shawl tightly as though to prevent my making off with it. Then followed a voluble stream of invective which I sidestepped and let run its course. As she paused for breath I said, as calmly as I could, "They're worth every penny of it." The Señora pointed a trembling brown finger against my chest. I was, she said, *"Sin vergüenza"* (without shame) to try to cheat her thus. At that point I came down ten cents.

"You need the shoes," I pointed out reasonably, "and you won't get another pair this side of Socorro." The ten-cent reduction had softened, not satisfied her. She wept. We were

coming to the closing minutes of the game. How could I do
this to her, she whimpered, a poor widow with no one to
protect her interests? Keeping my mind's eye firmly on her
sleek fat sheep and her sleek lazy son, I shook my own head
sorrowfully and continued to regard the price tag. In that
instant she reached the grand climax. *"Malhayas tu!"* (Damn
you!) she screamed, exactly as she often screamed at Father.

It was a fine compliment. I was satisfied. I reduced the
price twenty-five cents. She smiled. I smiled. It was a deal.
The Señora had her shoes—and a bargain. I had a profit—
and a raise. For as she left, Father came out from behind the
baling wire grinning broadly, his fat gold watch in his hand.
"Done like a gentleman and a businessman," he said, "and in
good time, too."

I have played variations on that scene throughout my
whole life, often with bigger chips, often over longer periods
of time. But the rules are always the same and I have never
lost the thrill of the game.

With my raise at the store came additional responsibilities. This too, I have found to be a rule, whatever the chips
might be. For $15 a month I not only clerked and cleaned
and bargained, but began to take inventory of the stock and
do some of the ordering.

One of the first things I ordered was purely personal, an
L. C. Smith twelve-gauge hammerless shotgun. It was a
beauty and I'd always wanted it. When it arrived Father gave
me merry Ned.

"You can have all the blank blank shotguns you want,
since you're paying for them," he said. "But the minimum
freight charge is on one hundred pounds. This gun weighs
about twenty. You threw away an eighty-pound opportunity. You could have gotten a keg of nails for the same freight
charge. You'll never get rich that way."

At the end of the summer when I wanted to buy Mother
a new tripod for her camera I also ordered eighty-five pounds
of whitewash. I was learning.

It would not be fair to leave an impression that I gained
nothing from the several years I spent at the New Mexico
Military Institute. I am sure that even as a mediocre student
some education rubbed off on me. And I learned one invaluable lesson. It was not taught by teachers, but by the boys
themselves.

"A gentleman told the truth." To lie was a disgrace!

To the cadets at Roswell there were no degrees about this. You either spoke the truth—or you didn't. I saw the same treatment accorded a sneak thief who tried to shift the blame and a boy who broke a window and then denied his guilt. I myself was a witness to the window-breaking. There was no question as to which of us hit the baseball that landed on the floor of the school chapel. When the culprit denied his act no one told on him. But from then until the end of the semester he was as frigidly ignored by his schoolmates as if he had been a shadow.

"That's about what he is, too," an older cadet sagely informed me when I timidly suggested we might be overdoing the frost, "a shadow. All a man has got is his word. If you can't trust what he says, how do you know he's there at all?"

If, in the course of my own life, I have lost some small things by carrying my regard for truth to an excess; if I have driven business associates, lawyers, public relations counsels, to a frenzy by an inability to dissemble, I can only believe I have gained greater things by it than I have ever lost—the Palmer House for one, I firmly believe—but that story comes later. One thing I know. I personally have been able to do business with some pretty rough characters; but I have never been able to deal with a liar. It is, as my cadet friend at Roswell would have put it, like shadow boxing. It isn't worth the effort. You can't win.

At fifteen I shot up suddenly as is the way of adolescent boys. Mother had quite a time getting into the habit of looking up to the six feet where my face now was. If the change in my outward appearance was sufficient to startle the family, there was an internal change going on that startled me.

I was beginning to think—or to try to. Till now my life had been one principally of doing or feeling. Any thinking I did was set in motion by an outer activity or need. And then another girl entered my life, a girl I was never to meet or even see, yet she had a decided hand in forming my thought processes. Her name was Helen Keller.

At that time Helen Keller was the "Eighth Wonder of the World." A young lady of twenty-three, she had been blind, deaf, and dumb since her second year, literally imprisoned in a universe containing no light, no sound. My imagination could scarcely encompass this picture. With the aid of a handkerchief and some bits of cotton in my ears I tried to simulate it.

To a healthy young teenager, just stumbling around my own familiar bedroom was enough to give a frightening glimpse of the world in which she lived. Yet somewhere she had found the courage and drive to learn to communicate, to turn her hands into eyes, to become a student at Radcliffe College at a time when most others so afflicted were still bearing the stigma of feeblemindedness. I regarded Helen Keller and her accomplishments with an awed admiration I have never lost. I even had a picture of her then, a lovely, poised girl in cap and gown, which I snipped surreptitiously from the front of a book she had written.

For she *had* written a book. Helen Keller, blind, deaf, dumb, had written a book called *Optimism*. To me, this alone was miraculous. I found it on my mother's sewing table and concealed it under my pillow for private consumption. I believe I was just a little ashamed of this new desire to think. I wasn't sure what Father or the girls would make of it.

After I had finished the slim volume, I knew I could talk it over with Mother. For the miracle of Helen Keller's optimism, although they were not members of the same church, had its roots in exactly the same soil as my mother's—faith.

She wrote that "Optimism is the faith that leads to achievement; nothing can be done without hope." And summed up by stating that "Optimism is the harmony between man's spirit and the spirit of God pronouncing His works good." *

I do not believe I fully appreciated her wisdom then. But I did recognize that here was a girl barely eight years older than I, calling out from a different world, a world that filled me with dread, and insisting that I personally must recognize pessimism as a sin. I hope I have been true to that particular lesson, for I knew she was right. I thought she was great. I still do!

My sixteenth summer was a big one.

Father had sold the coal mines for $110,000, which in those days made him one of the richest men in the Territory. In 1904 the dollar was worth something. Men worked for a dollar a day and on that lived decently and raised a family of five or six. A section hand on the railroad, a prize

* *Optimism* by Helen Keller. C. P. Crowell and Company, New York, 1903.

job, received exactly $1.00 per diem. Coal mining, a hazardous occupation, drew the respectable sum of $2.00 a day and put the miner in the moneyed class. With $100,000 Gus was a millionaire.

To celebrate he took the whole family to St. Louis to see the Exposition. We stayed at the Inside Inn, the first hotel ever run by E. M. Statler, but since I had yet to dream of one hotel and certainly could not imagine a day just fifty years later when I would buy the Statler chain in a $100,000,000 deal, I paid very little attention to our accommodations.

Carl and I were much more interested in the fact that the first Olympic games ever held in America, the third Olympiad of modern times, was a part of the Exposition and we could wander out on the horse trolley to watch the competition.

But the big event, for me, was that Helen Keller, now twenty-four and graduated from Radcliffe with a B.A., was to lecture in the main auditorium.

She was a world celebrity now, and I can still remember the great press of people trying to crowd into the hall. Gus and I stood with the throng, for it was impossible to get a ticket. But what Gus wanted, Gus got, and while one minute he was there beside me, pressed tightly against the restraining arms of the law, the next minute he was on the other side and waving to me as he disappeared through the doors into the audience.

I'm afraid I sulked. If I have since developed some force or drive, it is apparent I was not born with them, for I wanted to see Helen Keller with compelling eagerness, yet I hadn't the gumption to push past the first obstacle placed in my way. I didn't even have the courage to hang around the stage door and watch her leave. It was suddenly borne in on me that my grown-up-ness was obviously all in my elongated frame.

Back at the Inside Inn, I faced a moment of decision, the moment where the urge to be a man was frustrated by the limitations of the boy, where something had to give. Of what use were faith, hard work, honor, optimism, if I could not *do* something with them? Mothers sometimes have difficulty recognizing this age of rebellion that is part and parcel of the youth growing into the man. Fortunately for me, I was protected by the conditioning of habitual faith and work from the more hazardous doors through which it can lead. My direction was established. But when Father returned triumphantly from Miss Keller's lecture I had news for him.

"I am not going back to school," I announced.

"All right," said that surprising man, much as if I had announced that I did not intend to go to a parade. "I guess you'll be worth $25 a month on a full-time basis."

Mother, too, was surprisingly docile. Perhaps Gus had talked to her. Perhaps she just had a complete confidence that my Heavenly Father could wisely direct my impulses. Or perhaps I caught her at the right psychological moment. For when we returned to San Antonio, Carl had been left in boarding school while Eva and Felice went on to South Bend, Indiana, to acquire their "year of sound religious training" at St. Mary's. With only Rosemary, now four, and Boy, aged two, left at home I think Mother was perfectly willing to have one member of the Older Set underfoot.

There was no question that the next year in the store did a lot toward "growing-me-up." Olaf Bursum had become a wheel in Republican politics, full of talk of statehood, the non-partisan dream of every New Mexican, and I now qualified for the cracker-barrel discussions.

I made buying trips with Father which were an experience in themselves. It was not all business. Father had a method of spreading good will, a habit of appropriating bits of verse or words of wisdom that appealed to him, having them printed on brightly colored cards with his name on the bottom and leaving a trail of them in his wake as he made his rounds of the Territory. He would go fifteen or twenty miles out of his way to present his latest card to an old Mexican who spoke no English, or to an Indian scout who couldn't read, or to get the approval of Father Pelzer at San Marcial. He would recite them aloud to me in a sonorous voice as we lurched and rolled over the rutted trails and I strongly suspect when I was not along he recited them with equal relish to the prairie dogs and vultures.

One bit I remember to this day. . . .

> The man who wins is an average man,
> Not built on any particular plan;
> Not blessed with any particular luck—
> Just steady and earnest and full of pluck.

The man who wins is the man who works,
Who neither labor nor trouble shirks;
Who uses his hands, his head, his eyes—
The man who wins is the man who tries.

This was printed on a brilliant orange card with a black scroll around it and boldly signed, with no regard for the author, "A. H. Hilton." Where Father discovered it, I do not know, but striking the word "average" from the first line, it could have been written *about* him if not *by* him, and he considered its sentiments deathless. I do not know how he regarded the verse.

In the spring I was permitted to make my first trip alone. This was a milestone as it meant that Gus now recognized my ability, felt I knew the value of the wide variety of goods we bought and sold, and *could be trusted to make a profit.*

With a team of mules, the wagon laden to the groaning point, I set off at dawn one morning to be gone from ten days to two weeks. The tamarisks were in bloom, their feathery plumes of bluish-green topped by sprays of pink blossoms and as the day went on there was nothing moving as far as my eye could see but my wagon, the mules, and the wind in the tamarisks. It was easy to believe I owned the world.

At the haciendas of the aristocrats I was a welcome guest, sleeping in fine old canopied beds, doing leisurely business according to a tradition established long before I was born. Custom demanded a polite interchange, gossip about the weather, inspection of the *rancho*, several glasses of wine, before any hint was given that business was afoot. Finally we would go and look at the cattle, or mohair, or hides, while my host depreciated his wares. Whereupon, couched in language as flowery as spring itself, we would settle down to a garlanded but most hard-headed bargaining bout. Wares changed hands in a flutter of bows and courtesies. It was a pleasant way of doing business.

At many of the other ranches the dealings were much more slipshod, and I generally did more advantageous business, but it was not so pleasant. During the '80s a breed of Texas ranchers, the *Tejanos*, had turned up in New Mexico. Those who liked a tall tale would hint that they arrived at about the same time that the state of Texas announced she had rid herself of nearly every one of her outstanding desperadoes. But I didn't believe it. Not one among those I did business with could hold a candle to my friend, the bee-keeper. But, while they paid their bills and traded honorably, there were none of the trimmings that sparked the game as we played it at the Spanish haciendas.

Nor the hospitality.

After trading at the ranch of a *Tejano*, I would drive my wagon and its heavy load out into the open spaces and spend the night under the stars. After feeding and tying the mules I'd put on bacon and coffee, the two most comforting smells I know, and huddle over my campfire. I do not think I was ever afraid. I regarded it as a great adventure.

But I will admit that just after sundown, when the startling colors faded into black, there was a mighty loneliness over the land. When the night noises came alive, tracing the move-ment of things I could not fathom, I'd say my prayers, jump into my bedroll and hang onto the stars till I fell asleep. If sleep was a while coming I would think again of the lovely young girl, Helen Keller, and try to imagine if the world of movement and surrounding darkness had seemed as mysteri-ous and menacing to her as it did to me. Then with my mind firmly fixed on her courage and optimism, and with a little extra prayer of gratitude that I wasn't cooped up in a bunk-house with a *Tejano*, I would drift off.

When I returned from that first lone buying trip I felt my-self every inch a man. I was in for a rude shock. The next fall found me in Long Beach, California—a schoolboy again.

4. A PANIC, A HOTEL, AND THREE GIRLS

We moved to Long Beach because we were rich. In less than two years we weren't rich any more. But we made the most of it while it lasted.

The plan was for Mother to put away her cotton apron and play lady in the big beautiful house Gus rented for us a block from the ocean, to let the cool breezes wash away the strain of frontier living. Gus, too, had earned a little ease and would commute from San Antonio, although ease obviously drove him wild and he never stayed long.

For me, I was to go to Dartmouth and major in economics at the same time absorbing along with it that coveted eastern polish, and to this end I willingly took up my school books again. Eva was already in New England fiddling away for experts at the Boston Conservatory of Music, but the rest of the Older Set could now be recalled from boarding schools, the educational facilities of Long Beach being excellent, and kept under the matriarchal wing—and eye.

Very little escaped Mother's eagle eye. But there were a few things. For one, she never noticed that Carl, who had turned into a thoroughly mischievous, very attractive rogue, doted on teasing little Rosemary, while Rosemary, pretty as a picture but with a cleverness all her own, bided her time. The time came when she contracted mumps and struggled from her isolated sick bed long enough to pass her misery and swellings on to a sleeping Carl, whereupon they passed quickly from one to another until Mamma, money or no money, had to get out the apron again and wait hand and foot on a houseful of demanding invalids. Gus took the first train to San Antonio.

Nor did Mother ever know about me and Flora. Flora was a horse, a borrowed horse. I had a delivery route and I wangled her from my great-uncle Adam Wasem to pick up my newspapers. My delivery route I could manage on a bicycle, but getting the supplies was always a problem. On this particular day Flora and I nipped a pedestrian. We knocked him flat as he stepped off the curb and when he arose, muddied and most irate, we bolted, although I admit it was more my idea than Flora's. For several weeks thereafter, while the police, the papers *and* my mother had their say about the hit-and-run horse and driver, I sheepishly sold my papers on the other side of town, an inferior route I had gotten by swapping with a smaller boy.

Of course, nobody ever asked me if I did it. But at Roswell that would never have done. So far as I can remember this is the only time in my life when I didn't volunteer the truth and it caught up with me—fifty-two years later. A short while ago I was to address a civic group in Long Beach. I had prepared my speech and rehearsed it beforehand. But when I stood up nothing came. It was a frightening feeling yet there seemed to be something I wanted to say and I couldn't remember what it was. I hadn't thought of Flora in fifty years. But suddenly I did.

"I've got to get something off my mind," I blurted out. "I guess I've been carrying it too long." Then I told the story of Flora. "It was me. I know it's pretty late—but if that gentleman is in the audience today I want to apologize."

After that I felt better and was able to recall my scheduled talk. The only way I can figure it is that, even when we think we've forgotten, it's all there on the shelves, just barely below the surface, waiting. And if your brother has something against you—well, you're stuck with it!

If I didn't tell Mother about Flora I told her everything else. She had never lost her taste for romance and I decidedly recall coming in from a high school party at one A.M., charging into the room where she lay sleeping, and announcing fervently that I had found *the* girl. At *last*. I do not remember *the* girl's name—or face—but I remember that Mother was very sympathetic. By and large we had plenty of time for romance and were very well pleased with our new existence.

The whole country was pleased with itself. Teddy Roosevelt had been down to inspect his brand new Panama Canal. We all hummed the "Merry Widow Waltz" and the luxury era of the early twentieth century was evident in pictures we saw of the new Plaza Hotel just built in New York City. It didn't mean a thing to me then because I was busy with my newspaper business and high school but it was nice to live in a luxury era. It was very nice to be rich. We looked upon the Long Beach house as a true Hilton home now that a new baby, Helen, had arrived, and Mother was unusually relaxed, pretty and gay. Gus, too, when he was with us was expansive, with extra time for ball games and such.

And then, in October of 1907 it was, suddenly we weren't rich any more.

A currency panic started by a run on the Knickerbocker Trust Company of New York exhausted that bank's reserves in a day and a half. In a matter of weeks it had spread and banks throughout the country closed.

Gus, in San Antonio, was left holding a warehouse full of stock for which he had paid, or on which he still owed, more than he could get. He yelled for help. At once Mother gave up her lovely house, bade farewell to the sea breeze and, with her brood around her and a baby in her lap, headed for the Territory again.

Father never went bust. He bent, as I was to bend later, but he never broke. Money simply didn't exist in the fall of '07. He lost a lot. He owed a lot. He could sell nothing or, if he did, he was forced to extend credit he couldn't afford. We were certainly in a fix. Gone were Mother's dreams of ease. Gone were my dreams of Dartmouth. It was time to go back to work. We were right back where we started from.

And that's when we went into the hotel busines. My *first* hotel.

We had, we decided, four assets. The stock on the shelves, which we couldn't move. A lot of manpower for even with Eva, her tuition paid, still in Boston, and the other girls in school, Carl and I were distinctly of working size. We had the biggest, ramblingest adobe house in New Mexico directly facing a railroad station on a main line. And we had my mother's cooking. This added up to only one thing—a Hilton Hotel.

Even with business at a low ebb there would be salesmen, travelers, railroaders, miners covering the Territory trying to drum up business. "If they get a taste of Mary's cooking," Gus predicted, "we'll have more business than we can handle. Every traveling man in New Mexico will try to break his trip at San Antonio." Which proved to be exactly correct.

It was up to Carl and me to get them in for that first taste of Mother's cooking. It was "Family Hold Back" at table and sleep where and when you can, depending on how many guests we had. Carl and I met every train, at midnight, at three in the morning, at high noon. We hustled. We took morning calls to awaken sleepy travelers. We carried luggage and trunks and showcases. I opened the store at eight and closed it at six, for there was always a chance of selling a can of tomatoes and business had to go on. Gus was "mein host" and the ace gladhander of us all. Mother cooked. And cooked. And cooked.

I can't honestly say I fell in love with the hotel business as it was practiced by the Hilton family in 1907, or began to dream of the Plaza or the Waldorf. It was a case of urgent necessity and soon we were making a name for ourselves *and*, more important, at $2.50 a day with meals, a profit. I think, between the station at nights, the early calls for guests, and the store, I was probably too sleepy to respond to anything. Only once did I give serious thought to a future in the hotel business and then strictly as a bellboy.

A man tipped me *five* dollars.

Tipping was not a normal gratuity in those days in the southwest. Occasionally I got nickels and dimes for extra duties, but I worked hard for them. Or some easterner wandered out our way and gave up a quarter for nothing at all, as foreigners will, but the natives regarded the practice as neither necessary nor thrifty.

When I got the five dollars I took it straight to Mother, a speculative look in my eye. "He wasn't an easterner," I said, "and he wasn't drunk. Even if he thought it was a dollar . . ."

"He was just plain crazy," my mother said disdainfully. "You forget about him."

My mother, I might add, never did modernize her views on tipping. When she lived for some years at the El Paso Hilton, this was a source of some amusement and much conniving on the part of her children. I, myself, would take her twenty or thirty quarters with specific instructions that she was to give one or two to any bellboy, any waiter, anyone, indeed, who gave her special service, depending on the extra amount of trouble it gave him.

"I'll try, Connie," she'd say.

And I would find out from my sister Helen that, as soon as my back was turned, she'd trot down to the cashier and have the quarters converted into dimes, with which she reluctantly rewarded any service she absolutely could not do herself. Ten cents remained all her life the most she could bring herself to tip.

Gus, on the other hand, was a tipping fool, a trait which, along with his inability to spell, was duly manifest by my son Barron. But in 1907 when we were all hanging on to every nickel and dime it was a good thing Mother was such a careful manager.

Within a matter of months the hotel was doing well enough to hire help. The store was beginning to come alive. Once again, with a lot of work and a lot of prayer, the Hilton family could see daylight ahead.

Instead of Dartmouth I now entered the New Mexico School of Mines at Socorro. It didn't offer the polish but it was handy and cheap, and I could board with my cousin Olaf Bursum and be back in San Antonio over week-ends or at nights if they needed an extra hand. I wasn't interested in mining, even academically, but I was as determined now at twenty to study *something* as I had been determined at sixteen to study nothing at all.

As Mother said, when she told me to go and pray about it, it looked like "He did know what was best for me," for what I learned in Socorro has been invaluable to me throughout my entire career. I learned really to understand higher mathematics.

I'm not out to convince anyone that calculus, or even algebra and geometry, are necessities in the hotel business. But I will argue long and loud that they are not useless ornaments pinned onto an average man's education. For me, at any rate, the ability to formulate quickly, to resolve any problem into its simplest, clearest form, has been exceedingly useful. It is true that you do not use algebraic formulae but in those three small brick buildings at Socorro I found higher mathematics the best possible exercise for developing the mental muscles necessary to this process.

In later years I was to be faced with large financial problems, enormous business deals with as many ramifications as an octopus has arms, where bankers, lawyers, consultants, all threw in their particular bit of information. It is always necessary to listen carefully to the powwow, but in the end someone has to put them all together, see the actual problem for what it is, and make a decision—come up with an answer.

A thorough training in the mental disciplines of mathematics precludes any tendency to be fuzzy, to be misled by red herrings, and I can only believe that my two years at the School of Mines helped me to see quickly what the actual problem was—and where the problem is, the answer is. Any time you have two times two and *know* it, you are bound to have four.

Valuable as this was I didn't spend all my time at Socorro in the dizzy realms of calculus. I was twenty now, and had pushed up another two inches to exactly match the size of my feet. This meant they were finally mine to command, and command them I did. I fulfilled a dream born when I used to attend those marriage festivals at the haciendas around San Antonio. I learned to dance.

I also learned to play a reasonable game of tennis, a mediocre game of bridge, and improved my poker in the smoke-filled back room behind the Atlantic Bar, still called the "longest bar in the world," and serviced twenty-four hours a day by three shifts of bartenders. Socorro was a quieter town now, sedate and prosperous, but there were still miners and drummers, railroad men and students to fill the back room at the Atlantic with good' drinking, fair song, and a sturdy brand of poker.

But what I really liked best was dancing. I took pretty Edna Hammel to the dances at school. I journeyed to the ranches to bow over the hands of the lovely Montoya and Apodaca girls, as I had always hoped I would some day. At home in San Antonio I danced with Mother, or Felice, or even little Rosemary. I just plain liked to dance—and I still do.

In those days we did the waltz, the two-step and, to be fancy, the varsoviana. We, too, had music that caused our elders to sit up and wonder what we were coming to. St. Louis ragtime in the manner of Scott Joplin was popular, and from New Orleans "Jelly Roll" Morton had provided us with a heavy beat in ragtime by composing such classics as the "Black Bottom Stomp," the "Chicago Breakdown," and "The Perfect Rag." There was quite as much to make the ladies lift their eyebrows then as now if you happened to be looking through the vision of the day.

Popular songs were quaintly suggestive: "Mary Took the Calves to the Dairy Show," "This Is No Place for a Minister's Son," "If You Talk in Your Sleep, Don't Mention My Name."

New York City had been forced to prohibit women smoking in public places by a city ordinance and in Chicago, when the "sheath" dress, imported from Paris, with narrow skirt and no petticoat, was first worn, the police had to rescue the daring lady who wore it.

It was a great time to be twenty, as I suppose each succeeding generation concludes, and I was not at all put out when Gus decided I was not to return to the store that summer. He had other plans for me.

Eva, eighteen and definitely handsome, was back from Boston with her violin and Gus concocted the idea of a Hilton trio to bring culture to the New Mexicans whether they wanted it or not. Two of Eva's friends, Viva Head, a contralto from Prescott, Arizona, a western lass with red hair and a splendid dash of temperament, and Edith Chapman, a small pianist from Oregon, comprised the rest of the trio. I was to be the manager. It was my first experience at managing women and was not a success from any point of view.

The Hilton Trio, Conrad N. Hilton, Manager, opened its statewide tour in one of Colonel August H. Hilton's warehouses. More from curiosity than an avid interest in culture we drew a full house and at Socorro, our second stop, we were still among friends. At Magdalena, the mining town ten miles off in the bush, they would have filled the hall to see three live girls play hopscotch. Prematurely, I began to congratulate myself. All there seemed to be to managing a trio was to hire a hall, get the performers there on time, and take the tickets. The girls were having a lovely time climbing on and off trains and in and out of evening gowns. Chicago might be having riots over the "sheath," but my artistes were decorously covered from shoulder to ankle —wore high-button shoes, to boot. Still we seemed to be creating our own mild sensation.

Then we hit Las Cruces, eighty miles south, and in unknown territory.

Once again I hired a hall—$15—delivered the girls in their finery, and took my place at the door. But almost nothing happened. Forty-five minutes after curtain time there were six individuals huddled in the hall and I had taken in $4.50. The girls gave them one tune free and I gave them their money back.

Then I went directly to the telegraph office and wired

Gus: "Come and get the trio. I'm through." Father ordered us back to San Antonio for a powwow.

He argued me into taking my lovelies on west to Silver City for one last try. "After all," he said, "we're both Elks, and we have friends there."

Sure enough, those friends helped us sell our cultural package to the Elks Lodge for one evening show, and I helped the Elks by organizing a parade to announce our arrival in the manner tested and proven by Messrs. Barnum and Bailey. One ancient, as he tottered out of the Las Cruces fiasco, had whispered to me, "Nobody knows you're here, Mister," and I did not propose to make the same mistake twice. Our parade carried large banners announcing HILTON TRIO and CONCERT TONIGHT. At least they would know we were in town. We got $50 for the show, which more than met expenses. The girls had an enthusiastic audience and improved morale.

I then dragged them clear across the state to Carrizozo which was close to White Oaks, and where we were very well known because of Gus' now defunct stagecoach line. Here we were welcomed with open arms and I sold my beauties to the Chautauqua for another $50.

Suddenly Gus figured we were ready for the Big Time and ordered us to Albuquerque. What would have happened at this point had we not joined forces with a resourceful young reporter on the Albuquerque *Journal*, I do not know. But the reporter, Will Keleher, agreed to act as our "press agent" for our major appearances and we then sold the trio to the Elks in both Albuquerque and Santa Fe for $75 per evening, and returned triumphantly to Hilton headquarters in San Antonio with a sheaf of first-rate press clippings.

We had lost about $24 apiece on the venture, but we had seen a lot of country, met a lot of people, and the girls had their precious "notices" from the papers. I had gained a profound gratitude for the Brotherhood of Elks and a lasting affection for Will Keleher. It had been a profitable summer after all. While I had not yet discovered what I wanted to do with my life, I had certainly found out one thing I did *not* want to do. I did not wish to be a theatrical manager for a teen-age trio in the great southwest.

When I was twenty-one Gus offered me the management of the San Antonio store together with a share in the profits.

Prosperity was turning our corner again, the hotel could be abandoned, and Father began to look toward even newer pastures, namely the town of Hot Springs, sixty miles to the south at the tip of the Fra Cristobal Range.

Mother, once more having served cheerfully during the emergency, had put her foot down, and the whole family was moving to Socorro. "One, I wish to be near my church," she announced. "Two, I do *not* wish to send Rosemary and Boy and Helen off to boarding school for lack of a fifth-grade teacher—and Socorro has schools. Three, there will be decided social advantages for Felice and Eva."

As always when Mother finally made a decision, action followed immediately. Bag and baggage the troop was off to Socorro, first to a yellow house rented by Father while he built the gray stone "mansion" which had been so telescopically reduced in size before my more mature eyes.

The thought of having the Hilton enterprises in San Antonio all to myself was heady enough inducement for me to desert formal education forever. There now began a two-year period of running a very diversified business and shouldering full responsibility. I had to learn how to evaluate a credit risk, how to bargain, haggle, and trade with a variety of experienced customers. How and when to coast and how and when to push—and never to show urgency, irritation, or uncertainty. This was another form of discipline which served me well through the years.

The only fly in the ointment was Gus. Father either could not or would not back up his confidence in me by letting me alone. Partially because I was young, partially because his hand on the rein was uneven, I strained at the bit. I had always known my father as a man of moods, either sitting on top of the world, high with elation, or viewing it from a pit of black depression. Mother had usually insinuated herself firmly between the "moods" and the family. She'd say matter-of-factly, "Your father has the 'blues' today," and expect us to steer clear until the storm signals were hauled down.

Now I headed into the rough weather of his temperament with no buffer. As his store manager I actually preferred the "blues." When he was depressed he was very humble, came down on a special trip to tell me what a great guy I was—what a clever fellow. He needed me and was planning to give me stock in the store.

But the blues lasted too short a time. When he was on top of the world he'd yell at the thought of my sharing in the ownership. "By God," he'd chortle to anyone who happened to be within earshot, "this kid, this whippersnapper, thinks he knows as much as I do."

His laughter nettled me. "If only I could be thirty," I thought, "he wouldn't be able to call me 'kid' any more." Thirty seemed to me then a most desirable age, and as it turned out it was exactly that. But by then Gus was gone and I was many miles from San Antonio.

I learned at twenty-one how a man feels when he has been given a job but complete confidence has been withheld. It couldn't work. My "boss" drifted into the store like a floating leaf or a falling brick, depending on his mood, and I had the constant sensation that I was a minister without portfolio. Perhaps that is why, in later years, when I had carefully selected a man for a job I left him completely alone, knowing that either I had been *right* in my selection or I had been *wrong*. But he had to have a free hand to show which.

For myself, as Father's San Antonio manager, I wished heartily that he would devote more time to his new ventures in Hot Springs. I saw quite enough of him for business purposes each week-end.

Saturday night after I had closed the store I rode into Socorro for a dance or a party or an evening with the family. Sunday morning I took Mother to church. It wasn't hard to see that Mother liked Socorro—and her new house—and the schools—and the social activities.

"See," she pointed out complacently. "Felice is already in the social columns." And she was. Often. Annie Meyers, society editor of the Socorro *Chieftain*, to whom originality was an affectation, each week had one item about Felice, referring to her as the "amiable eldest daughter of Mr. and Mrs. A. H. Hilton." Carl promptly began calling her "AED" and this name stuck until she cried for mercy.

Felice was not only socially busy but was teaching in the Socorro grammar school where both Rosemary, aged nine, and Boy, barely seven, were pupils. Rosemary, much to her disgust, was in her eldest sister's class and with her usual resourcefulness made life so difficult for "AED" that Felice promoted her on nuisance value rather than merit to the next grade.

Much to Mother's delight both her older daughters were

romantically involved, Felice with Cony Brown, Junior, a brilliant young student at the School of Mines, whose father was a mining engineer much respected in our parts; while Eva, when she was not batting her long eyelashes at the local talent, was exchanging long letters with a Bostonian named Arthur Lewis.

Living now in this frontier Utopia, my mother sought to fulfill one of her dearest wishes: she invited Grandmother Laufersweiler and her several unmarried sisters to visit her.

New Mexico, as if to honor a beloved daughter, put on her finest sunsets, her outrageous moonlight nights, her most imaginative cloud formations. Socorro turned out in its best for tea, afternoon bridge, even dinner dances. But the visit was not a success.

"There aren't any green things growing," a maiden Laufersweiler shuddered.

"There isn't any water," groaned a second.

"Poor, poor Mary," lamented my grandmother. "It's so big —and so empty. It's Godforsaken."

Mary, who had heard that argument before, simply smiled. But I knew her heart hurt when she retreated into San Miguel's church and permitted me to speed her family guests on their way a full week before the scheduled time by taking them as far as Albuquerque. Fort Dodge, I realized, was Fort Dodge—and the Territory was the Territory—and the twain just would not meet at that moment. But what bothered me was the tendency of one faction to claim God exclusively for its own.

Once I had waved my grandmother and aunts on their way back to civilization, I gave my full attention to two important events then enlivening the growing town of Albuquerque. One was a musical, "The Gay Musician," playing one-night stands throughout the West and introducing an unknown actress. She had a magic quality, a rough dynamic warmth that seemed to reach out and set you on your feet rejoicing. Her name was "Texas" Guinan.

The second was a dinner at the Alvarado Hotel honoring the President of the United States, William Howard Taft. New Mexicans, after sixty-three years of Territorial status, were eager to be admitted to the union as a full-fledged state. President Taft, that night in Albuquerque, promised to support our pleas.

Less than a year later President Taft signed the bill admitting New Mexico to statehood. We had come of age.

At about the same time the President put his signature on the bill so much coveted by New Mexicans at large, Gus Hilton signed some papers much coveted by me personally. I, too, had come of age.

We had been fencing now for over a year, Father and I, with me a boy genius when he was depressed and a smart Alec when he wasn't. During the "blues" he would swear that he wanted to assign me stock in the store, and when he felt better he almost perished at the thought. I had ideas about the store but couldn't execute them because the owner wouldn't back me up consistently—only, say, on off Thursdays.

So I decided to catch him on an off Thursday and the next time he said, "Connie, you're doing a great job. I want to give you some stock," I was ready for him. I handed him a pen.

"Go ahead," I said. "Now is as good a time as any. Sign some over." And he did. Two weeks later I had put a few ideas into effect—the stock rearranged, a new line of plows on display—when Gus came thundering in. "What does a kid like you think he's doing—" he blustered.

"You've forgotten," I said serenely. "This 'kid' is now part owner of this store." That day I was a man. I had stood up to Gus.

The following year Eva, too, had grown up—and the first of Mother's brood was about to marry and leave home. Like that of Mary Laufersweiler herself, Eva's courtship with the Bostonian, Mr. Lewis, had been carried on by ardent correspondence.

"I like what I read in his letters," Mother told me.

"Does Eva let you read them?" I asked in astonishment.

"Now, Connie," Mother soothed, "a mother has to protect her children. You mustn't tell Eva."

Shades of my first girl, I thought, remembering my very proper mother and the scented pink envelope she had found in San Antonio.

"Yes, he writes like a lovely fellow," at which unconscious indictment she smiled happily. She was thoroughly pleased. Here was Romance, her beautiful Eva and a lovely fellow from a fine New England family, plans for a big wedding at San Miguel's with Father Pelzer coming from San Marcial to officiate. It was all as it should be.

Gus, not having the secret sources of knowledge open to Mother, was not so perfectly satisfied about his future son-in-law, and made the trip to Albuquerque to meet him and "look him over."

Next day he rode down to San Antonio looking puzzled. "Well, how is he?" I asked.

"All right, I guess," Gus said. "But he's a pretty fancy bird. I took him round for a drink, to sort of break the ice, and do you know what he ordered? A Gin Whiz. They didn't have one."

No, I thought, a Gin Fizz would certainly be outside the ken of a western bartender, whose chief function was to keep straight shots to the ounce so the house made a profit.

"Carl calls him 'Eva's Sunday School teacher,' but I don't think he is," Gus volunteered.

My brother-in-law-to-be. had certainly made a variety of impressions on my family. A lovely fellow. A fancy bird. A Sunday School teacher. I decided I had better go immediately to Socorro and, as the oldest brother, see him for myself. What I found was a very definite eastern specimen, complete with all the Dartmouth trimmings for which I had personally once yearned. I could see why Carl described Arthur Lewis as a Sunday School teacher. He was very correct. His manners pleased my mother, who continued to regard him as a lovely fellow. And he introduced enough Bostonian trimming to the wilds to be regarded as a very fancy bird. But underneath he was just a smart lad, very much in love with my sister, and I felt kind of sorry for him, having to pass, as it were, the inspection of the united Hilton clan.

Young Lewis was in the paper business in Massachusetts, and he was eventually to make a good many millions, to provide Eva with several magnificent houses, where Eva tucked away her violin and raised four children.

After the wedding, reported by Annie Meyers as "the social event of the year," we saw them off at the station. Watching them board the train, all eagerness to be off to independence and adventure, to a life of their own, I began to think.

I was twenty-three years old. I had been working for eleven years. So far I had earned a partnership in a store in the town in which I was born. But it was my father's store. A. H. Hilton & Son. A. H. Hilton & Shadow? a small voice within me was questioning. Wasn't it time I formulated a dream of my own?

I went to talk it over with Mother. She sent me to church. From there I walked around to talk to Olaf. I had an idea.

5. POLITICIAN, BANKER, CAPITALIST

My business with my cousin was political. H. O. Bursum had pole-vaulted right over the counter of the Hilton store into the chairmanship of the Republican Central Committee and the honored position as sheriff of Socorro county. Now I wanted a boost.

Republican-wise, things were popping across the nation. With our constitution accepted and our birthdate into the family of states officially set for January, 1912, Olaf planned to resign his smaller honors and go for the Big Plum—the governorship. Teddy Roosevelt, after four years of political retirement, had swung into action with a falsetto roar: "My hat is in the ring."

So was mine, I told Olaf—in a minor way, of course.

"I would like to run for the state legislature," I said.

My cousin sank behind his hand for a few minutes of deep reflection and then gave his verdict. "I think you'd run pretty good," said he.

I thought so, too. I knew every name and face in the country and, more important, they knew me. I had a fine case of political fever, my temperature so high I was sure I could do more than make a name for myself in Santa Fe. I could—and would—make the state better for New Mexicans.

Our first elections were spiced with the ruthlessness characteristic of a tough-minded, determined breed of Territorials who believed that "only the fit survive" and calmly expected each political contest to be rugged enough to prove which was which. My Democratic opponent entered fully into the spirit of the thing, with my own father in his corner. Gus wanted me to stay at home and tend to the mercantile business and he wasn't too particular how he accomplished his purpose, even to a steady supply of helpful hints on "how to beat that youngster."

I had a few ideas of my own, however, and when election day rolled round I piled up 1,821 votes to my rival's 1,578. Standing in the crowded Atlantic saloon on the night following my victory I overheard one of my valued constituents in conversation with an active Democratic worker.

"Don't think we don't know you voted a herd of sheep," said my friend.

"And don't think we don't know," said the rival camp, "that you voted the entire population of the Socorro cemetery."

Since the tone was one of awed admiration, I let it pass. The point was that I had won handily while my political mentor, Olaf Bursum, was defeated. It was very puzzling. I found politics like that.

Between my victory and my departure for the state capital, I dedicated my time to feverish efforts toward self-improvement. First, I tried to increase as rapidly as possible my life's savings. Second, I tried to better my elocution, the then current term for public speaking. Neither short course proved a spectacular success.

When Old John, a shaggy prospector who had haunted our parts for years, came into the store one night whispering sweet songs of a vast silver vein he had struck in the Oscuras Range, I listened. That was my first mistake. Then, my heady political victory having temporarily unbalanced my business acumen, I reckoned maybe my luck was running—that I could indeed "get-rich-quick" on another fellow's work. That was my second mistake. It cost me two wagonloads of supplies and several sleepless nights since Old John, queer and secretive in the way of many prospectors, refused to tell me exactly where our "fortune" lay buried. Later, when he hit town we signed partnership papers, still without Old John entrusting to me the exact location of our wondrous "colored" rock. "I'll take 'ee out thar tomorrow," he promised, "and we'll stake our claim." That was my third and final mistake. It cost me a coffin and several hours of manual labor.

For Old John's "tomorrow" never came. As he ambled from the store toward Bianchi's he suddenly dropped dead before my eyes, carrying with him the secret of our Golconda. For that I now thank him. A treasure map, or even one hint, had been the undoing of men older and wiser than I was. Why, to this day I might be looking for buried treasure, following another man's dream instead of my own.

In the absence of next of kin, I, as John's partner, drew the burial honors which I dispatched with all decency. If he was having a "mad dream," an hallucination sometimes granted old prospectors when their years run out in a kind of desperate frustration, I did not begrudge it to him. For a few weeks he had let me share his dream. I had the consolation of knowing that, for a small price, at least I laid him to rest with a full stomach. But when I dug Old John's grave I buried with him any will-o'-the-wisps that could lure me again into believing I could achieve an effortless fortune. For all I know —and for all I care—the silver may be there yet. But it was John's dream and John's silver, and in his own way he took it with him.

The dream of becoming a world-shaking public speaker was strictly my own. During my campaign, when the six hundred delegates to the Republican county convention nominated me in the Garcia Opera House, they called for a speech. I took one look at that sea of faces and ran like a desert pony. Individually, man-to-man, look 'em in the eye, I could talk to anyone. But lump those same individuals into an impersonal aggregate called a "crowd" and I froze. This could be fatal to a politician. So I bought a book, Grenville Kleiser's Course in Public Speaking, a "how to" book—we had 'em even then—which guaranteed to teach me in ten easy lessons how to enrapture any audience.

The author, however, had never met my audience.

If I expected the family at large to be impressed with my status as youngest representative-elect to our first state legislature—and I secretly hoped they would—I was disappointed. It caused scarcely a ripple. The grown-up members were busy about their own affairs.

My father, it is true, was actively furious, a positive reaction at least. But Carl had received an appointment to the United States Naval Academy at Annapolis and barely took time to look up from his packing to remark that "some folks want to be peanut politicians." I'll admit to being so hot under the collar I didn't shed a tear when he left.

Felice said it was "too sweet" and she had an appointment at the dressmaker, and did I think blue was her color? She and Rosemary were about to leave for what we regarded as a simple little visit to Eva in Massachusetts. Actually, for Felice, it was a very big trip, indeed. She already knew she would meet Cony Brown, Jr., in Chicago where he was at college and, if things went according to the dictates of her heart, she would not return to Socorro. Blue did seem to be her color, for Cony proposed to her in the blue dress and after the visit with Eva, Felice and Cony were married and Rosemary returned to New Mexico alone.

There must have been a tight lid clamped on Felice's fluttering emotions when we waved the girls off at the railroad station, knowing as she did that it might be a long goodbye. And so it proved, for Felice and Cony settled in New Jersey where she raised her four children, and she did not return to New Mexico to live until Cony's death many years later left her a widow. But our family ties were strong and it must have been with mixed feelings that the "amiable eldest daughter" boarded the train. Being Felice, she said little, except to remind Mother in her practical voice to take over her duties on the Ladies' Altar Society the following month.

It must have seemed to her then that life itself was tearing our family group into shreds for she could not foresee that the bonds of our affections were so strong that there was rarely to be a true parting in our family—and that beyond human control. In the years that have passed I cannot remember a single one that did not bring some of us together somehow, somewhere. Mother, the eternal matriarch, while never trying to clip a single wing, shuttled east and west, north and south, keeping our family ties a living, breathing, gossiping thing, while her offspring would cheerfully, without a second thought, jaunt a thousand miles out of their way to spend a few days together.

At that time I myself could not see that the clan was actually departing to follow their diverse destinies. I could see no further than Santa Fe and the fact that my political bomb had been a dud at home. I was truly hurt that no one seemed interested in my elocution. Even my dog Pancho, who accompanied me in the evening into the foothills where I could practice my oratory, was more interested in chasing rabbits than in listening to me.

It was Boy who soothed my ruffled feathers, who listened spellbound while I declaimed "The Midnight Ride of Paul Revere" and "The Boy Stood on the Burning Deck," my arms whirling like windmills, my mouth variously shaped like an "O" or warped to emit "pear-shaped tones." Together, my ten-year-old brother and I improved our diaphragm control by lofting a feather on a slow, even breath.

Had it been left to Boy, for whom everything I did still spelled magic, I hate to think what might have happened when I first addressed the dignity which was the state legislature. But finally Mother intervened, gently dousing my fervor with her cool common sense. The night she joined our practice session I recited with *feeling* my *pièce de résistance*, "The Charge of the Light Brigade," which I had practiced alone among the tamarisks trying to "fill space with my voice," as per Lesson Eight.

Mother listened politely and with scarcely a twinkle until the last of the six hundred rode valiantly into the jaws of death. "Very nice," she said, "for poetry. But if you ever make a speech, Connie, and up there in Sante Fe you might have to, you'll have to unlearn all this. You are not going to be a Chautauqua entertainer."

"But Mother," I began to protest, for most of the great speakers of that day were filled with rhetoric and oratory. Mother was ahead of her time.

"Connie," she said with conviction, "all those trimmings are sinful. You are hiding yourself behind a lot of gestures. If you're afraid to be *you*, son, you're throwing dust in God's face. He made you. If you have confidence in Him, you'll relax and be just what you are. You'd do better to pray about it than practice *this*." Whereupon she walked off with my book.

On the opening day of the legislature I did pray about it. I faced the crowd, kept my hands at my side and my mouth in a normal line, said simply what I had to say and sat down. It worked out very well that day. It has ever since. At any time, if I've been tempted to phony it up a bit, I remember that that's lack of confidence in *Him*, and I'll look pretty silly throwing dust in the face of the Infinite. My obligation, as far as I've been able to see it, is to be the very best *me* I'm capable of being, using the tools He's provided.

In Santa Fe I lived at St. Vincent's Sanitarium where the good Sisters, in those hardy, nerveless days, had more rooms than patients and offered excellent accommodations together with good food for a modest sum. Their unfailing cheerfulness and good humor was thrown in free.

Sometimes I needed the good humor more than the food for, during the early part of my stay, a week rarely passed without a nagging, unpleasant letter from Gus. My victory was his loss—and Father didn't like losing. Weekly he ordered me, in terms of picturesque abuse, to "give up that silliness" as soon as my term was over and "come home and tend to business." This only served to arouse my sense of manhood and defiance.

Finally, with as much dignity as I could command, I wrote to Mother: "Would you please explain to my father," I requested coldly, "that I have many important things to do, and I cannot do them if he keeps pestering me. I will not be writing to him again because I am very busy." I do not know what Mother said, but after that I did not get any more mail from Gus for quite a while.

How important the things I was doing would have looked to Gus, I cannot say. But I *was* very busy. That part was true. Starry-eyed, over-eager, and perhaps a little naïve, I was serving on eight committees, engaging in debates, and ultimately introduced nineteen bills of which only nine passed. I doubt that there is anything to match the enthusiasm and dreams peculiar to the very young politician except, perhaps, the frustration and disillusion when he finds himself blocked by precedent, procedure, "deals," and red tape, from setting the old world straight overnight. But disillusion set in slowly and at first I found the thought of having a hand in democracy in action stimulating and wondrous.

A state capital, even the capital of a fledgling southwestern state, was a great place for enlarging horizons. The Rio Grande valley had been my little world, the Territory of New Mexico my big world, for almost all my twenty-four years. Now, in Santa Fe, we talked casually of the eastern seaboard, the west coast, the Great Lakes, the North Atlantic, Washington, D. C. We were part of a family which extended from one ocean to the other and what happened in any state affected us all.

The *Titanic* disaster, with its loss of 1,502 lives, had such impact on this landlocked state where most of the inhabitants had never seen a wave, let alone an iceberg, that we walked the streets in mourning, carefully lowering our voices.

The advent of Teddy Roosevelt into our midst had a reverse but equally dynamic impact. As Teddy's hat flew into the ring, it sliced the Republican Party in two and when he whirled through New Mexico "feeling like a bull moose," he was campaigning as the presidential nominee of his own short-lived Progressive Party. His famous grin, his high falsetto voice, his advanced platform of woman suffrage, direct primaries, abolition of child labor dazzled us. When Woodrow Wilson, the rather colorless highbrow, defeated both the volatile Teddy and our old Republican friend Taft, we were mighty surprised. Why, the fact that Teddy, when shot by a fanatic in Milwaukee, the bullet penetrating his eyeglass case, the manuscript of his speech, and his lung, went right on, bullet and all, to make a scheduled appearance, was direct evidence of the "fit surviving." That alone would have spelled sure victory in New Mexico.

Strangely enough, it was our mutual interest in the amazing career of Teddy the Great that served as a bridge across the gulf which had estranged my father and me.

Gus had made a trip east to see the wholesalers who bought much of his wool and mohair. I got a brief, rather formal note asking me to meet him at a railroad station near Santa Fe on his return journey. Perhaps the invitation was a trifle stiff and self-conscious, but I could see through it. He wanted to be friends again—and so did I. I had an enormous regard for my father as well as a deep affection. So I met the train.

We had dinner together and, just at first, it looked as though there was no common ground on which to stand and offer the olive branch. I didn't care to offend him by discussing my political career in Santa Fe. He was reluctant to risk throwing fresh fuel on the old fire by talking of the business in San Antonio. It was probably one of the few times in our lives when my father and I were at a loss for words with each other.

Then we hit on Theodore Roosevelt.

After three courses of animated discussion on this seemingly inexhaustible and reasonably safe subject, the bridge was crossed, any friction forgotten. The handshake extended and taken following that meeting served to cement a new relationship between us. We were father and son—yes, but Father now accepted the fact that we were also man and man. He still wanted me back in San Antonio, but he had faced the fact that it would take honey instead of vinegar. He went away sure that he would some day find the honey—and left me to solve the deep things of politics.

Impressive as it might be to report that I spent my whole time in Santa Fe working for suffering humanity, the truth is that I managed to have a very good time as well.

What helped was that I was born an incurable romantic. It's just as well to face the fact squarely for it seems very often to go hand in hand with the dreamer. Whether I was interested in a hotel or a horse or a pretty girl, it was never to me just "hotel," "horse," "girl." The hotel was "the greatest of them all." The horse was a steed of nobleness and fire, whether it was Chiquita with her poor swayback or my latest elegant sorrel, MacDonald Streak. And the girl was Juliet or Cinderella or Mata Hari, and it was my firm intention to sprinkle stars in her lap. If she turned out to be, as she generally did, simply Minnie Jones in a new make-up, if she wanted nothing to do with stars but preferred "another strawberry soda" or "a man who turns over his *whole* paycheck *every* Friday," I was undaunted. Surely the next one would have better taste.

Truthfully I would not have had it otherwise. Being a romantic may bring some exquisite agony, but it also makes everyday things more fun.

When I went to the Inaugural Ball at the Palace Hotel honoring the first state Governor, W. C. McDonald, it was not enough for me that this was Santa Fe's most dazzling social event in years. It was not enough that I had finally, with the help of Will Keleher's brother Ralph, who ran a haberdashery in Albuquerque, laboriously assembled my first genuine dress suit. And lovely Jouett Adair Fall, vivacious daughter of Judge Albert Bacon Fall, star contender for our United States Senator—it wasn't enough that Jouett was one of the genuine belles of the southwest. When I led her out for the cotillion, the ornament of brilliants she wore in her hair became real diamonds. She was a princess. My dress suit was shining armor. And the Palace was not a hotel. As a polished, dashing courtier, I knew one day there would be something I could lay at her feet.

As it turned out, I was right. But it was, perhaps, an unfortunate choice.

These were very elegant dreams, not everyday things, to be sure, but not too long before I had been just as happy in Socorro with my dreams of the miller's daughter, Estelle Greenwald, ingeniously carving her initials, E.G., on everything from the oaken bucket to my wrist. One night I had the supreme thrill of thinking I had rescued her. We were driving through an Indian village in the buckboard when a spectacular lightning storm unleashed its fury right over our heads. Estelle was magnificently frightened. And I was magnificently brave, whipping my horse across those open spaces in a mad dash for the safety of the mill.

In Santa Fe not all my dreams were of princesses. With Jouett Fall I did the dignified dances of the day: the cotillion, the schottische, the two-step, the waltz. And she was regal indeed. But there was a girl come out from Chicago, a pert, frisky girl who knew the latest thing—the "animal dances," spawned by ragtime, which had scandalized the conservatives and caused mild eruptions from pulpit and press. From her I learned the fox-trot, the grizzly-bear, the bunny-hug, the chicken-scratch, the kangaroo-dip, and the camel-walk. They were not romantic, not graceful, but they made me feel worldly and sophisticated, and when the legislative session was over, I carried them triumphantly back to Socorro, the herald of the Jazz Age. With them I combined the newest in slang—Beat it! Getting your goat. Sure. Peachy. Classy. Nutty. Flossy.

If all this had the desired effect of dazzling the girls back home, it had quite the opposite effect on my long-suffering mother. She simply raised her eyebrows and asked, "Connie, didn't you learn anything *worth* knowing in all that time at Santa Fe?"

And so I told her what I had learned, the whole story. "But the important point, Mother, is that I've found something else I do *not* want to be. I do not want to be a politician."

From the Solid Seventeen in Santa Fe I had learned that there were "ways" of getting things done politically. In those days the election of a Senator did not lie with the popular vote, but with the legislature, and the Solid Seventeen were dedicated to catapulting Judge Fall into the Senate. I belonged to it partially from conviction, partially because Olaf was his strong supporter, but mainly because I thought the beauteous Jouett worthy of Washington. This I could do for her.

The jockeying for votes by over-eager senatorial candidates led to a riotous time, with four representatives being hauled off to jail, caught red-handed accepting bribe money. The House promptly dragged them out, "tried" and exonerated them. The Solid Seventeen resorted to no such obvious tactics in our efforts to elect Judge Fall. Instead, late one night, we invaded a joint session of the two Houses and marched into the Senate, announcing, "We will now elect Albert B. Fall to the United States Senate."

The Democratic leader had barely time to yell, "What's going on here," before Fall's nomination had been made, seconded and carried.

In the cold light of the following morning this procedure was regarded as more than unusual, it was declared illegal. But such is the nature of the politician that the waverers and stragglers had latched onto what they felt was an accomplished fact—and Fall was legitimately elected.

In view of what happened later I wonder now if I might not have done the Judge and his lovely daughter a greater service if I had kept myself to myself—or even campaigned for his opponent—but there was no way of foreseeing that the Judge would rise spectacularly from the Senate to the Cabinet, and fall in disgrace in the Teapot Dome oil scandal of the early '20s. Fall was convicted of accepting a bribe while Secretary of the Interior under President Warren Harding and spent the rest of his life in an effort to clear his name and save his family from tragedy and heartbreak.

I found out, too, in Santa Fe that, as there were "ways" of getting things done, there were some that could *not* be done, even by the President of the United States. One of the first things to offend President Wilson's sense of propriety after he entered the White House was a memorandum from the Indian Commissioner reporting the growth of polygamy among the Navajos. Wilson ordered it stopped.

"And how do you propose to stop it?" I asked the presidential agent who stopped off in Santa Fe.

"I've called a powwow with a dozen or more tribal leaders at Gallup. I shall simply tell them the Great White Father in Washington wants plural marriages to cease." He spoke with official nonchalance.

I knew the Navajos and the idea tickled me. "Let me know how you make out," I invited.

A week later he was back, his nonchalance sadly crumpled. "Well, I told 'em," he said, "and they just sat around on the floor in stony silence staring at me and smoking their pipes. So I asked how many wives each had. Some grunted 'three.' Some 'four.' One old boy admitted to seven. 'It's simple,' I told them, 'just pick the one you like best, then tell the others you're not going to live with them any more.

Isn't that a good idea?' The old boy with seven wives led the rest to the door in complete silence. Then he turned. 'Good idea,' he said, with no change of expression. 'You tell 'em.' "

I also found out that, while there were a few things the President couldn't do, there was practically *nothing* that an inexperienced young legislator *could* do. I knew real frustration from red tape and muddling, disgust at under-the-counter deals, and complete futility when I saw good bills, my own and others, defeated through self-interest, laziness or cumbersome procedure.

I got one adopted, probably because it didn't mean much then. But I had become convinced that the automobile would, indeed, be more popular than the bicycle, and offered some highway marking plans which are in use to this day. I got one idea turned down, truly a dreamer's dream, to prohibit motion pictures from depicting crime. But the one I cared about most, my public moneys bill, was shouted down for a reason that finished me forever as a politician.

I had studied very carefully the system of banking the public funds, and found that they were deposited as political favors in ramshackle banks all over the state. These banks, fly-by-night affairs, folded almost before the paint was dry, carrying the state funds into nothingness with them. Yet from the floor, the objection to my bill separating public money from political control, was that it was "against the interests of the poor people."

"After that," I told my mother, "I concentrated on learning the camel-walk until it was time to come home."

"And what are you going to do now, Connie?" she asked matter-of-factly.

"Mother, I know exactly what I'm going to do. I'm going to be a banker. That's the real ambition of my life. Some day, you wait and see, I'll have three or four banks all up and down the Rio Grande. You'll be proud of me. And I'm going to start right at home—with the New Mexico State Bank of San Antonio."

In the beginning Gus did not approve of the New Mexico State Bank of San Antonio.

"It's just more nonsense," he said crossly. "There's plenty to do around the business. What more do you want?"

"A bank," I said.

And since this nonsense at least would have the advantage of being directly across the dirt road from the store, he decided to humor me. Gus figured he had finally found the honey that would keep his wandering boy at home.

"Put me down for 10 shares of stock," he said grudgingly.

That was $1,000 worth of honey and I promptly threw in my life savings, $2,900, to sweeten the pot. My goal was 300 shares, and that left me only 261 shares to go. Dusting off my saddle, I mounted my horse to ride out on a new kind of selling trip. For the first time I was selling myself, my word, my integrity—stock in a scheme that was tangible only in my head.

It wasn't easy.

All summer I rode back and forth, up and down, pouring out a torrent of words, smiles, firm handshakes; pushing a few shares at a hacienda, a few more to barely accessible trappers' camps. I tackled the rich widow to whom I had once sold a pair of shoes and was again soundly "damned," but I sold shares.

I found out a lot about raising money. I found out, too, that once I had a handful of impersonal stockholders, I couldn't quit if I wanted to. I didn't want to, of course, but there was a yoke of responsibility that attached itself firmly the minute someone had trusted me with their capital. I carried this yoke easily, joyously, for I was young. I was confident. I was determined. But it was my first introduction to a strong feeling of protectiveness toward investors that has been one of the dominating forces throughout my life.

By September of 1913, I had reached my goal, 300 shares, $30,000. The New Mexico State Bank of San Antonio became a chartered fact and opened its doors in the small square building which today stands empty near the ruins of Father's store.

But if I thought it was "my" bank, I was sorely mistaken. The larger shareholders who attended meetings elected one Mr. Allaire, a seventy-year-old Hilton business rival, to the presidency. I was fobbed off with the nominal title of cashier—no salary.

"Wal, Connie," one old rancher tried to soothe me, "you're a good youngster and a smart youngster, but Allaire's had banking experience back in Peoria, Illinois. You want the bank should be run right, don't you? It's going to be a big thing for the community."

"And just who thought of that first?" I demanded. "Just whose idea was it? Who did the work?"

Sure, I wanted the bank run right. It was *my* bank. I had made a lot of promises to a lot of people to get it started. It was my dream—and my work—and my prayer—that had made it a reality. But how could I run it right, protect the investors who had trusted me with their money, if those same people froze me out?

I was bitterly hurt and I was fighting mad. I didn't know which way to turn. So I went across the dusty road to St. Anthony's and had a long talk with the Lord about justice and injustice. I inquired of St. Joseph if this was the way a worker should be treated. At first it was strictly a one-way conversation as I bombarded Heaven. When I had poured forth all my bitterness, I knelt for a while, empty of anger—calm, receptive to ideas. At the moment I had none of my own.

Then something became clear to me. It was not all the little people who froze me out. It was a small group of what was called the "smart money" boys. They had frozen the both of us out: me and the little investor who trusted me. There *was* something I could do about it. It would take a calm head, a quiet tongue and patience.

I waited for the annual stockholders' meeting. I watched the post office in the store until the notices began to filter in. That was on a Saturday morning. The meeting was scheduled for four o'clock Monday afternoon. Gus, whose sense of justice had been offended, who could deal with me personally as he saw fit, but was bitterly upset when I got the wrong end of the stick from outsiders, had watched with me.

"You know, they froze us both out," he said, his eyes glinting. "I don't like it one bit."

He stood by the corral, chewing a bit of hay, and watched me saddle my horse that Saturday morning. I didn't have to tell him what I had in mind.

"Good luck," he said.

I don't know how many miles I rode in those next two nights and days. I don't know how many people I talked to or where I cornered them. I remember being in some queer places at queer times. But when I galloped back into San An-

tonio just before the stockholders' meeting I had collected
enough proxies to control the bank.

Only there didn't seem to be a bank to control any more.

"There's been a line of depositors taking out their pennies
ever since the doors opened this morning," Gus informed
me. "I doubt there's two silver eagles left to speak to each
other in reserve. Now you don't suppose Allaire heard
what you were up to?" he grinned. "A man wouldn't start a
run on his own bank, would he?"

"Some men would," I said, stalking in to wash the grime
from my face, sick with disappointment, blind with rage.

I didn't give Gus a chance to tell me that he, too, had been
busy while I was gone. I saw his grin and, warped with emotion, it meant only one thing. Allaire had played right into
Gus' hands. He was glad I'd failed. Glad to have me forced
back into the store by fair means or foul.

I did my father a grave injustice.

When we entered the directors' meeting I felt I was going
to a funeral. . . . "A dream lies dead here. May you softly
go before this place, and turn away your eyes. . . ." * Mr.
Allaire knew I had come to take over the bank. And I
knew Mr. Allaire had left me no bank to take over. But neither of us knew that Gus, God bless him, was holding two
aces in his sleeve.

"The cashier," announced Allaire with satisfaction, "will
give you the closing statement. We're busted."

"Not quite," said Gus grimly. He dug around in his stuffed
pockets and produced two wires, one from the Texas Bank
and Trust Company of El Paso, promising a $3,000 cash de-
posit by the following morning, the other a pledge of a like
amount from the First National Bank of Albuquerque.

We *had* assets. Shortly, we had a new president, one agree-
able to Gus and to me. I was now vice-president. At twenty-
six I was a banker. It remained for me to become a successful banker. This meant work, work—and more work.

I had gotten stockholders. Now I needed depositors, more
assets, money with which to make loans. If the rancher, the
trapper, the small Mexican farmer wouldn't come to us,
we'd have to go to them. But this meant more than just a
house-to-house, sheep-pen-to-sheep-pen canvass to pick up

---

* From the poem "A Dream Lies Dead" by Dorothy Parker. *The
Portable Dorothy Parker* (The Viking Press, Inc., New York).

money for deposits. It meant a very concentrated job of educating our people to the advantages of banks. For most a teapot or a buried chest or an old-fashioned safe had proven a reliable repository for years. They knew nothing of savings, of interest. I had to show them that letting my bank guard their money would mean more money for them. It wasn't easy. They were suspicious of the idea. To some it didn't sound logical. To others it wasn't safe. And actually there wasn't a lot of money in the teapots, the chests, the safes. Father still banked the most plentiful commodity in New Mexico in his warehouses, their produce.

But little by little, $5.00 by $5.00 deposits, the bank grew. Two things I did not have to worry me. Bad checks. And bad loans. The rubber check was something my careful customers never thought of and, while the ability to borrow, the function of a co-signer who owned property, had to be explained to many of them, once they got the idea they were scrupulous about their payments.

It took a lot of time. It took a lot of effort. But day by day we prospered until at the end of two years we could show assets of $135,000. Then I considered myself a great success.

Although it was hard for me to admit, there were other things of importance happening in the family, in New Mexico, in the world.

Gus had acquired the first automobile to be seen in our parts, a Model "T" Ford touring car with a hand crank, no top and hard tires. At first this was piloted by an imported chauffeur—not an elegant fellow, but a mechanically minded youth versed in the ways of this sputtering beast. Then I learned to drive and found high adventure even on the journey from San Antonio to Socorro over the rutted roads designed for wagons. When Father himself learned to drive, which he always did with great gusto and very little respect for his car, the chauffeur became a mechanic and Gus opened the first garage in San Antonio.

The Colonel was the first person to drive an automobile over what he named the "skyline route" which followed the wagon road from Magdalena over the Black Range, through Winston, Hermosa, Animas Canyon, Cave Creek Hill, and into Hillsboro—a route which up to that time was used only for horses and wagons. The journey, which Father made alone, was a perilous one. When he reached Cave Creek

Hill, always a terror for teamsters and horse-drawn vehicles, he was almost forced to give up the trip. Finally Gus solved the problem of ascent by putting the Ford into reverse and going up the hill backward so that the gasoline would feed from the tank to the engine.

From this and like adventures, Father developed a definite concern for the development of proper roads. "These things," he remarked to me sagely, "are going to change the transportation world entirely."

When Gus got hold of an idea, he did something about it. Once convinced that the future of New Mexico was bound up in her ability to build good roads, he began going about the countryside, from town to town, ringing a cowbell up and down each main street. When he had attracted a goodly crowd he stood in the front of his Model "T" and made speeches. "Improve the roads," Father would exhort. "We must have new and better roads!" And when the state didn't build them fast enough to suit him, which I could have told him they would not do, he built one himself.

The first decent dirt automobile road through San Antonio was the handiwork of *El Coronel* and some of his men. It was known for years as Hilton Boulevard.

Over the newly built Hilton Boulevard, a short time later, I drove the bucking Ford to the railroad station in Socorro and met my mother's old friend from Fort Dodge—Em. Emma Rank had finally decided to come west and marry Mr. Buell, the stationmaster. She was past fifty now but had all the charm of a bright new Valentine, and was chockful of the gentle flirtatious ways of the 1880s and the very latest gossip about what was going on "back home."

She bridled and blushed to report the newest "novelty"— twin beds—which my uncles were now selling, over my grandfather's protests, in the Laufersweiler store. Aunt Em further described the tango, but balked at instructing me in this newest dance to reach the advance posts of culture.

She and I got along famously. She was young in heart then; and, since I saw her only the other day, I can report that she is young in heart at ninety-six. Aunt Em was actually more in sympathy with my role as a gay blade at this point than my beloved mother.

It is true: I did work, work, work. But I also, as usual, found time to play, play, play.

In Albuquerque a group of eligible bachelors had formed

the Thirty Club and since I was not only a bachelor but a capitalist and banker, I was one of the select thirty who were considered eligible as well. Once a month we held a dance at the Odd Fellows' Hall which had the best dance floor in town. The Club developed a reputation as a short cut to marriage—and if you squired a girl to dinner at the Alvarado Hotel before the dance it was tantamount to announcing your engagement.

Will Keleher had been induced to join, protesting rather violently that now, as a struggling young lawyer, he was quite ineligible. Here, too, for the first time, I met Joe Goodell, who was to prove a staunch friend—and Alice Herndon, whose brother J.B. was to become one of my most valued associates. But my most constant date was pretty Eleanor Vaughey. It was Eleanor's father Emmett, once a successful clothing merchant in Illinois, who gave me an order on his deathbed several years later that was to change the entire course of my life. I not only took Eleanor to the dances, I took her several times to the Alvarado for dinner. But, alas, she married someone else.

I thought very well of myself romantically in those days. Also, I must confess, much to my regret, that I was a bit of a wag. I remember having cards printed:

Conrad Nicholson Hilton

Heart Broker

Beware of Fakes, as I am the Original "Honey Boy"

Love, Kisses and Up-To-Date Hugs a Specialty

I also fancied myself as a versifier and recall sending invitations to a dance I gave at the opera house in San Antonio, which I composed myself. I think it went:

> We oft meet with reverses and
>   disappointments too,
> And often get to feeling sad no
>   matter what we do.
> But cheer up, make the most of life,
>   be happy while you may,
> And be our guest for an evening to
>   dance dull care away.

But by 1916, there were a good many serious matters to be sandwiched in between banking and romance. Germany had begun her march of terror through Europe and cast a long shadow over the whole world. The war had played havoc with the mercantile business and Father took a substantial loss before he gave up and sold out. He was thinking of a bank himself now, in Hot Springs. Carl graduated from Annapolis so Mother with Rosemary and Helen went to Maryland for the exercises. Mother returned with pride in her eyes, but something else as well, something we began to see in women's eyes more and more, apprehension, tension, the shadow of sorrow. The *Lusitania* had been sunk by a German U-boat and to a man, Americans were shuddering over German atrocities. We were feverishly near war.

At about that time I made a trip through the southwest contacting other banking interests. I was dreaming bigger—that chain of banks again, Lordsburg, Deming, Roswell. But everywhere there was talk of war. Would we get in it? Could you be too proud to fight?

Closer to home, south of the border, Pancho Villa still played tag among his native mountains with General Pershing and there had been several definite clashes between United States and official Mexican troops. Many expected outright war to be declared on this front.

I stopped at the Grand Canyon en route back to San Antonio to sort my thoughts. How did I personally feel about the war? I was very interested in my bank. I was doing well. I talked it over with a young man I met there in the hotel, Ira Casteel, another young banker from Denver.

"I just can't make up my mind," said Ira, "how I feel."

"I can't either," said I.

We were together when the fantastic news was released that the British Secret Service had intercepted and decoded a message from the German Ministry of Foreign Affairs to the German Ambassador in Mexico, instructing him to offer Mexico an alliance as soon as war broke out between Germany and the United States. Part of the promised plum was Mexico's right to "reconquer the lost territory in New Mexico, Texas and Arizona."

"Well," I said to Ira, "they just made my mind up for me. I want to be a banker. But I don't want to be a Mexican banker. Right now I want to be an American first and a banker second."

We smiled and shook hands and I went back home.

It took a little time to sell the bank. But by the time I did,

America was at war. When I enlisted, I think I was doing it to make the world safe for bankers. Yet the war was to change my whole life. While I dreamed of banks for two more years, they were pointless dreams. Past dreams. When I came back from the war I finally found my life's work. And it wasn't in the banking business.

6. TO TEXAS VIA PARIS, FRANCE

It would be simple to say that as a soldier I was neither a heel nor a hero and dismiss the whole matter. After all, "our" war, World War I, is an old one now and all that can possibly be said about it has long ago been said. Yet when a man has been to war, however passé and obsolete that war may become, however small a part he may have played, the experience is part of him. Some things he gains. Some things he loses. Some he learns. To some degree he suffers.

Whatever happens it changes him. He may be better or worse, but he can never quite be the same man he would have been. I know I wasn't.

When I enlisted in 1917 I was a fat young frog in one of the smallest puddles of the world. But I didn't know it. I honestly didn't. I was accepted for Officers' Training Command and the minute I took the train for the Presidio, San Francisco, I began to find out.

There wasn't much family left to bid this soldier goodbye. Carl was already on his ship somewhere "out there." Rosemary, at seventeen, had determined to become an actress and taken her pert prettiness to Boston where she was studying at Emerson College of Oratory under Eva's wing. Mother, whose memory seemed made of less elastic fiber than most women's, made no fuss when Rosemary took it into her head to do her own kind of pioneering. And she made no fuss when I joined up. She looked me squarely in the eye and said: "All right, Connie, but you'll have to take some of the prayer load. I can't do the praying for the whole family."

Mother, Gus, Boy, and little Helen waved me off at the Socorro station. Three days later I was in San Francisco.

San Francisco was my first metropolis. Sophisticated world travelers have fallen in love with the Golden Gate and the gleaming city that climbs up and down the surrounding hills. To a young man from the vast emptiness, the deserts and wastelands of the southwest, it was a vision of another world.

92

We had our own beauty, our browns and purples and reds, our dryness and brilliant sun, but I could not have dreamed San Francisco, for the images necessary were foreign to my imagination. Tall, tall buildings, parks and trees, a blue finger of water that widened to an embracing sea, gentle fog and mist, the tang of salt sea air with no sand between the toes, flower vendors, violets on the women's coats, the women themselves with wispy hats, furs, spotless white gloves, businessmen in faultlessly tailored dark suits and derby hats, and for laughs streetcars that climbed crabwise up the steep hills, and fat ferryboats that bustled across the Bay.

The first friend I made at the Presidio belonged to this incredible city. His name was Bill Irwin and he sat beside me in officers' school. Irwin was a graduate cum laude from the University of California across the Bay in Berkeley. He knew every pigtail in Chinatown, every pirate along Fisherman's Wharf, and most of the lovely young ladies who had tea at the Palace. He also knew the answers to all the most difficult questions on our examinations. I found him an invaluable friend.

Bill, like all San Franciscans, enjoyed showing me his town and liked my wide-open enthusiasm for everything from Alcatraz Island, a stern rock in the middle of the Bay to the elegarit ladies who graciously wore our violets.

When we were both shipped to Camp Lewis, Washington, Bill was convulsed at my reaction to rain. Never, in my entire twenty-nine years all put together, had I seen as much rain as I did in a single month in the state of Washington. I could not believe then that there was not some freak fault in the heavenly plumbing. But I had never been in France. That came later.

We both applied for overseas duty and were transferred to Jacksonville, Florida. En route to Camp Johnson we had an hour stop-over in Denver and a hasty letter brought my banker friend, Ira Casteel, to the station. We talked of our last meeting at the Grand Canyon and Ira said he had been rejected by the Armed Forces because of a heart condition. Now he was trying to join a Red Cross unit. "I'll get there yet, Connie," he said, "and when it's all over we'll do something big together." He didn't know how right he was!

At Camp Johnson there was nothing to do but wait—and we waited. That's one thing you learn in the Army for sure. We brushed up on our poker and our French and shined our brass. And then we waited some more. One night I heard the young lieutenant, Don Weber, in the next bunk muttering over a letter. "Lucky France!" he said. Then he launched into a lyric description of a YMCA singer who was sailing to entertain "the boys" that brought the whole barracks to what looked like battle alert. But Don wouldn't part with her name or address.

I got them though. I found a way. Her name was Ruth Bush, and before very long I got to use both name and address. For on Valentine's Day, 1918, we were ordered "over there."

Bill and I took our embarkation leave in New York. This was my second metropolis, but most of the sagebrush had fallen from behind my ears while looking up Nob Hill, and New York didn't scare me a bit. It was bigger. It was taller. The people seemed in a greater hurry and there were more of them. While San Francisco had welcomed me, New York was hidden by an impenetrable armor. "I don't think an outsider could crack this town," I observed sagely to Bill as we strode along Broadway. "It has been done," he said, "but would be mighty difficult." This decided, we registered at the Astor and had a beer.

Twenty-four hours later I left Bill and went to Boston. Rosemary met me at South Station and I was plunged into another city, a city so marked by the past that I could almost hear Paul Revere clattering through at midnight. We lost ourselves in crooked streets, saw Boston Common, the Old North Church, Bunker Hill Monument, Beacon Hill, the permanent imprint of another kind of pioneering that was done in America long before the West was more than a wild dream.

We came back to the present when we arrived at Eva's and I said hello and goodbye to some brand new nieces and nephews. From Eva's I went to Franklin, New Jersey, and saw Cony and Felice. This sister had some interesting advice on how to keep out of *trouble* in Gay Paree. I met another set of new nieces and nephews and then, on March 14th, Bill and I boarded our ship. The ship was blacked out and camouflaged, but under the wartime masquerade Bill assured me, she was the *Matsonia*. We waited twelve hours in New York harbor just to keep in practice and then the *Matsonia* sailed for France.

From the day we sailed I kept a diary, a small red leather-bound book whose first few pages contained such useful bits of information as the population of Canada, the antidote for arsenic, apothecaries' weights, and the eclipses of the sun for the year 1918. On the first night out I found a section for my personal description and duly entered it: Height—6'2". Weight—160. Hat size—7⅝. Shoe size—11½. Coat—38. Shirt collar—16. Drawers—34. I am pleased to think that I could almost, not quite, be outfitted from this list today. The hat size, at any rate, is exactly the same.

In the back of the book I noted down when my insurance premiums were due, the dates on which I owed money on some coal land leases which I had held over from my banking days, a few French phrases that had been suggested to me as useful, and Ruth Bush's address.

I was very faithful to that diary although there was little outstanding in my own activities to report. Basically most of it could have been included in the life of every ordinary Yank soldier in the American Expeditionary Force.

"*Four days out to sea:* An awful lot of ocean, a lot of wind, cold. *Five days out:* Storms. Seasick. I want dry land. Anywhere including No Man's Land. I prefer dodging bullets to the ocean. *Five Days Later:* I have learned to sleep in my clothes with my life preserver on. *The Greatest Day of All:* We are well inside the submarine zone and we meet our convoy of six destroyers. That night Bill and I sit on deck in the moonlight on a glassy sea and I pen a letter to Ruth Bush to be posted when we land.

"*March—France:* We have landed. I am in *Blois*. The champagne is cheap. $1.50 American. Nobody drinks water. They all drink 'vin' which is cheaper still. I never dreamed there was so much wine in the world. And three Armies are drinking it. I do not like it very much so I will never be a proper Frenchman. . . . Rain! Mud! The people here wear wooden shoes. Many widows. Much mourning. Those French phrases are not the right ones. I got lost today and couldn't find my way for hours. Streets like Boston. Nobody seemed to know I was asking for directions. Worse still, Madame, the lady of the house where I am billeted, simply cannot understand when I ask directions to the 'chamber.' . . . We are all getting lectures and physical drills at the Caserne preparatory to going up. A Second Lieutenant was leader of a squad consisting of a complement of Captains. How's that??? Rain. . . . My cousin, Joe Hilton, showed up at the Caserne with a bottle of something very special from Bordeaux. The AEF is a small world. More Rain.

"*April:* Bill Irwin and I are both ordered to the 304th Labor Battalion at Bordeaux. We leave at the right time. Cooties have been discovered in the straw sleeping mats at the Caserne. . . . *Bordeaux:* We are here. But where is the 304th. After some inquiries we are advised that our company has moved on to the front. We set off to join them via Paris. . . . *Paris:* In April. Rain! Hotel Continental. Big Bertha shells the city all night. St. Joseph's Church. Beautiful! Cafe Paree. Maxim's. The American Bar (note to Gus: they would know how to make a Gin Whiz here!). . . . Arrive at *Toul.* It takes two days to locate our outfit at a French Caserne a mile from town. See our first aerial dog fight. We are fourteen miles from the front. . . . Our job, handling freight and supplies, transferring goods from standard to narrow gauge railroad which runs on up to the front. Rain! Mud! Those trenches must be knee-deep. If New Mexico had rain like this it would be Paradise. . . . I wish I would get some letters from home. . . . There is a beautiful Cathedral on a hill overlooking town. You can see it from every point of the compass. But try and get there! I did today for early Mass. The streets are so crooked you go right on seeing it but don't make any headway. More rain. . . . We start a Checkers Tournament. It is not fair to play 'pokaire' with the Frenchmen. They simply do not understand 'bluffing,' and we take their money.

"*May:* Ruth Bush is coming to Toul. Oh, for the sight of an American girl. . . . *Mother's Day*—I send off a letter and a cable to mother from the officers' YMCA. I wish my mail would catch up with me. . . . Ruth Bush arrives. She is very pretty. We walk along the canal in the center of town under the Catalpa trees. . . . Ruth sings a concert and we have a romantic ride by night watching the signal rockets go up to light No Man's Land. . . . Ruth and I walk in the country. . . . The mess plans a picnic. Eggs eighty cents a dozen. One chicken, $3.50 American. No more picnic. More rain. . . . We watch Major Lufberry, famous ace with the Lafayette Esquadrille engage a German fighter plane directly over Toul. Other planes show up. They chase off toward the German lines. Later we hear that Lufberry has been shot down and killed. All day long the French brought flowers to lay on his casket. . . . Ruth leaves. More rain. . . . A Big Offensive about to start. Trains pass back and forth. Every kind of troop, Italian, Algerian, Sikhs, French, American. These dinky little trains sure do the business after all and how they do it is more than I can understand. . . . Troops trains every fifteen minutes. I go up to the front around Dead Man's Corner. I know now how it got its name. . . . One of our Majors marries an Army nurse. We tie cans to the car just like at home. The Frenchmen think we are crazy. Maybe. . . . *Mail! Letters from home!* I leave the scented envelopes go. Gus is full of talk about *his* bank now, the First National Bank of Hot Springs. Mother tells me about all the nieces and nephews although I can't keep them straight yet. Helen writes that Boy is taking the lead in the Socorro high school play and is very funny; whether this is by accident or intent she does not say. She liked the sewing kit I sent from New York and they both enjoy the periscope. Socorro seems to be growing bigger, says Helen (she should see New York!) with a new theater completed, Mr. Brown building a hotel with a swimming pool, and the Ocean-to-Ocean Garage about to open. She has learned a new prayer which she copies off on the back of a Third Liberty Loan application. It makes me out a hero. I get a little choked up and walk under the Catalpa trees alone, in the rain, and wish I was as noble as they think me. I can hear the guns at the front where the heroes are. . . . More mail. Ira Casteel is in Wales with the Red Cross. He made it, bless him! Rosemary is coming along famously, she says. Next stop Broadway.

"*June:* Sixteen planes overhead at one time. Moonlight night later and more aerial visitors. Irwin can sleep through it all. . . . Another moonlight night and Ruth won't be back for three days, by which time it will be raining. Pvt. John McCall from a plantation way down North Carolina says: 'If dem Bushes don't come over tonight deys outa bombs.' But the 'Bushes,' which seems to be North Carolina jargon for Boches, 'is not outa bombs.' They even wake Irwin up. . . . I am getting complaints about the food. A heavy day at the yards and Billy Richards can't work. 'I'se got indigestion, Lieutenant.' 'How come, Richards?' 'Yesterday it's pork an' beans fo' breakfast. Last night pork an' beans fo' supper. This mawnin' pork an' beans agin. And I never *was* no hand at eatin' vegetables.' . . . I hear they are using 500,000 carrier pigeons for delivering messages over here. They fly a mile a minute thru all weather and any barrage and ninety-five out of a hundred get through. I'll write that to Boy. I'm glad Boy is only sixteen. . . .

"*July—Sorcy:* I have been transferred. Bill has gone to Mononcourt. I miss the old outfit. The First Division comes back from Château Thierry, what's left of them. The Second Division comes back. The Marines are still with them. Joe is with the Second. These are *men.*

"*September:* We are notified of a Big Offensive. Hospital trains pull up on the sidings. From one to five the Big Guns. At five the Infantry advances. You can hear it but you feel so helpless. . . .

"*October:* I am shifted to Battalion Headquarters at *Raon l'Étape* in the Vosges Mountains. Our Captain at Raon is Jay C. Powers. This is a fellow I'd trust. . . . Riding into Toul in the side car to meet Ruth we are hit by a *Chinaman.* I receive a minor cut. My single battle scar! *A Chinaman!* . . . Captain Powers is now Major Powers. He's a great guy. . . . The mademoiselles of Raon play tennis! Maybe I'll be here long enough for my mail to find me. . . . No such luck. I am ordered to Paris to the office of the Chief Purchasing Agent. . . . *Paris*—Our offices are in the Hotel Elysee Palace on the Champs Élysées. My assignment is liaison work (with *my* French) and takes me to all the offices in the city. . . . Move into an apartment with three officers from Camp Johnson at 11 Rue de Bassano. We have a French cook. This is going to war in style. Mother should see this! But Paris does not seem like war and I wish I was back up there somewhere in the trenches. . . . The last day of October: Armistice with Turkey.

"*November 5th:* Armistice with Austria. *November 11th:* Armistice with Germany. Signed at five A.M. Effective at eleven A.M. The greatest sight I ever expect to see! About two million people throng the streets, yelling, cheering, mad with joy. Flags are waving, innumerable processions, everybody kissing everybody, jumping up and down. Anything goes. The Americans celebrate too. Without a word they leave their place of business and join the crowd. . . . The celebration has lasted all night and will go on all day. Words can't describe the feeling of joy for these people who fought four long years and all of a sudden realized their hope of victory and peace. I am glad, however, that I won't be in any more celebrations for some time to come. Joe Hilton must have heard about the big doings in Paris for he rolled in tonight. . . .

"King George of England arrives in Paris. . . . King Albert and the Queen of Belgium arrive. . . . A few days later it's King Victor of Italy and his son, the Prince of Piedmont. All of them roll up the Champs Élysées right under my office window through the cheering throng. If the miller's daughter from Socorro could see me now! . . . My brother Carl turns up for a few hours before leaving for Brest. His ship will be part of the honor guard going ninety miles out to meet President Wilson's convoy. . . . Major Powers is in town. So is Bill Irwin. The apartment is bulging. We do the Folies Bergère and the rest of Paris but somehow I have no taste for it. I want to go home. The Major says, 'Some day, after this is all over and we are back in America, we'll get together. Don't forget.' All over Paris, all over France, buddies are saying this sort of thing. But I have a hunch we three will do it. . . . I get a letter from Gus. He has paid, on my instructions, $1,200 out of my funds on those blasted coal lands, and I'm beginning to think we won't get enough coal out of them for mother's living room grate. Gus has been buying mohair at eighty-two cents which seems to me too much to pay. He has been to Boston and wants me to come home *via Cape Town, South Africa*, which is, he says, the biggest producer of mohair in the world now that Turkey has been knocked out. Rosemary has a friend, says Gus, whose father owns a large goat farm. I wonder if my father knows how far Cape Town is? I answer the letter simply saying I am fed up with Paris, and foreign lands, and I wish now they would send me home *tout de suite*."

But Gus never got that letter. I dropped it in the mail on my way to midnight Mass at St. Joseph's on Christmas Eve. Eleven days later I made my last entry in the red diary.

"*January 4th, 1919:* Cable from mother received telling of father's death."

"Father killed auto accident. Come. Mother." That was the cable. Five weeks later I was at Camp Dix, New Jersey,

U.S.A. and got the details. Gus in the old Ford, on his way down Hilton Boulevard to keep a business appointment on New Year's Eve, skidding on some ice, turned over in a ditch and was gone in seconds. After thirty-six years of high adventure in the West, sixty-four years of active living, Gus had died on his way to work. He would have had it that way.

On February 11, 1919, I got my discharge from the Army at Camp Dix and took the first train for home.

If I hadn't gone to war—

If Gus had lived—

If Emmett Vaughey had chosen another man for his confidence—

If a stranger in Kansas City had stuck by his word—

If!

But I did go to war, and Gus died, and Mr. Vaughey chose me and the man in Kansas City turned out to be an angel in disguise. All those disconnected events worked to shape my life.

For three months after my return to Socorro my life seemed completely without pattern or purpose. I was in fact restless, impatient, depressed for the only time I can remember when my digestion, my credit, and my romantic life were all sound.

It was spring. The tamarisks were in bloom. But I saw no romance in anything. Something had to be very wrong. And this is what it was. I had come home from France unscathed only to find I was a Displaced Person.

It was a paradox. I was home, yet it wasn't home. I was the same man, but changed. I had gained a vision of a wide, wide world beyond my native river, my native state. My former dreams were bound up in past limitations.

Nor was I alone. From San Francisco Bill Irwin wrote, "So here I am admiring my sheepskin cum laude and wondering what on earth to do with it." And Major Jay C. Powers in Chicago complained, "I simply do not know whether to go on to California and practice law—or what?"

We were only three among thousands of uprooted ex-service-men. The whole country was asking, "How're You Gonna Keep 'em Down on the Farm, After They've Seen Paree?"

A distant cousin who had been plodding along unhappily

as an office accountant hung up his uniform and electrified the family by becoming a pioneer airmail pilot. A young Spanish rancher near San Marcial disposed of his magnificent but heavily mortgaged family hacienda and moved his family to Albuquerque where they huddled quite happily in cramped quarters surrounded by the comforts of city civilization. Irwin reported meeting a private from our outfit, a New Yorker born and bred, once afraid to venture off city pavements, who couldn't get those neat French farms off his mind and was working on a turkey ranch in Sonoma County.

This was the tune of the times. The interruption of normal life had sent many men back to view the limitations of their former life, to search restlessly for their own adventure, their own destiny.

What was mine?

To me, Socorro had become a toy town of adobe and wood surrounded by emptiness. Was I content to become a fatter frog in this puddle?

I was not. That much war had done to me . . . or for me.

And the sudden death of my father—

With Gus' going there was no business left. If I had lost my first partner, San Antonio had lost something too. Already the town had begun to crumble. I spent some time on the old familiar ground trying to untangle the numerous business matters that had been stuffed in Gus' pocket (for he never learned to use a desk) on the night of his accident.

He didn't die at the top. He didn't die at the bottom. In property, real estate, investments, and cash, Mother could realize roughly $40,000. Boy, grown two inches taller than I, was headed for Dartmouth. That left only Helen, the baby, now a young lady entering high school, at home. Gus had left enough to protect them. But that $40,000 was his entire material legacy. The town he had helped to build seemed to lose heart with his passing.

There was an emptiness up and down that portion of the Rio Grande that Gus had staked out thirty-six years before as his own. Like a house whose owner has gone away, the doors began to sag, the shingles to fall, and soon the structure itself would collapse. This was sensed and mourned beyond the limits of his family.

On the main street of San Antonio one morning, an old Mexican stopped me, his Latin emotions, always close to the surface, spilling over in tears. Reverently removing his sombrero, he spoke in halting English: "Oh, Señor Conrado, how much we miss *El Coronel*. Everybody grieves. It is a so great loss."

It was true. It was also the tribute that Gus, lying in the rugged graveyard of Socorro beneath the blue Magdalena Mountains, would have liked best.

But here I was very much alive, thirty-one years old, trying to rebuild with the tag ends of my father's dream. Day in and day out, I sat in a small $30 a month office in Socorro's Val Verde Hotel, trading a carload of mohair. A few furs. Some cattle. A bunch of hides.

After eighteen years of work—clerk at thirteen, then trader, merchant, speculator, politician, banker, soldier—I had wound up playing penny ante with somebody else's chips!

It didn't spell success.

I had wanted to be a banker before the war. I wanted to be a banker still. But I hadn't got a bank. All I had was $5,011, my accumulated savings. And big ideas.

"I just can't seem to get started," I told Mother.

Once again my mother's faith was like a rock. One word from her that she needed me and I would have played out my hand in Socorro. But she gave no such word. She could lose her husband, her companion of thirty-four years, and turn right around and send her oldest son, who had just come home, away again. She loved us both. She knew grief. But she did not know the meaning of fear or loneliness or dependence on human agencies, because her Protector would "never leave her or forsake her."

And so it was my mother who said very firmly, "You'll have to find your own frontier, Connie."

When I hesitated she added, "A friend of your father's, a great pioneer, once said, 'If you want to launch big ships, you have to go where the water is deep.'"

So I went to Albuquerque.

The fact that Albuquerque was where Emmett Vaughey lived never crossed my mind.

I knew Albuquerque was only a pond, as Socorro was only a puddle. But it was a starting place. There were fifteen thousand people there now, and the number of easterners who sought its healthful climate had brought it something of a cosmopolitan air. I took with me my $5,011, plus a determination to some day see New Mexico wear that chain of Hilton banks. It seemed a good, sizeable dream . . . and I was used to it.

It turned out to be a nightmare.

I took none too gentle abuse from my friends and outright ridicule from businessmen. This wasn't the time. This wasn't the place. My bankroll was too small.

"I *started* a bank once on $2,900," I protested.

The most courteous thing I was told was to forget it. Times had changed. Business was full up. Like Gus when he hit Santa Fe in the 1880s, I found existing merchants had most of the opportunities well packaged. They assured me the same would hold true all over New Mexico. Why didn't I go back to Socorro where I had a good thing, where I had established the first American Legion Post and been its commander, in short, where I was known, had a reputation, and be grateful that I already had a niche cut out for me? It was discouraging.

And then Emmett Vaughey sent for me.

Mr. Vaughey was dying, and we had always been good friends. In the days when I took the lovely Eleanor to the Thirty Club dances, I had developed a warm admiration and respect for her father. Now the gay places saw little of Eleanor who, with her mother Tess, was caring for the dying man. Her father saw few people. But he wanted to see me.

I was pleased. Perhaps there was some small thing I could do for him, something to repay him for his generous friendship. Instead he wanted to do one last thing for me, possibly the single biggest thing that was done for me in my career. Raising himself on his pillow, Mr. Vaughey said in an urgent, clear voice:

"*Go to Texas, Connie, and you'll make your fortune.*"

It was an order. Just like that!

Suddenly, for the first time in months, I felt vitally alive. Not only my mind and my nerve ends responded, but my enthusiasm, excitement, sense of adventure stirred to instant alertness.

Something within me agreed. "He's right!" it said.

I didn't believe in oracles or crystal balls, nor had I liked taking orders in France where someone "back there" who had a lot of facts you didn't suddenly upended your plans and set you off in an unexpected direction. I learned to take those orders because it was the voice of authority. And it saved my skin several times.

Now I was hearing the voice of experience. And I had a hunch these were my new marching orders. True, I had never thought of Texas, but I thought about it now. Emmett Vaughey had facts I didn't. In the '90s he had given up a conservative business in Illinois for the oil fields of Oklahoma. He still got reports from wily, experienced oil men.

Oil! That brought me up short.

"You're talking about oil, sir," I said. "What do I know about oil?"

"Just what I know. Only you've never *seen* it. Where there's oil there's activity. Money. Business. Building. Merchandising. Banking. You name it!"

I tried to visualize a state booming under the fabulous oil flow from the Burkburnett and Ranger fields. Oh, we'd heard about them. The $200,000,000 yielded in two years from the Ranger fields alone had sent everyone scurrying about leasing oil lands right here in New Mexico. Only it had come to nothing. But certainly down there there would be activity. A Texas oil town would be as wide open with opportunities as Socorro had been when Gus hit there during the mining frenzy.

Mr. Vaughey and I were riding the same train of thought. "Texas is the new frontier, Connie. It's only the beginning. . . ."

What had my mother said? "You'll have to find your own frontier."

"My stake is pretty small," I was thinking out loud. "If they laugh at $5,000 in New Mexico, it's probably cigar money in Texas."

"That part's up to you. The difference is, there's nothing to put it into here. Granted it isn't much, but it's a start. If you've got what I think you've got, you'll make it grow."

There was the challenge, the adventure. Could I go into Texas with $5,000 and make it grow?

I looked at the older man and noticed the bright spots of excitement on his cheeks. I remembered how ill he was.

"It's a good idea," I said, standing up. "I'll come back tomorrow and we'll hash it over."

"Sit down," said Mr. Vaughey. "I haven't got all the time in the world. I can't get up and go myself; I would if I could.

But I've got a partner for you. L. M. Drown. I've known him longer than I've known you. He hasn't got capital but he's got savvy. He's been a small-town banker in Oklahoma, and in San Diego. He wants to go down but he's got a wife and kids and can't do the prospecting."

"Suppose I go down and look around and report back to you," I suggested.

"I'm not apt to be here. You find a good thing, you sit on it and holler for Drown. He's got contacts. He'll come. I'll tell you how strongly I feel, Connie. I'm leaving Tess some insurance money. Everything else is tied up. But I want her to send part of that down to you after I'm gone. You ride herd on it. Put it where it will do something big. I know you can. I have faith in Texas and I have faith in you."

Did I have that much faith in myself?

I had been looking for my dream. A big one. The pieces suddenly fell into place. Here it was. My own frontier. . . . Where there's oil there's activity . . . banking. . . . A string of banks in *Texas* . . . If you want to launch big ships, go where there's deep water. Go to Texas, Connie, and you'll make your fortune.

"I'm sold," I said. "And . . . thanks."

I went to Texas on the next train.

If a stranger in Kansas City had stuck by his word— I would have bought a bank in Texas.

Granted that's what I set out to do. Granted I tried my best, in Wichita Falls, in Breckenridge, in Cisco. And if I had succeeded I would, I know now, have been a very mediocre banker and gone broke besides. Within a few years when oil, the banker's security, dropped from $3.00 to $1.00 a barrel, most of the banks went broke.

I didn't buy a bank. I bought something better. The minute I stepped off the train in Texas I knew Emmett Vaughey had been right. There were fortunes to be made in Texas. You just had to find a good thing.

Will Keleher was with me when we hit Wichita Falls. Even the conservative Will, with a growing law practice, had heard enough about Texas to want to have a look around. The first thing we saw was a town roaring like a blast furnace. It was hard to get meals, next to impossible to get beds, and inconceivable that a man could think of buying a bank.

I put the question squarely to the president of the first bank I saw. I was eager.

"The price?" the man said icily. "Why, it isn't for sale at any price."

I should have been discouraged. I wasn't. Evidently business was as good as it looked—and it looked good. Here was boom town vitality, jostling crowds, a whirlwind of excitement that was as stimulating as an icy shower after the drowsiness of the Rio Grande Valley.

There were oil men in laced boots and flaring trousers, each one a potential millionaire. The nearby Burkburnett fields were pouring black gold into their veins. There was the colorful riffraff that follows in the wake of sudden money, smooth-faced gamblers, smooth-tongued promoters, a sprinkling of painted ladies, more obvious than smooth. Between the two, catering to all, were the banks, false-front emporiums, over-crowded restaurants and hotels.

There were no saloons. The Eighteenth Amendment had closed the package store. But there was a seemingly endless supply of corn liquor, quite disreputable stuff, and alcohol with which those lucky enough to have a bathtub made what they deceitfully called "gin." Men were still protecting their lives and possessions with guns.

It was lusty country. Tall men. Tall tales. Giant laughter. Feverish work. Fierce fighting. I wanted in!

Will Keleher didn't. "I'm shoving off, Connie," he said. "I've got a nice growing law practice and nobody to look after the office. This is mighty interesting, but a little high on the hog for me."

Wichita Falls was too "high on the hog" for my bankroll and when Will pulled out for home, I moved on to Breckenridge, west of Fort Worth and not far from the Ranger fields. It was the same story in Breckenridge. Even the drinking water was loaded with oil. And there was nothing for sale at any price.

I headed for Cisco, farther south but comfortably close to the Ranger fields. Here was a new kind of Romance, a search that knocked everything else from my mind. I thought, dreamed, schemed of nothing but how to get a toehold in this amazing pageant that was Texas.

It was waiting for me in Cisco.

Cisco was a cowtown gone crazy, but basically still a cowtown. I had a feeling it had been there yesterday and would be there tomorrow, that there had been citizens on the street when only children bothered to dig holes in Texas dirt. Besides, it looked closer to the size of my stake, and it had four banks. Call it hunch again, but Cisco *felt* right.

I went straight from the railroad station to the first bank I saw. It was for sale. I had a mounting sense of excitement. There was no trouble about examining the books and from what I saw there the price was right. The absentee owner wanted $75,000. Better and better. A bank, at the right price, in Texas!

The difference between the price tag and the amount pinned inside my coat didn't bother me. You could, I thought confidently, always get money on a good thing. For once I was too impatient to bargain. I dashed back to the railroad station and wired the owner in Kansas City that I was prepared to buy at his price.

Then I cruised around town. I was dreaming big. I had visions of laying the cornerstone of my banking empire right here, and went back to wait restlessly until the owner should deliver it into my hands.

He did nothing of the kind. Instead, the telegrapher handed me a message which read: *"Price up to $80,000 and skip the haggling."*

There it was. The telegram that changed my life. The stranger who went back on his word . . . and in such an arrogant fashion that I saw red. "Skip the haggling?" Why I'd already, against all my instinct and training, skipped the haggling. I didn't like that kind of a raise. Once, many years later, I was to stand raise after raise from a man named Healy to get the biggest hotel in the world. I didn't like it then. I didn't like it that day in Cisco. In fact, I wasn't going to stand this raise.

"He can keep his bank," I informed the startled telegrapher vehemently. Then I strode out of the station and across the street to a two-story red brick building boosting itself as the "Mobley Hotel."

The Mobley Hotel, when I first saw it, looked like a convenient place to sleep. Nothing more.

I wasn't through with Cisco. I was playing out my hunch. But I figured I'd play a steadier hand if I could rest in a bed for a few hours. The milling press in the hotel lobby acted like sardines clamoring to get into the can. From behind, from the sides, the crowd tried to push into the tiny funnel around the desk clerk. Since I was tall, in excellent condition and determined to get a room, I plunged right into the spirit of the thing and was within speaking distance of the clerk, when that harassed individual slammed his book shut and hollered: "Full up!"

For a stunned moment the crowd milled in a circle, I with them, and then, like children playing musical chairs, dove for the few seats the lobby boasted. I wasn't expecting it and lost out. Leaning against a painted pillar I tried to decide what to do next.

A granite-faced gentleman was making his way methodically about, giving here a push, there a push, trying to clear the lobby. Finally he worked his way to my side.

"Sorry, fella," he said, looking anything but sorry. "Come back in eight hours when we turn this lot loose. You may have better luck. But we don't allow loitering in the lobby."

I was hot under the collar. First I couldn't buy a bank. Then I couldn't get a place to sleep. Now I was accused of loitering. I was about to explode when a thought struck me.

"You mean you let 'em sleep eight hours and then get a complete turnover?" I demanded.

"That's the idea. Three times every twenty-four hours, day in and day out. They'd pay to sleep on the tables in the restaurant if I'd let 'em."

"You own this hotel?"

"I do," he said bitterly. "I am tied to it with an anchor and chain. Every nickel I've got is sunk in this glorified boarding house when I ought to be out there in the oil fields making *real* money."

"You don't seem to be doing so bad."

"Not," he said shortly, "if you're willing to settle for the hotel business when guys are turning into millionaires overnight. If I could get my stake out of this place . . ."

"Are you saying," I spoke slowly, fighting to keep any trace of excitement out of my voice, "that this hotel is for sale?"

"Fifty thousand cash and a man could have the whole shooting match including my bed for the night."

"Mister, you've found yourself a buyer," I said.

He gave me a suspicious look. "You don't get the bed 'til I get the cash."

"I don't want it," I retorted. "I want to look at the books."

Three hours later, after a careful inspection of the Mobley books, I thought a man would be crazy to want oil. If they told the story, this had banking beat all hollow. I watched the lobby for another hour, wary of planted "guests." But if Mobley had salted this mine, everyone in town and his brother had to be in on the act.

I wired L. M. Drown that I'd found something and then slept on a bench in the station. As Mr. Vaughey had predicted, Drown came running, arriving on the noon train. He was pretty excited. When I explained the deal his eyebrows went up. "I'm a banker, man. I don't know a thing about hotels."

"I've had a little experience," I said, possibly stretching a point, considering the size of the family hotel in San Antonio, "and when you've had a look at this, you'll be ready to learn."

I escorted him to the street and pointed proudly to the Mobley. "*That*," said Drown, "is a hotel?"

"It is a cross between a flophouse and a gold mine," I replied. "Just be glad the people around town have so much oil in their eyes they can't see it."

After looking things over carefully, Drown shook his head. "The man who'll sell this is either a crook or he's crazy."

"Oil-crazy," I said.

"It's a good thing," Drown said. "I'd sure like to get in on it. But I can't swing it."

"You are in. I'm cutting you in," I told him. "You can be manager of the Mobley. What we've got to do first is buy it."

We needed to know exactly how much we had to raise. That meant bargaining and I rolled up my sleeves. Mobley was a gem, a worthy opponent. He knew when to howl, when to run, and when to clamp down. It was a first-class bout and we could both enjoy it because we never let the deal get out of hand. He wanted to sell. I wanted to buy. At $40,000 we shook hands. Mobley gave us one week to "transfer funds."

"But not one day more. I mean it!"

Then I began to put together my first buying group. I had one-eighth of the money on me. Drown moved another $5,000 when he turned up with an oil man, one C. P. Smith, who was looking for an investment. Mother mailed a check for $5,000 and a rancher friend in Socorro came in for another $5,000.

We had used up four days. With half the purchase price in my hand, I approached the Cisco Banking Company. I had rehearsed my sales talk on Smith and Drown. I could have saved myself the trouble. The president knew all about the Mobley, his bank was loaded with money and, since we would outright own a half-interest, they were more than prepared to give us the necessary loan. It was almost too easy.

Then the rancher's check bounced.

When the notice came to me by mail, we had twenty-four hours to close the deal in cash, or bow out. It looked like we were through. We couldn't find another $5,000 in town, and it would take too long to get it from New Mexico, even if we should turn up another partner.

One thing I knew I had to do immediately was inform the Cisco bank. Their loan was being made on our $20,000. We didn't have $20,000. I set off for the bank feeling as if I were going to a wake. I could taste again the bitterness, the defeat I had felt when I'd worked hours on end, ridden miles to gather proxies for the San Antonio bank only to have Gus announce that the president had started a run on it.

But that time Gus pulled a rabbit out of the hat. I didn't have a rabbit, nor even a mouse.

Anyone following me to the bank would have thought I'd gone crazy. First my steps lagged, while I tried to make the dream last. Then I'd increase my pace almost to a run, to get it over with. Lag. Run. Lag. Run. Finally, there I was. There was nothing to do but go in.

I sent a fervent, if confused, prayer to St. Joseph, approached the bank president, and dropped my bomb.

Nothing happened. He didn't throw me out. He just pressed the ends of his fingers together, swung his chair from left to right, and thought. I was thinking, too, feverishly.

Finally he spoke. "It's rough. You had a bonanza right in your hand."

Then an idea came. Startling, but worth a try.

"This rancher friend of mine," I said. "He owns his ranch in New Mexico outright. A conservative valuation would be $20,000. Why don't you loan him the $5,000 on his ranch 'til he gets in a liquid position? I'll wire for his power of attorney to act for him. The money'd be here. The check would be good. We could go through with the deal."

For a moment he didn't say anything. The Mobley was hanging in the balance. Then he said, "Fair enough."

And that was the way it happened. I raced off to the telegraph office, leaving Smith and Drown in a coffee shop gazing steadily at our hotel, as if it might vanish if they took their eyes off it.

The following day, at noon, the Mobley changed hands. I was in the hotel business. And I hadn't been in the hotel business five minutes before I knew this was *it*.

I sent Mother a gleeful wire: "Frontier found. Water deep down here. Launched first ship in Cisco."

"Mister," drawled the telegrapher. "You sure you know what you're saying? There's never been a boat in Cisco. I've lived here all my life. There ain't even any water."

"You can launch ships in oil," I said sagely.

"Boy, you sure musta struck it rich."

I thought how right he was. Back at the Mobley, Drown reported we were full up . . . even and including his bed and mine. That night we slept in the office and I dreamed of Texas wearing a chain of Hilton hotels.

It took some doing to make that dream come true.

7. INNKEEPER, TEXAS STYLE

My first five years as an innkeeper in Texas involved me in murder, suicide, reunion with wartime buddies, my first flier at buying diamonds for a lady—and a series of romances in which girls played little part.

I found myself developing a real crush on each prospective hotel.

Love, of course, had its blind spots. It made no difference to me if the hostelry in question was past her prime, down at the heels, her tattered slip showing. In those early years most of the hotels that could be courted on my bankroll were exactly like that. The first gift my dowagers got from me was usually a face lift.

Romance blossomed the minute I could see through a frowsy façade to potential glamour—the inherent ability to make money. I had no interest in hitching onto any hotel without a dowry. Satisfied as to this, after a careful check of her background, books, location and asking price, I would go a-wooing despite grime, soot, ragged carpets and sagging furniture.

Bankers and businessmen, asked to sweeten the courtship with a loan, were known to suggest a funeral instead of rejuvenation for some of my finds and I got quite accustomed to hearing my latest flame labeled a "dead or dying dump." I must have been a positive thinker because none of this daunted me. If these men didn't share my imagination and vision I knew some who did and I got the money elsewhere.

After my first three dowagers showed their true beauty in healthy bank accounts and neat profits, when my investors (including myself) could count on getting our money back in two years, or even one, my romancing commanded more solid respect in banking circles.

The Mobley in Cisco, my first love, was a great lady. She taught us the way to promotion and pay, plus a lot about running hotels. She was indestructible, the ideal hotel to practice on. L. M. Drown and I did just that.

It was at the Mobley that I tried out two principles that have been basic in every one of my subsequent operations from Waco to Istanbul.

The first came to me as the result of a nightmare.

Drown and I continued to sleep in the chairs in our cramped office to free more bed space, and it made for restless nights. Drown, who had shown a remarkable aptitude for hotel managing, carried his problems into his dream world and murmured fitfully in his sleep about having no room but providing a bed "with three *other* gentlemen." Since I awoke frequently with the need to refold my long legs and rid myself of cramps or pins and needles in slumbering members, I suppose his murmurings sparked my nightmare.

I dreamed old man Mobley was back nudging guests with a billiard cue to settle them on the tables in the restaurant and saying to me, "I told you they'd pay to sleep on the tables if I'd let 'em." And my father, old Gus, was waving my L. C. Smith twelve-gauge hammerless shotgun, the one I had bought in San Antonio with my first major wage increase at the age of thirteen, and saying, "You lost an eighty-pound opportunity. You could have gotten a keg of nails for the same freight. *You'll never get rich that way.*"

I awoke wide-eyed and perspiring, shook the weary Drown to semiconsciousness and said excitedly, "This hotel's got too much waste space."

"So *that's* why I'm sleeping in this cracker box," Drown grumbled. "I wondered."

"Come on and I'll show you." I dragged the protesting man out into the lobby.

The drowsy night clerk jerked to alertness and eyed us with amazement but said nothing as I pointed toward his long desk. "That desk is too long by half. And that dining room would take twenty more beds."

"So . . . they could eat off the beds and sleep on the desk," Drown said. "You crazy, Connie?"

"You wait 'til morning and see how crazy I am," I snorted.

"Okay," said Drown. "Now could I go back to sleep 'til then?"

Drown went back to our cubbyhole but I prowled the main floor. By sunrise I knew exactly what we'd do. For us, the profit was in beds. There were plenty of hash houses in Cisco to cater to the undemanding palates of our guests.

I ordered in carpenters to close the dining room and split it with partitions, just space enough for a bed and a dresser. Then I had the main desk cut in half and a news and tobacco stand installed. Another corner of the lobby surrendered an ill-used potted palm to make way for a small novelty shop which we rented immediately. Inside of a few weeks our books showed that we had taken on a good thing—and made it better.

I decided there and then that the trick in packing a box is to pack a full box. This had nothing to do with crushing or crowding, only the intelligent use of what is available. I have never had reason to change my mind. Truthfully, the manner in which waste space is unearthed and utilized can mean the difference between a plus and a minus in an operation. And a very exciting part of the game.

Why, I found waste space even in "the greatest of them all." The four giant columns in the Waldorf-Astoria's beautiful New York lobby were phonies, decorator's items, completely hollow and contributing nothing to the support of the building or the stockholders either. When we had *vitrines*, shiny gold plate and sparkling glass display cases, built into those columns, discriminating perfumers and jewelers fought for the privilege of displaying their wares there.

After revamping the first floor of the Mobley, I had the second idea that has become basic in all Hilton hotels. I was pleased with it but even more pleased that I, who a scant month before had been too muddled to deal with the simple problem of a carload of mohair, seemed to have come alive again. "I know something else that would make us a better hotel—and eventually more money," I told Drown. "*Esprit de corps.*"

"I'm all for it," said Drown. "How do you get it?"

"Same way we got it in the Army," I said. "Pride plus incentive. Wages won't do the whole job. We had to sell the idea that our men belonged to the best durn outfit in the A.E.F. and they were the ones who made it that way."

I grant that our twenty-odd employees were stunned when I assembled them for our first pep talk. They liked the attention, however, and they were very pleased to hear that Mr. Drown and myself, while able to front for them at the bank and in the lobby, were completely at their mercy once a guest got beyond the front desk. "You're the only ones who can give smiling service," I said. "Clean rooms, spotless halls, plenty of fresh soap and linen. Ninety per cent of the Mobley's reputation is in your hands. You get steady jobs, good money, pay raises, *if* Cisco means the Mobley to travelers. It's up to you."

Self-interest plus pride added up to increased efficiency and we simply blossomed with *esprit de corps*. That is, Drown and I and the staff did. We had one holdout. Our partner, C. P. Smith.

Here was a mistake we had made even before we took possession of our first hotel. A silent or absentee financial partner does not need any talent for the hotel business. But C. P. Smith was neither absent nor silent and, while he was a good oil man and a decent fellow, in our line he was strictly no-talent.

C. P. Smith did not like people. He did not even like people who paid to stay in our hotel. And he was not backward about saying so.

"It's a risk every time I go out to lunch and leave him behind the counter," Drown informed me. "Why I come back and he's been hanging on to room keys and cussing at the customers. Why? 'He only does it to annoy because he knows it teases.' There *ain't* no reason."

One of our early discoveries was that our guests were mighty sensitive along purely social lines. Emily Post's troubles ended once she had decreed which fork was correct for baked Alaska—but ours had only begun when we realized that, whether our guests used the right fork or no fork at all, each one looked to us to uphold their precarious position on the social ladder.

I made this discovery personally when, during the lobby renovation, a practical painter with no aesthetic sense designated the twin doors off the lobby simply MEN and WOMEN. Before the paint was dry, one of our female guests informed me she was a *lady* and had never been so insulted in her life. And one of our male guests, who outnumbered the ladies four to one, glaring at the offending doors, told me we were "ruining this joint." From that day forth through our portals passed only *Ladies* and *Gentlemen!*

Except, of course, in the eyes of C. P. Smith.

The climax with Smith came one night when Drown and I were holding down the lobby, Drown listening with the animated sympathy of the born hotel host to a homesick middle-aged salesman while I, overdue at an important date with our banker, grew restive as the head engineer of a big oil operation favored me with the story of his life. Just at the point where I felt I would have to insult our friend or take him with me, Smith, glowering and champing on an unlit cigar, strode through the front doors. I signaled him for a lifeline and he purposely missed the signal. Somewhat annoyed, I called out, "Come over here a minute, C.P. Here's a fellow I want you to meet."

Deliberately C.P. looked the engineer over, rolled his cigar several times and replied coldly, "No, thanks. Already know all the people I want to know."

So we bought him out. The bank shied at our giving him $10,000 on his original $5,000 investment. But the Mobley was willing and able to pay for our mistakes and I, for one, thought it was cheap at the price.

With one smooth-running hotel under my belt, I was well aware that two would be better. But I had a couple of things on my mind before I could devote myself to finding the next one.

One was a girl. The other was a working partner. The girl, Ruth Bush, my thrush from No Man's Land, was in Indiana. The working partner I wanted, Major Jay C. Powers, was in Chicago. I tackled them in that order.

I hadn't danced so much as a cake-walk since I hit Texas and the heavy moonlight made me long for a real waltz with Ruth. That much I got. One waltz. It had been almost two years since I got her name from Lt. Don Weber in Florida and then beat him overseas to make use of it. But Don had beaten me to Indiana and staked his claim, a permanent one. I got a single farewell dance with the bride-to-be.

When I said goodbye to Ruth I was saying adieu to the ladies for a good many years until, in fact, I was thirty-seven and saw a little red hat in church in Dallas. But that takes me ahead of my story. From the minute I left Indiana 'til then, except for an occasional date, my hotels took all my time and attention and females were just lady guests.

In Chicago I had better luck. The Major and I sat over dinner at the Blackstone Hotel, and I drew word pictures of the hotel trail in Texas, using many of the same sales points Emmett Vaughey had used with me.

"Texas," I said, "is the place to make your fortune."

I am glad to think now that I told my Major the whole

truth, not just one side of the picture. For my invitation to Texas turned out to be, for him, an invitation to tragedy, although neither of us could foresee it then.

"The stakes are big," I said, "but it's a risky business."

The Major, still suffering as a Displaced Person, tended to find risks appealing.

"I'll tell you how tricky it is. Emmett Vaughey is dead now, God rest him," I told Major Powers. "But Tess' financial advisors think the risk is too high for her to invest any insurance money with me. *And*, if I were one of her advisors, that's just how I'd feel."

"First you sell me, then you unsell me," the Major grinned. "You don't scare me a bit. I want in! I haven't got much stake but you tell me where to start and I'll be on my way."

"Start in Fort Worth," I said. "That's the best oil town in Texas. Find us a hotel and wire me."

The Major was off for Texas the next day, while I hung around Chicago trying to learn more about our business. I wanted to familiarize myself with the supply markets so no salesman or purchasing agent could razzle-dazzle me.

Chicago was jumping in the summer of 1919. A daily air-mail service had been started between Chicago and New York. Hogs on the hoof, much to my horror, brought $23.50 per hundred-weight at the stockyards, the highest price known until that time. As I poked around I didn't feel any hankerings toward this metropolis. Texas was big enough for me and had a special excitement all its own.

I thought I was about the luckiest fellow there was. Funny, I think so still. I do believe in luck. But the kind I believe in has to do with people, and being in the right place at the right time, and receptive to new ideas. I thought I was lucky to have won Emmett Vaughey's friendship, to have Major Powers on my team. Jay was still not only a man I liked, but a man I respected. A man whom, as I had written in my diary at Raon l'Étape, "you could trust." I was lucky to have men of his and Drown's caliber with me. I was lucky always to have steady, courageous backers like my mother and Ira Casteel. The value of buddies was something you learned in the Army where your life depended on how well a hundred other men carried out their assignments. In the Army you were as good as your buddies. In Texas you were as good as your partners. Later, when I reached the rarefied air of Big Business, I learned to call them "associates." The facts remained the same. All my life long I have only been as good as my associates, and in them have found my good luck, my fortune.

Major Powers found a hotel. I was debating traveling from Chicago to Texas by way of Toledo, Ohio, to see Jack Dempsey and Jess Willard fight for the heavyweight championship of the world when his wire came. It was a good thing, for it would have been a long detour to see Dempsey win in three rounds on a technical knockout. Jay's message left me no choice. "Have struck pay dirt. Come running."

When I arrived in Fort Worth I sent for Drown. Drown's reaction to the Melba Hotel, the Major's find, was the same he had awarded my Mobley.

"*That*," said Drown, "is a hotel?"

"Don't judge by appearances, boy," the Major rebuked. "She has sixty-eight rooms and you should see her books."

Drown liked those books well enough and admitted cautiously that the Melba appeared to have sixty-eight rooms. "But how *long* will she have them? Might tumble in a heap tomorrow. This one could get us in trouble with the sanitation department. Connie, even with second sight I cannot see buying this hotel."

"We don't aim to buy," I said soothingly. "It can be leased for $28,000 or less."

The Melba was our dowdiest dowager. Her original color was forever lost beneath a thick coat of grime, her interior wore a half inch of grease, her carpets threaded away to bare floors, her sooted window curtains looked like last night's false eyelashes. Her general air of shiftlessness cried neglect through the years.

"I don't see it," said Drown. Neither did the Texas State Bank of Fort Worth. I had got the lease down to $25,000. The bankers advised me to raise the full amount, "So you'll have something left over to pay for having it hauled away." They were quite positive I would get no bank money. "One success has gone to your head, man," said the president. "Don't push your luck. Not here anyhow."

"You just never heard of soap and water," I said in disgust and went over the way to the telegraph office. Mother came in again and Ira Casteel from Denver. What had Ira said before I went overseas? "When this is over we'll do big things together." This was the first of them. Within a matter of days the astounded Drown was turning down cash money from patrons in the lobby of the Mobley. We had already raised enough. The Melba was ours.

"What this old lady needs, Jay," I told the Major, "is a new type of management."

"What this old lady needs is soap and paint and Lysol," he said wryly.

Eighteen hours a day, then, the Major and I rode herd on the bucket brigades, a platoon of scrub women, a company of window washers, a division of painters and carpenters. When we were through the Melba *was* a hotel. And, under Powers' management, she made money as a hotel should.

At the end of three months the old-fashioned safe in the office was stuffed and bulging and we were forced to open a bank account. I banked the money at the Texas State Bank of Fort Worth. A bank wouldn't want to miss the same boat twice. Each deposit slip helped prove to them that my ships came in!

The Waldorf, my third hotel, was undoubtedly named for the élite rendezvous. *The* Waldorf, at 33rd Street and Fifth Avenue, New York City. Right there all resemblance ceased.

My first Waldorf, in downtown Dallas, Texas, was a six-story semi-fireproof building, 150 rooms with a sprinkling of baths, and a fifty-room annex, no baths at all. It was, however, our biggest venture to date, and I went on over to Dallas as acting manager. Following my basic rules I converted every waste nook I could find, and began to build that old *esprit de corps*. Then I joined the chorus of Powers and Drown, leaning happily over the desk saying, "I'm so sorry, we haven't a single. But I could let you have a room with three *other* gentlemen . . . two *other* ladies."

It was very satisfactory. Once again that element of "luck" that was so important in my life was functioning for me. Mother and Ira Casteel had come in on the deal. I had gotten a loan from a young banker, R. L. Thornton, at the Dallas County State Bank. Bob Thornton was to play an important part in my business life, to be a loyal friend and, conservative banker that he was, to offer me one of the greatest gambles I ever took. It was Bob who suggested during the Depression that I play double or nothing with

$55,000, when I hadn't money enough in my pocket for car-fare. When we made the deal on the Waldorf lease, however, the country's economy was behaving harmoniously and we were all looking along toward an unlimited horizon.

One other friendship came out of the Waldorf deal. Harry Siegel, one of the partners from whom we bought the lease and who eventually bought it back from us, quite literally saved my business career one day six years later and prob-ably kept me from jail as well.

Yes, that name Waldorf has always brought good things my way. It was at the Dallas Waldorf that I was joined by Bill Irwin, my closest wartime buddy, who threw up his prospects in sophisticated San Francisco and cast his lot with ours in the rugged future of Texas.

Along with the manager's suite at the Waldorf I inherited from some unknown benefactor a set of books which had a profound effect on me. As a youth I was certainly proof against any attempts to make a reader out of me. But now that I was older, and vastly busier, I found a lot of things I wished I knew. The set of Elbert Hubbard's *Little Journeys to the Homes of the Great* turned up just at the right time.

Bill would take over the desk and I would fold up in my single easy chair and travel to these homes with Mr. Hubbard doing the amusing, instructive narration. I am sure I gained mightily by a close-up of big businessmen (Meyer A. Roth-schild, Stephen Girard, Andrew Carnegie, Peter Cooper). I know I was fired with the *feel* of success, an expanding hori-zon and a lot of powerful new dreams. I liked the sections on great philosophers (Socrates, Marcus Aurelius, Henry Tho-reau), scientists, orators, artists, and the like. But my absolute favorites, the ones I read over and over again, were the tales of American statesmen and "great lovers." I dreamed of do-ing something some day for my country and of finding a woman who would love me as Kitty O'Shea loved Parnell or Emma Hamilton loved Lord Nelson. Not since my teen-age discovery of Helen Keller had I sat still so long or been moved so profoundly as I was by Mr. Hubbard. He is, I am told, rather passé now and all I can say is, more's the pity.

Between my reading, greeting, and counting our profits, I was actually thinking I'd got egg in my beer. I was begin-ning to be a fat frog in an expanding oil pool. Even when oil took a nose dive in 1921 and brought a sharp reces-sion to Texas, when the Cisco bank I had once tried to buy collapsed on the hands of the rude owner in Kansas City, I went right on collecting $6,000 a month as my share of three hotels in those "happy days before big taxes."

I think maybe that fact went to my head a little. I think maybe I was verging on complacent self-satisfaction and I do not know of any single thing that will halt a business career so rapidly. A further facet of my "luck" has always been that, when I was riding a little too high, something or someone dragged me back to earth again. In this instance, as in many others, it was my family. My family and those durn diamonds.

I bought those diamonds for my mother—a big brooch, the most showy affair I could find. And the expert gentleman in the swank jewelry shop encouraged me to buy it!

It was not, I will confess, entirely his fault. He assumed they were for an entirely different type of lady. And I let him. I, who had all the confidence necessary to walk right in and buy a hotel, found the delicate matter of women's jewelry left me blustering on the outside and quaking on the inside. It was one thing to do bold business with a banker and another to have this gray little fellow, dressed in clothes I had always associated with undertakers, eyeing me slyly and whispering confidentially what diamond line was conquering the ladies of New York and Paris.

Anyhow, I walked out with a conquering type of brooch nestled in a bed of satin and blue velvet, imagining my mother's delight when I casually dropped it in her lap as "a little something to wear to church." Cagily wrapping it in a brown paper sack, I took the first train for Socorro.

While the Cisco bank folded, Mrs. Hilton's oldest son bought diamonds for his mother!

At thirty-four, I still had a lot of rough spots. I had poured myself vigorously into a hearty Texas mold, the mold which produces a rugged man's man, a driving, concentrated dynamo upon whose consciousness any subtleties intrude as a kind of waking dream.

I know perfectly well that Bill Irwin, with his San Francisco sophistication, was forever trying to polish me, prod me, dress me, remold me, in short, and not getting very far, either. I had more important things on my mind! I shudder to think what that distinguished group who later placed me several years running on the list of America's ten best-dressed men, would have thought if they could have seen me then. My clothes I can only describe as "quick clothes," the quickest to buy, to clean, to climb into and out of. I had two suits for the very good reason that it was hard to keep a press in my pants if I slept in my office, as I still did upon occasion. While I had not succumbed to high-heeled boots, being already as tall as comfort permitted, I cherished a slightly battered broad-brimmed Stetson as the most practical head covering. I might say that I still wear one although the one I wear today, white and dashing, a gift from Mr. Amon Carter, is a very distant cousin only to my first one.

If Irwin despaired of influencing me in the matter of dress, he did occasionally give me helpful hints on dealing with the fairer sex, which I took. I recall one dilemma I offered him for solution. It concerned the matter of the exit lines on a casual date.

"We drive back to her house," I told Irwin. "Obviously she doesn't expect me to come in. I lean over very gentlemanly, open her door, and what happens? Nothing. She doesn't get out. She sits. Now she can't want to talk any more. And she can't be wanting to be kissed good night. I don't know her that well. And if I wanted to ask her for another date I'd have done it already. So what are we waiting for? I feel real foolish."

Bill gave a knowing smile. "Just *you* get out of the car, walk around to her side, open the door and stand there. She'll get out. She'll have to."

Bill's little plot worked very well. My own to dazzle my mother did not.

First off, when I arrived in Socorro I found myself catapulted into the midst of a family gathering. If I considered myself a rising wheel in the Texas hotel scene, in the bosom of my family I was still just a spoke. My dramatic entrance was lost in a happy hubbub. Carl had returned on a surprise leave from the Navy. Boy was on vacation from Dartmouth. Mother was busily filling us in on Eva's new mansion in Massachusetts—"and it's going to have a private swimming pool" —and Rosemary's success in a stock company of "The Gold-diggers"—"they're playing the big cities, you know." My baby sister Helen was practicing her valedictorian address preparatory to graduating from Socorro High School. Boy, with Carl's help, was trying to learn to make a baa-ing sound like a sheep, "because," said he, "they call me 'Shep' at Dartmouth, short for sheepherder. They think everyone in New Mexico raises sheep. . . . Baaa."

"Baaa," responded Carl. "And everyone in Texas is a millionaire, right, Connie? Are you into your second million yet?"

No, there is nothing as leveling as a large family. I replied, with some dignity, that I wasn't quite a millionaire but that I *had* just happened to bring a little something home for Mother.

That got me on stage, front and center, and I dropped my package carelessly in her lap. There was complete silence as she unwound the brown wrapping and pressed the lid on the box.

"Wow!" Carl breathed.

And Mother burst into tears. Then fled to her room. Women, I have found, even mothers, will react most strangely to gifts. Uneasily I turned to Carl. "Have I done something wrong?" I asked.

"Too soon to tell," said Carl. "She's overwhelmed. Wait and see if she wears it to bed tonight."

She didn't wear it that night. She didn't wear it to church on Sunday. She didn't wear it to a dinner party at the Val Verde Hotel where the clan gathered to bid farewell to a member who was certainly getting on in the world, cousin Olaf. He was now the Honorable H. O. Bursum, United States Senator from New Mexico, filling a vacancy created when my old constituent, Albert Bacon Fall, was elevated to Secretary of the Interior by President Warren Harding.

When we got home from the dinner party I asked Mother straight out. "Don't you like the brooch?" I said.

Being Mother, she couldn't give me anything but an honest answer. "I like it," she said, "better than anything that has ever happened to me. I'll always cherish it. I may not wear it though, Connie. It's a little . . . well, outstanding, for a woman of my age."

There it was. She cherished it for twenty-six years. And never wore it once. And it didn't take me long to figure out what she meant. The thought was right. She cherished that. The gift was wrong. I had picked out something that pleased me . . . and not something to please her. It must have cost her a lot to tell me the truth and I was hurt, but I've been grateful since, because I've always liked giving gifts and she set me straight on it in the beginning.

A year later I gave her a more expensive string of small matched pearls. They didn't look like much to me in the way of jewelry. But they looked like Mother. Much later still, I gave her an old-fashioned watch to pin on her dress, set in a single gem. And that, I'm convinced she *did* wear to bed.

From that time on I began collecting and storing away little preferences which would make me a better gift-giver, both personally and professionally. It is not sound procedure to send baskets of fruit to friends or guests who are allergic, candy to women on diets, whiskey for Christmas to an AA, or American Beauties to a lady who suffers rose poisoning. I know that when the late and wondrous Gertrude Lawrence was a guest at our Los Angeles hotel some years later, I was tickled that I had overheard her at a theatrical party tell a friend that the tiny white roses in her corsage were her favorite flower. And that gift, thoughtful rather than expensive, made such a warm impression on her that she recommended that same hotel to her close friend Noel Coward. I knew he was interested in the bizarre plants from tropical countries. So we put a living, odd type, green and brown orchid tree in his sitting room during his stay.

I honestly think all this came about because of my diamond fiasco and my mother's absolute refusal to compromise the truth to spare my momentary feelings.

She did, however, apply some immediate salve by proposing herself and Helen as my guests in Texas for a month.

The Dallas Waldorf did not roll out the red carpet for my mother. We didn't have one. But the staff rose to greater heights of *esprit de corps* and became practically delirious when Rosemary, a real live actress, got as far as Arkansas with her stock company, gave notice, and came over to join us.

The three Hilton women patronized culture in a big way, even and including the exhibit given by the Dallas Art Association at the Adolphus Hotel, and our own hotel went ritzy with luncheons and teas.

I was glad to be thus represented, for my partners were sound family men. L. M. Drown's wife and three children had settled in Cisco. The Major's wife, Lena Budd Powers, a tall, handsome, efficient woman, was the leading light in the Little Theater of Dallas. I have still a yellowed program from the play—"'Green Stockings,' produced under the direction of Lena Budd Powers"—which got me into hot water. Rosemary, the graduate of Emerson College of Oratory, thought that program a riot. To brighten the intermissions, in a booklet devoid of advertising, the Dallas Little Theater had inserted timely jokes. One I recall, "I haven't written a word of my election speech except 'Gentlemen,' and that's a lie," sent Rosemary into a fit of giggles. But the production of "Green Stockings" was no laughing matter.

Rosemary there smelled grease paint again, felt the nice, hot footlights, and heard about Mother's brooch. "If you can buy diamonds you can produce a play," she hinted winningly and I, forgetting the results of another sister, a violin, and a cultural trio, plunged right on in. I hired the Hippodrome Theater, picked up a stranded stock company, starred Rosemary, and took my trimming like a benevolent brother.

I am given to understand that this helped Rosemary to a Broadway career. I feel she would have gotten there without my help. I would not have considered it a financial loss if it had cured me of playing at the theater. Unfortunately, it didn't. I had to take one more, larger trimming before I finally confessed I was strictly a hotel man.

But the fate of the Hippodrome was only a ripple on the water. A major tragedy was in the making. Fate was carving out a pattern for murder. It was time for the curtain to rise on the first act.

I first heard the name, D. E. Soderman, from Major Powers over the phone. The Major, speaking from Fort Worth, described him as an "angel."

"I've found another hotel," Jay said, "a great one. *And* a backer. Come running."

The hotel, the Terminal in Fort Worth, was another dowager, two hundred rooms, a fine potential dowry. D. E. Soderman, the "angel" backer, was a short red-headed fellow who had started his career as a cook and parlayed his talent into a sizeable chain of eating houses. Now he wanted to branch out. Soderman seemed a reasonable fellow, thrifty, hardworking, and the Terminal was better than a reasonable deal.

"We can get a lease for $60,000," I announced after a preliminary skirmish. "Part of that we can get from the bank."

"It's a steal," said Powers. "But I'm afraid I can't swing my third without selling out of the Melba."

"You'll have to manage both," I said.

"Borrow what you need," Soderman volunteered, "and I'll sign your note." He certainly acted like a good angel at that point. The deal was closed and I went back to Dallas leaving Powers in charge of two hotels.

If C. P. Smith, our partner at the Mobley, had been a mistake, Soderman was a disaster. The Terminal, under Powers, began to coin money and Soderman spent his share on corn whiskey. His thrift and industry went up in alcoholic fumes and so did his reasonableness. Enough corn likker and our angel sprouted a long tail. His imagination fired a third-rate thriller plot to the pint. One of them was that Powers had stolen his money (the exact amount of the note he had signed for the Major), and this Jay deeply resented. The next was that Powers had stolen his wife, which added the resentment of Mrs. Soderman and Mrs. Powers to the combustible pile he was building in Fort Worth. Soderman had a positive talent for stirring up trouble.

The Major bore all this with as much dignity as he could command, and that was a lot. Then one night he called me and I knew he'd had it. "That little grub-slinger is now threatening to call my note," he announced. "Connie, I do not know how much more of this I can take."

"Hold tight," I said. "I'll come over and see what I can do."

Experience had taught me there was only one thing *to* do. If you get a bad partner, buy him out. I tried. I offered him a fat profit. Soderman was greedy. He wanted the Terminal. I was astounded when he countered with an offer to buy us out. Powers and I talked it over. There was no way to cut this plum and no way to get along with Soderman. We agreed to sell.

Powers bought into the Waldorf in Dallas and moved over there to manage. Bill Irwin and I went to Fort Worth to look after the Melba. Soderman was exclusive owner-manager of the Terminal. Everybody should have been happy. But everybody wasn't.

As a hotel man, Soderman was a good cook. Maybe he could mix corn whiskey and an angel cake at the same time. He couldn't mix it with a hotel. The Terminal, under Soderman, was sinking into a last decline.

When it was about on its last legs, Soderman came to me crying—with an offer to sell. He asked $35,000. I didn't like doing business with him. The man was insistent and the Terminal still had a glamour potential. I bought. But, for one of the few times in my life, I not only didn't bargain, I padded the deal. I was beginning to understand the man. He was an adept at twisting the truth to *himself*. I gave him $38,500, throwing in a few extras.

Soderman went away. I hoped we had seen the last of him.

A few months later I bumped into him in El Paso. He was drunk and ugly. He informed me that Powers and I were sharpies and had bilked him. I was twice his size and sober. I crossed the street. I didn't want any more trouble.

Soderman did.

On April 18, 1922, D. E. Soderman entered the lobby of the Dallas Waldorf, walked to the house phone and called Major Powers. A bellboy heard him say, "I want to see you. I'll wait down here."

A few minutes later Powers stepped from the elevator. Soderman shot him once, through the temple. The Major died instantly.

How does a man feel when an ex-partner, a crazed fellow, shoots down in cold blood a permanent partner, a valued, respected friend?

It's hard to say. You can't put it into words.

For the first few hours and while rushing from Fort Worth to Dallas on the interurban, I was blessedly numb. Stunned. Speechless. I don't even recall any desire for revenge. It didn't seem real. Powers would be there in the Waldorf lobby to greet me.

Only he wasn't.

Even then it didn't become real. I saw his widow. I made arrangements to attend the trial. Then, in court, in a sensational case which rocked Texas, I suddenly realized that the impersonal being referred to as "the deceased" was my friend Jay C. Powers.

I looked at the stubborn red-headed figure at the defense table and even then there was no desire for revenge, only a cold loathing disgust.

I sat with Mrs. Powers throughout the entire ordeal. She seemed still a dynamic woman, self-possessed, capable, but empty. Like myself, she found little to say. And then, when the trial was over, a Texas jury returned a verdict of manslaughter. The defense attorney had convinced them that the defendant was crazed by drink—and I suppose he was. Soderman was sentenced to five years.

Almost immediately he was out on bail. Lena Powers told me about it. I had called on the phone to tell her I had raised the money to take over Jay's interests.

"You won't have anything financial to worry about," I said.

"I'm not worried for myself," she said. "But Soderman is out. And this time, Connie, he's looking for you."

You always have friends who want you to run—get out of town 'til the thing blows over. I had my share. The Major never had a chance to run. I don't think anyone ever really has. I know myself I couldn't live wondering if a fellow who was "looking for me" might be just around the next corner.

"All I want to do is face him," I told Bill Irwin, "and get it over with. Then I can get back to work. Will you get word to him, Bill, that I'm here—and waiting?"

An hour later Bill was back. "I saw one of his pals," he said. "He'll pass the word along. Being practical, Connie, shouldn't we make some slight preparations for this visitor? Have you got a gun?"

I had, of course. My old army service revolver was in my bottom desk drawer. I opened the drawer and looked at it. Across the years came the picture of my father staring down the barrel of a gun trained on him in a saloon by a drunken rancher and my father saying to me, "If I'd had a gun one of us would be dead." There'd been too much blood already. I shut the drawer.

"Let's turn our desks around, Bill." Without a word the two of us shifted our desks, which had faced the windows, until they faced the door. I had a strong feeling I'd rather Soderman saw my face than my back. Then I sat down to wait. Irwin settled down in his chair.

"This is my beef, Bill," I said.

"That's right," agreed that gentleman, putting his elegant feet on the desk and lighting a cigarette. "But it might be a long wait. You might get bored."

It was a long wait. We waited until dinner time and the next morning we took our places and started waiting some more. I'll admit I was jumpy. "Maybe he won't come," I said.

"He will," said Bill calmly.

About eleven o'clock we heard shambling footsteps and a

figure cast a blurred shadow against the door. The shadow hesitated, then the door opened and Soderman stood there. He didn't look drunk, and he didn't look sober. He didn't look particularly belligerent either, but I'd heard he was smiling when he fired at Jay. Bill stiffened and I spoke.

"I hear you want to talk to me," I said.

Soderman sat down, his hands in full view, a weak smile on his face. "I just wanted to say—well, I got no hard feelings for you, Connie."

I didn't say how I felt about him.

"I've appealed," he said, "and I'm going to beat this thing—"

That made me mad. "Maybe," I said. "But I'm not going to help you. Major Powers was my friend."

"Well, no hard feelings," Soderman said again. He didn't offer to shake hands, which was a good thing. He grinned again, kind of self-consciously, and ambled out.

"Now what," said Irwin, "was that all about? A courtesy call? No hard feelings."

I thought maybe now I had heard the last of Soderman. Again I was wrong. He had no hard feelings while he was out on bail, but when he lost his appeal and began serving his time at Huntsville, the rumbles started coming in again.

"He's going to get you, Connie," I heard over and over again.

"Not for a while yet," I said. "He's pretty cozy behind those bars. In the meantime I'd better get back to the hotel business."

A murder in the lobby had in no way affected our business at the Waldorf. We had, in fact, put cots in the hall and run curtains around them to accommodate our ever-increasing guest list. Taking the Major's place behind the desk I was soon saying briskly, "We can let you have a room with three other gentlemen," but I had no heart for it.

Providentially my brother Carl elected to take a long leave from the Navy just about then and give the hotel business a trial—maybe his wife wanted a diamond brooch. I don't know. I didn't ask any questions but gratefully turned over the Waldorf desk to him and went courting again. What I needed, I decided, was a few more hotels.

I got a lease on the Beaton at Corsicana, a jumping little town, for $20,000 and L. M. Drown came over to manage. With only sixty rooms the Beaton started to make money, good money, immediately. Funny thing about Drown. He was a topnotch hotel manager and a sound businessman, but he was very conservative. We hadn't had the Beaton two months when he was sending me along a blue check every ten days for $1,000, my share of the profits. But Drown never wanted to buy in. He made a good living the thirteen years he was with me, without ever once being tempted into a big plunge. When his sons grew up one of them, Joe, had all his father's acumen plus an eagerness to back his judgment by taking a gamble. Young Joe Drown and I did some exciting things together. It's heartening to see everyone around you getting a little bit rich when the getting is good, but I was never able to talk Drown into climbing past the security level.

After the Beaton I did a little risky speculating on my own. It wasn't a howling success but, as I told Drown, you can't win 'em all.

It looked good enough.

There were rumors of a big oil field coming in at Wortham, a fork in the road south of Corsicana. After nosing around a bit, those drillers had me sold on the boom that would come to the town as the wells came in. I decided to climb in on the ground floor.

Wortham didn't boast a hotel, but I got a lease on a rooming house and began to build it up. The oil rumors plus my hotel sparked a real estate boom and pretty soon the town had everything but money.

I opened my hotel the day they brought in a gusher. The well gushed all right. Salt water. Three guests registered across my desk. That was all. No other guests came so I boarded up the doors. It was my first dry hole.

In disgust I retired to Socorro to contemplate my next move. Frankly, although I couldn't complain, looking over a tiny domain of 530 rooms, representing an investment of $220,000, of which I could claim $100,000, I was getting vaguely tired of transforming "dowagers."

A wire from Carl at the Waldorf pinpointed this vague feeling. "Fellow in 202 bumped himself off last night. After looking at his room I don't blame him. We have got to fix up those rooms."

I somehow doubted that the décor in 202 had driven the poor fellow to suicide. Unfortunately tired people, discouraged people have sought the impersonal solitude of a hotel for their unhappy business since time immemorial.

However, Carl had a point. It was time to redecorate. Yet nothing roused the ire of our public, our ladies and gentlemen, more than to have us close off rooms even to rejuvenate them. Suddenly I knew I didn't want to stay in the face-lifting business all my life. I wanted a modern love, young and shiny and streamlined.

Sitting in Mother's living room I began to doodle. A tall hotel, the newest of the new, with the name Hilton on it.

Mother looked over my shoulder. "Something new, Connie?"

"I'm putting a dream on paper, Mother. Maybe it's time to go all out," I said softly. "This time I am really going big. And the first thing I'll need to do is raise a million dollars."

"If you're serious, son, the first thing you'd better do is pray about it. A million dollars is a lot of money."

"I'll take it over with St. Joseph," I promised. "This should be right in his line."

8. A MILLION DOLLAR MOUNTAIN
AND A RED HAT

A man's first million dollar deal may come under the heading of Big Business. To me it spelled Big Adventure—comparable to sailing around Cape Horn, or climbing Mount Everest. Anyone who brushes business off as a tame occupation revolving around a conference table and poring over figures with corpulent gentlemen, is just plain wrong.

There is nothing tame about raising a million dollar building from a standing start.

If you climb Mount Everest, no matter how carefully you plan, anything can happen. Your ice axe slips, your oxygen gives out. A concealed crevasse swallows you up. Well, that's about the way it was building my first Hilton Hotel.

I hung over precipices, gained a promontory only to have my rope break, got within sight of the top and, before I could plant my flag, all but perished for lack of money, the lifeline used to build my mountain ahead of me, one floor at a time.

Story by story, I fought my way toward the summit—and there was never a dull moment.

Halfway up I met a girl, *the* girl this time, and all but lost her when it looked like I'd crash to the bottom, pulling my self-made mountain down on top of me.

No, if you want the dull, tame life, if you have no compelling dreams or head for excitement, stay on the ground, away from big business.

This first mountain I decided to climb is a pretty good example of the high adventures that have gone on, one after another, in my business life.

I began with some long talks with St. Joseph, that Patron of Builders, and then I went around and talked to a firm of architects. The exact spot for my new dream girl stood on the corner of Main and Harwood in the Dallas business district and I had optioned it from the owner, George W. Loudermilk, onetime liveryman and undertaker, now real estate rich.

132

The architects estimated they could put my new hotel on that site for exactly the sum I had foreseen, one million. I do believe that under his breath the man may have said, "or more." I now know all estimates have that inherent possibility. But I wasn't listening.

"Go ahead with the blueprints," I ordered. And then I set out to raise a million dollars.

It wasn't easy.

My first move was positively naïve. An advertisement in a New York paper caught my eye: "Need money? See us. We will finance you." So off I went to New York. The company sold me an insurance policy and lent me exactly nothing.

Back in Dallas I decided I'd better do a little more thinking and a lot more praying. I was around the impressive cathedral on Ross Avenue so much I suspect Father Diamond thought I was permanently unemployed. I figured I could probably realize $100,000 on my own, one-tenth of what I needed, and two-tenths more from my regular backers. But what was three-tenths of a million? And there was nothing to invest in it at this point but a wild dream. If I raised the money and gave it to Loudermilk I'd have nothing left to erect a building.

The more I thought, the more I decided that Loudermilk was the key man in this deal. I had an idea, a startling idea, but it was worth a try. I worked the whole thing out in my head, and then carefully thought up all the possible objections. Loudermilk was known as a difficult fellow and old-fashioned in his ways. My idea, while beginning to be accepted in the East, would be brand new to him. And Porter Lindsley, Loudermilk's real estate advisor, was a hard man to do business with. I'd need all the answers.

When I thought I had them, I broached Loudermilk.

"I'm going to pick up that option," I announced, "and build a million dollar hotel."

Loudermilk beamed. He allowed Dallas needed a new hotel. That was just the sort of talk I wanted to hear.

"Of course a hotel like that is going to tie up all my capital, so instead of buying your land, I want to lease it. . . ."

Loudermilk beamed no longer. He snorted. "You're crazy. You're not about to build anything on land I own."

"Lease it," I continued, "on a ninety-nine-year lease. It's really a sale in installments. . . ."

"I'm not Methuselah," Loudermilk shouted. "I won't *live* ninety-nine years."

"And you go right on owning the land. If I don't pay, you get the land back. . . ." My man was beginning to look interested, so I gave him my biggest gun. "And my building, too."

"I'd own the land . . . and the building, too," he repeated. He thought a minute. "I'll talk it over with Lindsley."

Lindsley had heard of the ninety-nine-year-lease practice. He worked out a figure of $31,000 a year, a total of some three million dollars, all of which would be protected by my hotel.

Loudermilk decided he'd been very clever. I agreed with him. Then I discharged a cannon. "I'd just like that lease to have a clause authorizing me to float a loan on the real estate," I said quietly.

You could have heard Loudermilk's yelp out on the Panhandle. But eventually I got it. Not enthusiastically, I'll admit. I recall his saying something about getting rid of me while he still had his gold cuff links, but I got that all-important clause.

I had something now to build my mountain on and I began stringing the lifeline that would carry me to the top. I had the land. I still needed the million. I went to St. Louis where W. L. Hemmingway, president of the National Bank of Commerce, agreed to lend me $500,000—to be paid in installments as each story of the building was finished, but with the understanding that at all times I must have enough money on hand to finish the building or they would stop advancing money.

Hemmingway was talking turkey. But I was thinking positively. I was halfway home. So far, so good. I picked up another $50,000 from my friend Bob Thornton, who was now with the Mercantile National Bank. When it came time to accept bids on the building, I borrowed another $150,000 from the contractor. Seven-tenths of a million. Now that three-tenths I figured I could get, would lasso the top for me.

I put up my own hundred thousand first. Harry Siegel, one of the partners from whom we had originally gotten the Waldorf, bought it back as sole owner-manager. Cisco was returning after her boom years to the cowtown she originally was and we let the Mobley go. I raised my hat in salute to my first and most gallant "dowager." In the fashion of businessmen I have been true to her, for I've used everything she ever taught me. But I had a new love now and that hundred thousand represented everything I had, plus all I could safely borrow on existing hotels.

Once my capital was up, I was in a position to invite my friends in. I have never once in my life asked anyone to follow me financially into an adventure when I was not willing to take the lead. And I did then exactly what I do today. I wrote to or talked with people I knew were interested in investing and told them what I had to offer. The $200,000 of venture capital I needed came in quickly. There were old backers among them, including my mother and Ira Casteel.

On July 26, 1924, for the first time, I spaded up a bit of earth and threw it over my shoulder, breaking ground for a Hilton Hotel.

Almost immediately my life assumed a new pattern. I stepped out of the "leased dowager" circuit, forgot about three or four guests to a room, bought a brand new Stetson, danced, played tennis once again, the first time since the days in Raon l'Étape, France, when I found the "mademoiselles" interested in that game. I joined a golf club and began to play golf. And, perhaps the most personally pleasing thing that happened, my youngest brother, Boy, after a year with the United Fruit Company in Nicaragua, joined me in Texas.

I almost felt I'd raised Boy because of those summers when he was a toddler and I was a grown man of thirteen. There was a strong bond between us and I was as proud of him as if he had been my personal handiwork. He was the handsomest young man I had ever seen. Taller than I, with Dartmouth manners and New Mexico warmth. It added up to a very fine fellow, and I was proud to have him with me. He would be a great addition to the new Hilton Hotel.

Perhaps I was counting chickens ahead of time? No "perhaps" about it. I was. Why, I was feeling so good that I succumbed to that old temptation—and leased a theater.

This time it was the Circle. I thought it would keep me busy while they were building my hotel. And it did. Oh, it did! I picked up a stranded stock company and began producing plays. Sam and Ella Flint were a part of that troupe. I like to remember that. They were good friends then and later. They live in Los Angeles now and when I made my television debut in "Eloise," Ella and I were in the same cast. I am glad to think something good came out of my Circle Theater venture.

I was pretty pleased with life and with myself when I took the Circle in Dallas. It was a nice cultural activity for a prominent man. I thought I had already reached the summit and planted my flag. I had my land. I had my million dollars. The building was started. Everything was going my way.

And it was then that *the* girl came into my life.

All I saw of her at first was a jaunty red hat and a few curls several pews in front of me at church. The hat was dark red and the curls were very black and there was something about the way she wore the hat, the way she carried her head, that was very attractive. When I saw her face, pretty, vivacious, alert, with laughing eyes, in my excitement I did something worthy of a college freshman.

I followed the red hat out of church to try to find out where she lived. For once I wished I hadn't so many friends to greet. I'm afraid I was abrupt. But as it was, the red hat got such a long start on me that, after seeing it bob up and down in the crowd for a couple of blocks, I lost it.

For a month of Sundays I amazed that congregation with my piety. I attended every Mass from six 'til noon. But I didn't see her again.

Suddenly nothing was going my way.

I had half a hotel when the rope slipped. I was running out of money. Starting with the foundations everything cost more than I had figured. My bankers were the first to sense trouble. That's their business. A surprise visit from Hemmingway caught me with all my bills paid, but very little besides. Bob Thornton's bank began to get curious. I spent most of my days slashing at the blueprints trying to eliminate unnecessary refinements, watching to see that no builder slipped gold leaf into the interior and, above all, trying to get a sense of speed across to the workmen.

The contractor protested. "Mr. Hilton, we're not slowing down," he insisted. "I've got a stake in this, too." He certainly had, a $150,000 stake. But still it seemed to me to drag on and on.

When I wasn't harassing the workmen I was getting after

my theatrical company over at the Circle. "We've got to get a hit," I announced each week as I watched a few dollars dribble into the theater box office and a lot more dribble out supporting my venture. We weren't breaking even.

Every Saturday night, our biggest night, it was touch-and-go whether enough would come in to enable us to go on. The only reason I didn't just darken the house was that I couldn't afford to. I'd have to give two weeks' notice, and right then I didn't have the money. Sam and Ella Flint did their best to cheer me with the easy optimism of show business, but I couldn't see the bright side of anything.

Until one afternoon I left a rehearsal and walked straight into *the* girl again.

There she was, in a different hat, and I'll admit right now that only the saints saved me from accosting a stranger right there on the street. It seemed an omen that she was walking with Mrs. Beauregard Evans. And I knew Mrs. Evans.

"This is Mary Barron," Mrs. Evans said, "a relative of ours from Owensboro, Kentucky."

For a while then everything took a back seat to the girl with the laughing eyes and the soft Kentucky voice.

Mary was visiting and a feeling of urgency pervaded our courtship. We danced a lot and laughed a lot, and for a little while the weight of my mountain didn't seem to be on my shoulders at all. I would find myself forgetting my worries while an orchestra played "I'll See You in My Dreams," or "Lady Be Good," or even "Yes, Sir, That's My Baby." But in the back of my mind was always the knowledge that Mary would be leaving Dallas, that I had a hotel to finish, and I couldn't get on with my work until our business was settled. While I was with Mary it seemed the most important business in the world.

Before she left, she promised that when the hotel was completed she would come back and marry me.

She also, at my insistence, gave me the red hat.

There was the incurable romantic coming out again. It was now my firm intention to sprinkle stars in Mary's lap, and I would go back into the fight, climb my mountain, as her champion. In the days when Arthur was King, I would have worn her colors on my sleeve.

In Dallas, Texas, in 1924, I had to content myself with flying the red hat from my bedpost.

Then I went back to my mountain with renewed vigor.

I needed it.

On one hand I got a lifeline. On the other a large crevasse opened up ready to swallow me.

The lifeline saved me at the Circle Theater. As I was going through my weekly debate as to whether I could best afford to close the theater or best afford to keep it open, a man strode into my office and demanded that I sell it to him.

"And I'll tell you right now," he said stormily, "that if you don't, I'll build one in direct competition down the street."

Obviously he didn't know that I'd practically give it to him. And obviously I wasn't about to tell him. A business game is a business game and I automatically played it. I couldn't resist a bluff. "Give me," I said, "forty-eight hours to think it over."

In forty-eight hours, with a sigh of relief, I let him have the Circle. Then I had some more serious bluffing to do.

Bob Thornton and the plumbing contractor both hit me at once. Bob called my $50,000 note. And the plumbing contractor demanded another $50,000 due him for plumbing bills.

Bob was polite, even joking. "The bank just needs the money, Connie," he said. "Nothing personal." But I had to promise it to him or I knew Hemmingway would have more than a suspicion I was in trouble.

The plumbing contractor wasn't polite at all. He picked a Saturday morning to demand his money "or my men walk off the job next Monday." So I had to promise him, too.

I had only one $50,000 to use, and until Monday morning to dig up the other $50,000. My two days for digging, Saturday and Sunday, couldn't have been worse.

I flipped a coin to see whose $50,000 it was I had to raise. Thornton won the dubious honor. I made out a check for the plumber, addressed it, and then left it propped up on my desk. When I mailed that, if I didn't raise the other and right then I hadn't even an idea where to start, my decision was final. I would have kept the builders building—and cut off my supply of money.

Then I went for a walk.

Walking is a great device for clearing the head, for keeping the body so busy that ideas can come through. I walked that Saturday like the furies were behind me. I don't know where I went. I remember stopping in a church, being joined for a while by a friendly dog, and halting abruptly in a residential section as a quite unwelcome idea broke in. It was, in fact, a terrible thought.

I started looking for a pay phone, again with the furies behind me, because if my idea was right I had only until noon to check it. At noon my secretary went home.

I got her on the line. "There was a letter on my desk . . ." I began.

Her voice came back, efficient and poised. "I found it, Mr. Hilton. It's already in the mail. Don't worry."

Don't worry! I could feel the landslide starting. Thornton closing in. Hemmingway closing in. And Loudermilk! I'll admit I wasn't thinking clearly, but the only thing I wanted to do right then was get that check back.

And Harry Siegel was a friend of the postmaster.

I dashed into Harry's office with my wild request. "I've got to get that letter out of the mail," I insisted, "or I'm ruined."

Harry informed me that the procedure was highly illegal and not a good idea at all. He tried to calm me and eventually I told him the whole story. "There just isn't any other way," I said flatly.

"I think there is," Harry said.

He drew out his checkbook and wrote a check for $50,000. "Pay 'em both, Connie," he said with a grin.

"Harry, you know perfectly well I haven't any security for that," I told him.

"Did I ask for any?"

"And if I go down you've thrown it away."

"Pay 'em both, Connie," he repeated. "I trust you."

It was one of the most moving moments of my life.

"I just can't seem to get started," I told Mother.

Suddenly I remembered my father's story of the Catholic Archbishop of Santa Fe and the Jewish merchant, Abraham Staab, who saved his cathedral. Here I was, a Catholic hotel man, saved by the friendship and trust of a Jewish hotel man, a man whom the world might call a rival.

I was able to repay Harry Siegel the money. There was no way to repay him personally for that gesture of brotherhood, real brotherhood. But this vote of confidence from my friend did more for me than help build a hotel. It filled me with a living gratitude for a country where we can all work together as children of one Father. And a desire to promote understanding between us all.

In the early '30s, when a rabbi, a priest, and a minister first attempted a cross-country speaking tour together, launching the National Council of Christians and Jews, we were in the midst of a depression. To say that money was tight with me would be an understatement. But I found enough to help with their expenses and sponsor the idea in Texas and New Mexico.

Perhaps I would have done as much for an impersonal ideal. I do not know. For in my mind this was very personal. The conference was "building for brotherhood." Any small part I played I meant as a living tribute to men who already lived it.

As I believe in my own Faith, as I believe in America, so I honestly believe that Brotherhood is the platform on which a lasting peace must be built—in business, in a nation, in the world at large.

Men like Harry Siegel and Abraham Staab, any man of any faith who tries to do his daily business in God's name, in God's way, is, to my mind, a pioneer of peace. That makes it a very personal thing. It means we can each have a hand in building peace on earth.

I was four floors from the top, ready to plant my flag, when I ran out of money again.

It just didn't seem possible—but there it was. The closer I got to my objective, the more everything seemed to cost, the higher the wage bills, and the longer it took. Hemmingway's installments were still coming in, but they no longer met the expenses and I was all used up. There seemed no place to turn.

I went full circle, back to my original idea.

Loudermilk was the key man.

Would Loudermilk protect himself, and indirectly me and my investors, by taking over and finishing the building and then leasing the whole thing back to me?

He would not! This time his cries of injury and wrath must have reached San Antonio.

I talked. I sold. I exuded confidence. I explained that this way he would own both the land and the building. Finally he said what he had said before. "I'll talk it over with Lindsley."

Porter Lindsley, however, had taken this awkward time for a vacation. He was driving to Denver and back and there was no way to reach him for ten days. In exactly ten days I had to meet my payroll or quit. If I failed, my partners failed with me. Harry Siegel's trust was misplaced. I could not ask Mary to be my wife. I would be worse than starting all over. I would be at thirty-eight a man with no money, no credit, no future.

Well, there it was. So I went off to visit Mary.

Bill Irwin thought I was mad. In the ten days I was gone he lost a pound a day. I came back eight pounds heavier, refreshed, all ready to take on Porter Lindsley.

"You," I told Irwin, "are a worrier."

"And you're a phenomenon," he replied. "I just couldn't have done it. You know Lindsley's decision can make or break you . . . and you go dancing."

I'll admit this is a happy faculty but I deny that it is phenomenal. If more people would practice not worrying over their worries they wouldn't need happy pills. It says in the Bible, "Have done all—stand!" And I believe you have to do just that. When I had talked to Loudermilk, I had done everything I could. There was nothing to do but stand for ten days.

Then I took on Lindsley. I lost the eight pounds in a hurry but, in the nick of time, Loudermilk took over the payroll, agreed to complete the hotel, and I signed a lease for $100,-000 a year.

Boy was being schooled to act behind the desk. I had a slogan, a new operating slogan, one word—Minimax. It stood for "minimum charge for maximum service." I had the furniture selected. So I bought a new suit and broke a hundred at golf and sent for Mary.

On August 4, 1925, the Dallas Hilton opened with great ceremony. It was an immediate success.

I had climbed Mount Everest.

Mary Barron and I were married very simply at six o'clock Mass at Holy Trinity Church. Word of Ira Casteel's sudden death had not put us in the frame of heart for a more lavish affair.

My mother was there, pleased as she always was at a wedding, and very proud of the new Mary Hilton. I can remember a few other faces as I stood frozen at the altar—Boy and

Helen, and Harry Siegel, Bill Irwin, and Mary's mother. Mrs. Thomas Mason Barron, mother of the bride, was a small, sweet southerner with a youthful face and winning manners. She became my firm friend then and has remained so until this day. Perhaps because of my affection for Mrs. Barron, I have never been able to laugh too heartily at mother-in-law jokes. Certainly I was never to know what an "in-law" problem was.

Mrs. Beauregard Evans, Mary's cousin, had arranged a bridal breakfast at her home following the ceremony, and directly afterward Mary and I drove to Fort Worth in my old Franklin to catch our train. We had made a hasty change in our honeymoon route to give us a few hours in Denver with Ira Casteel's father and mother.

From Denver we went to San Francisco, and I introduced Mary to the city whose elegant beauty had captured my imagination as a young army officer. Then we traveled to Canada and Lake Louise. It was at Lake Louise that I bought my wife, a strict product of the prohibition era, her first bottle of wine. From Canada we swung down to Chicago, for I wanted Mary to see another kind of American city, a swarming, hustling, commercial city that could also stir the imagination.

In Chicago we attempted to register at the La Salle Hotel. The lobby looked like the Mobley on a good day and we had to take our place in line. I was not above trying to impress my bride; summoning a bellboy, I handed him one of my brand new cards: Conrad N. Hilton, President, Hilton Hotels. It did the trick.

An assistant manager came beaming to our rescue and whisked us off to a room. "I think I'm getting to like Chicago better and better," I said with satisfaction.

Mary liked Chicago, too. There has always been a lustiness about this particular city, a seething with life, and in the roaring '20s it managed to roar just a little louder than any place else. Each time we crossed a street we dodged more Ford cars than Mary had ever seen in her life, one explanation being that the price on the Ford had dropped so low, $290, with self-starter; about the price of a washing machine in these, our quiet times.

We didn't see a live gangster, but we saw more night clubs in one place than the whole of Texas would have supported. Gone were the sentimental ballads of our courtship or even the more recent "Rose Marie" and "Indian Love Call." Instead, we heard "Show Me the Way to Go Home," "Collegiate," "Thanks for the Buggy Ride," and "Don't Bring Lulu."

We saw shows and movies—I particularly remember "The Gold Rush" with Charlie Chaplin because Mary cried when he gave a dinner party and nobody came; and Harold Lloyd in "The Freshman," and this time I cried from laughing too hard. Outside the theaters during intermission and all day long on the sidewalks, the children of Chicago would dance for pennies, a new, vigorous dance called the Charleston. Before we left, Mary and I, to our surprise, found ourselves doing on dance floors a variation of it only slightly more moderate and sedate than what we saw on streets.

Yes, Chicago had charms. "Some day," I told Mary, "I'm going to come back and find a vacant lot. I'd like to build me a hotel here." I didn't know that someone, right that minute, was saving me the trouble; had found the vacant lot and was putting up the Stevens, the largest hotel in the world. It would be twenty years before I embarked on the adventure of buying the Stevens. And it was quite an adventure. But the mere thought of vacant lots made me hanker to see the Dallas Hilton and climb a few more mountains in Texas.

So Mr. and Mrs. Conrad Hilton headed for home.

Our first son, Conrad Nicholson Hilton, Jr., was born on July 6, 1926.

To celebrate the event, we Hiltons moved from the Stoneleigh Court apartments to a four-bedroom house on St. Johns Drive in Highland Park. There's no sense dwelling on how I felt, because every man who's had a son knows this is a main event.

If I listened to his grandmothers, who hastened to Dallas to view him, little Nick was something pretty special. If I listened to my wife, little Nick was something very special indeed. Actually I kind of thought so myself. He was not unduly red, had big eyes, curly hair, and was quite a howler. I did my share of the night duty and diaper detail without too much fuss. It reminded me of that summer when I spent my time trailing around after young Boy.

Mother, I do believe, was glad to see me settled down. And I know that she was pleased when Rosemary married Dean Carpenter, an eastern businessman and a great friend of my sister Eva. In fact, Rosemary and Dean met in Eva's mansion at Medfield, Massachusetts, and Eva played cupid for that romance.

"High time, too," my mother commented on Rosemary's wedding. She still felt that women were happier with a home and family. She hadn't been quite pleased when she heard my pretty sister was making the big time on Broadway in a play called "Pigs"—"*What* kind of a name is that for a respectable play, Connie?"—and was positively upset when she heard that Rosemary had taken my eldest sister Felice to a 52nd Street speak-easy—"What kind of a place is that, Connie, for two respectable young women from New Mexico?"

So she was glad Rosemary had "settled down." But disappointed to find that I hadn't.

I was busy looking for more adventures. Why, I couldn't pass a small vacant lot without a speculative look. This time it was Mary, my wife, who caught me dreaming on paper.

"What's that?" she demanded.

"A list of places," I said, "where I'm going to build hotels."

Over my shoulder she read: "Abilene, Waco, Marlin, Plainview, San Angelo, Lubbock, El Paso. . . . So many, Connie?"

"A hotel a year," I vowed solemnly. "Starting immediately."

I did not, however, start immediately. Some unpleasant business from the past cropped up. Convincing reports reached me that D. E. Soderman was making ugly noises from the state penitentiary at Huntsville.

This was nothing new. I had heard this intermittently for four years. What was new was that Miriam "Ma" Ferguson, then Governor of Texas, was generously granting pardons to many and had included Soderman in her latest list.

Now a killer making threats behind bars is one thing. That same killer running loose is quite another. I found that I myself was not in the exact frame of mind I had been four years earlier. Then I'd had the single man's easy courage, the "only one life to lose" philosophy of the fellow with no responsibilities. Now there was Mary at home and young Nick still crib-size. I couldn't take the same semi-casual view of an attempt on my life.

I called the warden at Huntsville.

"No doubt about it," he confirmed. "The redhead is up for a pardon and he sure doesn't like you. He swears he'll get you when he's released."

It was a cheerful thought.

"Can you keep me posted?" I asked. "I don't like surprises."

"I'll let you know the minute he walks out," the warden promised.

I had one more card to play. There was a missionary priest, Father Schmidt, who had known Soderman before the Powers shooting and I called on him. "I don't want trouble, Father," I said honestly. "On the other hand, I won't run from it."

"It sounds an evil thing he has in his mind," the priest said thoughtfully. "Maybe I should go down to Huntsville. Maybe if I talked to him when he got out, I might be able to reason with him."

"Maybe," I said. "And, look, I wouldn't offer any man a bribe and with a crazy man it wouldn't do any good, anyhow. But a man with a stake might be more able to see reason than a man who was broke and bitter. So maybe, anonymously, you could give him something to start again."

I handed Father Schmidt some folded bills and thought how ironical it would be if they were used to buy a gun. But I had done all I could. There was nothing to do but wait—and pray.

Three days later the phone on my desk rang. The warden's voice crackled over the wire. "Soderman's out," he said. "Keep your eyes open—and good luck."

Then I waited some more. I didn't go home. I didn't want this particular caller to ring Mary's doorbell. Late that night the phone rang again. It was Father Schmidt. "Soderman has just left," he said, "on a bus for California. He's going out there to make a fresh start."

"Amen," I breathed. And got back to work.

The Abilene Hotel was completed and the one at Waco launched when on October 23, 1927, our second son, William Barron, was born. This was another main event after which I settled down to building hotels, one after another, constantly learning something new about my business.

Christmas Day, 1928, on my forty-first birthday, I was well ahead of my self-imposed schedule of one hotel a year. Besides Dallas, Abilene, and Waco, I had added Marlin (eight stories, one hundred rooms, costing $400,000), Plainview (eight stories, one hundred rooms, costing $400,000),

San Angelo (fourteen stories, 240 rooms, costing $900,000), and Lubbock (twelve stories, two hundred rooms, costing $800,000).

Bankers Hemmingway and Thornton had given me constant support along with my old backers. New bankers and new friends seemed eager to come in on my ventures. I myself was in to the point where now and then I didn't have much pocket money, but my Texas hotel system was growing with a fine, healthy look to it. From Dallas and Abilene I had learned that it was most unwise to lease a dining room concession. If the food was poor, the management took the blame. On the other hand, at Lubbock I found that Texas had no use for an imported French chef. A sauce, they felt, was unnecessary, or a means of covering inferior meat. At Waco I discovered that air conditioning was not only a novelty but almost a necessity.

I made a business trip east to see what I could learn back there and had time for hurried visits with my sisters, Eva, Felice and Rosemary. I was with Rosemary who was expecting her first baby, and her husband Dean Carpenter, when Mother's letter came.

Boy, she wrote, had been coughing a lot and, during a violent attack, showed traces of that bright red that meant one thing, tuberculosis. They had taken him to a sanatorium in El Paso. He was doing well and I was not to worry.

I did worry, though, and so did Rosemary. Giving her my word that I would write her the whole truth, I went home at once.

It is always a terrible thing to see a young man whom you have left active and hearty, immobilized beneath sterile white sheets. For me to see Boy that way sent a sharp pain through my heart. Boy himself was cheerful, even gay, and did his best to reassure us. "Just keep my job for me, Connie," he joked, "and I'll be back before the ladies miss me." The doctors assured us "everything was being done" and what he needed was rest and quiet.

With that Mother and I had to be content, and we returned to Dallas.

Then came a letter from the doctor announcing that he suspected tuberculous meningitis. They were making tests. They would know within twenty-four hours and would call. They did, and confirmed the awful suspicion. Immediately we left again for El Paso. On the long drive we didn't talk much. Mother clasped her beloved rosary between her fingers and I knew as the miles rolled by she was telling her beads in an agony of love and anguish.

The doctor, when he had sized my mother up, told her the truth. "Your son is going to die, Mrs. Hilton," he said.

Boy, too, knew the verdict, although he never let on to Mother. I sat by his bed during long days and longer nights for over a week and watched his body fail. But, as I wrote Rosemary, his spirit never failed once. I told her of his courage, his even cheer, his little jokes. I reported his jest with his doctor on a day very near the end. "Doctor," he demanded, "why couldn't you have found me a little old tropical disease instead of this?"

When he'd look straight at me with questioning eyes I'd say, "Don't give up, Boy," just as I used to say when he was a little fellow learning to walk and kept falling down. And he'd smile and say, "I won't give up, Connie." And he didn't. But this was no "little old tropical disease." Within ten days Boy was gone.

Mother heard the news erect, silent, her fingers clinging to her rosary. I wanted so much to comfort her. I remembered the day in San Antonio after baby Julian died, when the old Mexican woman had come into our house with her shawl over her head. What had she said? "You have lost a little boy. I have lost a grown son. To you it will be a memory. To me always a *dolor.*"

Now my mother, too, would always have a sorrow besides the memory of her little one, and I would share it with her. In Boy I had lost not only my brother, but a cherished companion—my very good friend.

Once again we both clung strongly to our rope, our Faith. And our rope held in the crisis. When that was over and the emptiness set in, I tasted again that compulsion to turn from my grief and plunge into work.

I decided to build another mountain, this one bigger and more challenging than ever.

El Paso is the gateway to Mexico. It has all the color of the rugged Old West plus the romantic flavor engraved on it by the Spanish dons. It was smaller than Dallas but it was a big Texas city even then, with a tradition and traffic all its own.

In the middle of town, facing on the historic Pioneer Plaza, was a piece of ground where an old hotel had burned down. I wanted to build a new one there, something special, with buildings and décor embracing the best of the town's Spanish and western legacy.

I signed a ninety-nine-year lease on the site and prepared for my new venture. At about the same time I was joined by J. B. Herndon, Jr.

Herndon, Texas born and New Mexico bred, was the brother of Alice Herndon whom I had known at the Thirty Club in Albuquerque during our dashing youth. I had known his father as well, for Herndon, Sr., owned a bank there that crashed in the early '20s. J.B., Jr., was trained in banking, a graduate of the Missouri School of Journalism, witty, outspoken, and straight-thinking. Until his death in 1953, he remained one of my most valued associates.

His coming in at the time I started in El Paso was particularly opportune.

Ira Casteel, Major Powers, and Boy were gone. Carl had given up the hotel business and returned to active duty with the Navy. Mary was busy with our toddling sons. My mother had traveled east to be with Rosemary when her baby, a daughter named Constance Ann, was born. Then, with her sister Bertha, Mother sailed for a trip around the world. She sent me occasional souvenirs: a ticket from the Passion Play at Oberammergau, a franc note from Nancy, post cards from Interlaken and The Hague, and a long letter about her audience with the Pope. When she got to Cairo she wrote the redoubtable Annie Meyers, still society editor of the Socorro *Chieftain*, announcing that she was staying at the world-famous Shepheard's Hotel. Annie, who had never heard of it, translated the item to read: "Mrs. A. H. Hilton is enjoying herself at a well known Sheep Herder's Hotel in Egypt."

And so, as I headed into one of the most dangerous adventures of my life, it was good to have the steady, friendly, business-wise Herndon at my side.

I was dreaming bigger and bigger. I had organized Hilton Hotels, Inc., to consolidate all the properties into one group. I was getting ready to move outside Texas, with an option on a hotel in Oklahoma City and plans to build in Wichita, Kansas, and Mobile, Alabama. It was an expanding program and nothing alerted me to the fact that I was expanding on the brink of disaster.

The project closest to my heart, the one that came first, was the El Paso Hilton. In the fall of 1929, I announced that we would build a hotel on Pioneer Plaza costing $1,750,000. Nineteen days later the stock market crashed.

9. THE ONLY GILT-EDGED SECURITY

If I had climbed tall mountains, looked at wide horizons, and
felt myself equal to anything I could dream, the time had
come now to walk through a long, dark valley. I was not
alone. The whole of America went through that great Depression. And on each of us it left a mark.

For me the heights had bred vision and confidence. But it
was in the valley that I learned true humility—found that
when everything material failed, faith remained the only gilt-
edged security.

In over forty years I had never, without good reason,
missed a Sunday Mass. Now I started every single day on my
knees in church. To me there is nothing shameful about praying when you're in trouble. If prayer has been the habit of a
lifetime it's the natural thing to do. If you have never prayed
before it's a good time to start. Either way there can be times
when you are overwhelmed and there is no place else to
turn.

Such times now came to me. And each time the walls were
about to close in and crush me, when there was no light for
even one step ahead, "something" happened—a bellboy thrust
his life savings into my hand, a difficult business rival took
everything I had with one hand and gave it back with the
other, a promise that meant my business life was broken by
one man and seven others stepped in to fill the breach.

Could I take credit for personal cleverness in things like
that? I could not. To me they were answered prayer.

I myself am incapable of pulling a single rabbit out of a
hat. Yet throughout the Depression, when I desperately
needed a rabbit one seemed to appear.

The panic that paralyzed the East in 1929 and sent men
leaping from windows did not immediately engulf the southwest. It swept toward us slowly but inevitably. It was not
like a sudden plunge off a steep precipice but like slipping out
of control down a rocky hillside, bump, bump, bump, getting
sorer and weaker all the time.

We had only started to slide when, on November 5, 1930, managed to complete the El Paso Hilton.

It looks so simple written down like that. Yet building any-hing just then was not a simple matter at all. You cannot rect a hotel without money any more than you can make ricks without straw. And you could say that J. B. Herndon nd I picked up each wisp of straw by hand to make this ream a reality.

When the El Paso Hilton opened, the newspapers reported 5,000 people coming to share in our victory. That is a slight xaggeration. But this is solid truth: more people came then rom all over Texas, from all over New Mexico, than were register as paying guests for many a long year.

They came only partially to see the hotel. True, they were wed by such wonders as penthouses ("exclusive suites on the oof," as we called them), a building that climbed nineteen tories into the sky, and three hundred rooms carefully dec-rated in the tradition of the Indians, Spaniards, and pioneers.

But they came, too, to participate in a miracle of hope, a lag flown confidently in the face of adversity. For by then lmost everyone was talking doom. The people who came to ur opening wanted reassurance. And we gave this to them.

They were disheartened and wanted a party. And we gave hem a party as well. Our kitchen fed twelve hundred chick-ns to invited guests in one evening. Invitations were at a pre-nium. Sam D. Young, president of the El Paso National ank, one of our solid backers as well as one of the most im-ortant men in town, almost missed the main event when he ost his tickets. On opening night I got a frantic call from am. He had been barred at the threshold. Would I please ome down and let him in? As part of the festivities I hosted stag dinner for three hundred fifty. Five hundred danced t our ball.

Publicly and as often as I could I stated my faith in Amer-ca . . . the Golden Land . . . the Land of Opportunity. This "thing," I said, couldn't last. Our guests believed it. I be-ieved it. And we were right. But at that moment no one could foresee how far down a man could go before the 'thing" was over.

There were obligations contracted in normal times—and we tried valiantly not to betray that trust. We made promises in good faith and could not know of the myriad events, great and small, that would arise to prevent our keeping them.

I made a promise to myself the night of the El Paso opening. It was an important promise. I vowed that I would neve
let any hotel come between me and my wife. Ironic that i
was only then, when things were already slipping beyond m
control, that I recognized such a possibility.

It was my sister Rosemary who alerted me to the danger
Rosemary and her husband had come from New York an
my sister Eva from Boston for my party. Mother, too, bac
from her world cruise, came for dinner at the El Paso Hil
ton, fell in love with it, and made it her headquarters for th
rest of her life. We were all agreed that this opening was
brave and beautiful party. All, that is, except Mary.

Mary, of course, was there. In the brief glimpses I caugh
of her between my hundred duties as host, I thought sh
looked lovelier than ever, and perfectly happy. Then, on th
night of the banquet, when the major speeches were com
pleted, I saw her gather up her wrap and go upstairs to ou
rooms. Rosemary noticed it, too.

"Connie," she asked earnestly, "have you ever wondered i
hotels bore Mary?"

I was aghast. No one could be bored with hotels, least o
all a hotel man's wife. They were the substance of the stars
wanted to pour in Mary's lap.

"One hotel," said my sister sagely, "could mean a living
Two, luxury. But more could combine into a bitter rival
They could take up too much time. Don't forget Mary i
young and used to a lot of attention."

I protested. Didn't I build the hotels for her, for our sons
for our future security? Wasn't I attentive about bringing he
gifts, a dress usually, since she liked my selections, when
had to be away any length of time? Didn't I spend every fre
moment with my family?

"Well, maybe your free moments have been getting
scarcer. Maybe she'd rather have more of you and fewe
dresses. Maybe she's more interested in the present than th
future. . . ."

Right then I promised myself that I would never let my
business interfere with my home. I, who from that night on
was running before a tidal wave carrying my investors' fate
as well as that of my family's with me, vowed that one young
lady with laughing eyes should see more, not less, of her
husband.

Looking back on it now I can see it for what it was, a futile, wistful wish. I had about as much chance to keep such a promise as has a soldier off to war.

Like the Depression itself, what happened to Mary and me didn't come all at once. But, as I floundered through my valley, fighting desperately day and night to keep my footing, little by little the laughter went out of Mary's eyes.

After the El Paso opening I went broke by inches.

There was no thought now of *more* hotels, or *new* hotels. The constant struggle was to keep the ones I had, to hang onto a few, or finally, even one. My plans to be more attentive to my family were eventually swept away beneath a frenzied effort to keep them fed, clothed and housed.

What happened first was that hotel occupancy fell off. People weren't traveling. Salesmen weren't selling. The rolls of unemployed mounted steadily. J. B. Herndon and I would sit late at night in our office at the Dallas Hilton and go over the ailing books. Marlin, Lubbock, San Angelo, El Paso, each of our eight hotels, told the same story.

Week by week the income was a little less than before. Yet each week the operating costs remained constant. J.B. and I dashed from one to the other trying to cut those costs. Here I would close off a floor to save light and heat. Over the way I would take the room phones out and save fifteen cents on each. It took a good deal of talking to bolster the flagging *esprit de corps* of our personnel and teach them to smile while reducing menus, serving half pats of butter, turning off every possible light bulb.

"Clean beds, towels, fresh soap, always," I said over and over. "We will not economize on linen. But guard the luxuries—even the pen points, stationery, ink."

And still the revenues fell—and kept on falling.

And still the land leases, interest on loans, taxes, had to be met. Those land leases, which had not tied up valuable capital, and the fact that I had always done business with conservative banks, helped prolong the inevitable, but that was all.

Our reserve went first. Then J.B. and I, with the proverbial towel cooling our aching heads, would go over and over those hotel books to see where we could draw a few dollars for operating expenses, payrolls. I actually recall a week when we decided Marlin could afford to contribute $25 and El Paso $35, a pitiful intake balanced against a staggering need.

I had used up my personal funds and borrowed on my insurance. I remember still with gratitude the day I talked this drastic step over with Mary. "Of course you must do it, Connie," said my wife stoutly. "This won't last forever. If you can borrow enough to stagger through you'll come back stronger than ever."

How gallantly she rose to the big things! And how I valued her faith in me! But when I had gotten the insurance loan and had to dash off to Plainview to meet pressing obligations, she was bitterly disappointed because she had counted on me to make a fourth for bridge.

Possibly there was something I could have said that I didn't say. Possibly I should have taken more time to explain. But time, just then, was pressing me sorely. I never had enough of it. I would barely stave off disaster in Plainview when Marlin would be in trouble. And so it went. With me dashing all over Texas—and Mary alone at home.

Soon I was failing to meet interest charges. Here and there taxes became delinquent, nor was the end in sight. We lost Waco when we couldn't meet the land rent. Obviously I needed to pull out a fair-sized rabbit, and the hat looked empty. Who at that time had the kind of money I had to have, and would lend it? There was one prominent family in Galveston, the Moodys, who came to my mind. They had it. But they were careful with it. Still, my need was urgent and so, with a prayer, I went off to Galveston.

Riding over the "Katy," as the Missouri, Kansas and Texas Railroad was affectionately called, I reviewed what I knew of the Moodys. It didn't raise my hopes.

The name Moody and the name Galveston were practically synonymous. They owned the Galveston baseball team, banks, hotels, insurance companies, the newspapers. Unlike the Long family of Baton Rouge, they had somehow continuously failed to corner the political field, but in all else they were supreme. They even had their own separate Chamber of Commerce and refused to belong to the ordinary one.

The important Moodys were W. L. Moody, the father, and Shearn Moody, his son. I knew neither of them well. I was to know them better, to my sorrow, before my valley was traversed.

I knew enough of them then to regard them as a strange pair. Shearn, at thirty-five, was the dominant personality and those who secretly called him "King Midas" had hit the keynote of his character. Once when his father, in a burst of soft-heartedness contributed $200 to the non-Moody Chamber of Commerce, Shearn was reported to have burst into the senior Moody's office in a towering rage. "Papa, what do you mean," he demanded, "by giving money to our enemies?"

Shearn Moody was a man who did, indeed, love his enemies. He doted on them. He freely and openly claimed that he could never have as many as he wished. When a friend of mine had asked Shearn for a loan to keep his insurance company afloat, he was not surprised when Shearn turned him down. But he was angered by Shearn's manner in doing so. Barely able to keep his temper, my friend said: "Shearn, I've always wondered why nine men out of ten who've done business with you call you names."

"I can tell you why," Shearn grinned. "Because that's the way I like it. I'd like it better if it was ninety-nine out of a hundred."

These, then, were the men who controlled the American Life Insurance Company of Galveston from which I hoped to borrow $300,000. The closer the "Katy" carried me toward my destination, the more I wondered.

My business with the Moodys didn't take long. They heard me through, conversed briefly, and agreed to the loan. I had prayed and I had hoped. But when I signed ny name to a note putting up the Hilton Hotels, Inc. stock as security, and received in return the money I so sorely needed, I couldn't have been more surprised if a cottontail had suddenly hopped out of my old Stetson.

I had been in real danger and, at the eleventh hour, "Something" had happened to give me a new lease on life.

With that $300,000 judiciously spread around I bought time. And of course prosperity and paying guests should have followed before that time ran out. Only it didn't work that way.

Time was all I got out of it. Time and a brief period of refreshment with Mary and the boys. It was a blessed relief to deal for a while only with the normal, homely problems that arise within a family circle. Barron, I remember, at the age of three, worried Mary and me terribly by refusing to eat. Mary would cajole and I would threaten and Barron would sit there and stare at us. Eat he would not. The two boys were very different. Barron on the one hand was careful, quiet, single-minded. Nick was mercurial, outgoing, spontaneous. Nick got into more mischief, but Barron was harder to handle.

Nick and I celebrated my brief respite by going together to have our tonsils removed. We came home with very sore throats and the certain conviction that we were minor heroes. Barron was scheduled for the same adventure shortly and watched us with interest.

Mary had been firm that we must set Barron a good example and for Nick, who thoroughly enjoyed the whole affair, this was easy. I, who had enjoyed no part of it, had aroused Barron's suspicions. Trying to reassure him I croaked painfully: "Nothing to it, Barron. Nick had his out. Daddy had his out. . . ."

"And Barron ain't," said that young man. Walking out of my room he had made up his mind and later, when his turn came, it took Mary, me, my mother, and Mary's mother, two doctors and the floor nurse to change it. Barron was like that.

"Nick," my mother summed up the two from her wide experience, "has charm. Barron has determination." And at that age it was certainly true.

This was not a vacation period for me. I worked steadily trying to drum up business for our hotels, making rates to groups, proposing deals to electric light companies, laundries and the like, whereby they would purchase stock or suspend payment in return for long-term contracts. But at least I had time for a little golf, time to play bridge with Mary, to come home for dinner. There was harmony between us for a while, something like harmony in my heart.

Actually we were pretending, in a bit of sunshine that had crept into our valley, that everything was all right, everything was normal. But we couldn't keep it up very long. The sand in the hourglass was running low on my borrowed time.

Once again there were payrolls, taxes, land leases, interest on notes to meet. The $300,000 had gone out and nothing had come in. There was, quite simply, no money. I needed another $200,000 to keep going. Banks shied away from me like I had the plague; hotels were, as someone put it, a "drudge on the market."

I remember sitting in a sort of blank despair in my Dallas office one afternoon and looking up to see my mother standing there. She had come, I knew, all the way from El Paso to find out how things were with me. I tried to grin reassuringly but she must have seen right through that grin because it was one of our few awkward visits. We talked of this and that. She showed me a clipping from the Fort Dodge paper announcing the seventy-fifth anniversary of the Laufersweiler furniture store, the store my grandfather Conrad had built from nothing but a tool chest and a pair of skilled hands. It had lasted through thick and thin for three-quarters of a century. And here I was, after a mere twelve years, about to go under at any moment.

"Maybe," I said ruefully, "I'm in the wrong business. Maybe I should have learned to make cradles and coffins."

Mother got up and she looked every inch a Laufersweiler, every inch a pioneer. It was then she said, "Some men jump out windows, some quit, some go to church. Pray Connie, pray harder. And don't you dare give up!"

When she left I put on my hat and went to call on Bob Thornton. I told him I *had* to have $200,000. Bob looked out the window. "You see that Baker Hotel over there? Sixteen stories of it?"

I nodded grimly, wondering what he had in mind.

"Connie, I could just as easily jump over that hotel as let you have $200,000." Cotton, he said, was down to five cents a pound, "and that means only the katydids and the lizards are going to enjoy this summer."

He was just about right. But he did manage to let me have $55,000 and the hotels devoured it among them like locusts. Again the debts piled up and there was no money. I thought we had hit rock bottom. There was worse to come.

There were humiliations that have a sting in them even now—and mixed among them some of the finest memories I have, of the faith and loyalty of a handful of people who continued to believe in me.

Perhaps my sense of time betrays me, but the end seemed to come so fast, one thing on top of another, blow upon blow, that I couldn't catch my breath.

A sheriff's deputy paid me a business call at the Dallas Hilton office. "I've got a judgment here I've come to collect. Pay up or I'll tack it in the lobby," he said.

"Tack away," I said in a burst of fury born of helplessness. "You can use my ladder."

In a matter of minutes he was back. "It's marble," he said sheepishly. "You knew perfectly well I couldn't put it up."

"And you know perfectly well I'll pay that bill. All I need is time—time to get the money." I got time on that one.

Immediately a furniture company in North Carolina sued. This one hit me between the eyes. Originally I had owed them $100,000. Even during the past few years I had kept painfully nibbling away on that bill until it was reduced to $178. And for $178 they hauled me into court.

Right then my attorney began talking bankruptcy. "You're behind to the Moodys. You're behind to Thornton. You owe Mathias on the land lease in El Paso, Loudermilk here in Dallas," he said. "Connie, you're over half a million in debt. You won't get out in a thousand years. Wipe it off, boy."

"And lose the only thing I've got left?" I demanded. "My credit? Credit is my life's blood. I can't go bankrupt."

I couldn't, either. There was a stigma about it, an admission of defeat. It was quitting and I wasn't about to quit.

"That would be having no faith," I told Bob Thornton. "Running out of hope. If I run out of those I'm dead and I know it."

Every morning when I left church I was always full of both. Sure that something would happen. Why, only a few weeks before, when I'd been out of carfare and everything seemed unalterably black, a young bellboy, Eddie Fowler, walked resolutely up to me in the lobby and thrust something in my hand. "Just eating money, Mr. Hilton," he blurted out and fled, leaving me with $300, his life's savings.

"And I took it, Bob, because I needed eating money," I told Thornton. "And because Eddie has confidence that I'll come back. And I will. If I went bankrupt I'd be betraying people like that. Who'd ever trust me with a dollar again?"

"I would, Connie," Bob said, looking straight at me. "I would."

I'll never forget the way Bob looked nor those five words any more than I can ever forget Eddie Fowler and what he did. Those two men held a mirror up and said, "This is the way you look to us."

And there were others.

One morning when I drove into the gas station where I had a charge account and asked to have my tank filled the embarrassed attendant stammered out, "I'm sorry, Mr. Hilton, but I'm not allowed to charge any more gas for you." For a minute I couldn't think of anything to say. Until recently I'd been a good customer. Now I didn't pay my bills regularly. Word had gotten around. It hurt.

"It's not that I don't trust you," the man continued. "I sure do. Why, I've had that order for a week and I couldn't bear to tell you. Those last two tanks were on me." He filled it up again on him and grinned. "I ain't worried," he said.

But I was. A few days later I didn't have the rent money and Mary and the boys had no groceries in the house. I borrowed enough to drive them to the El Paso Hilton where they would have a roof and food.

But for how long? How long could I hold the El Paso Hotel? I didn't know. And then what? Again I didn't know.

Mother was still at El Paso, still independently managing her properties, collecting $4.00 a month on the building in San Antonio which had once been my bank and now housed the post office, something on the house at Socorro, a little on a ranch she had bought in Texas. She told me not to worry about her. But Helen, after a brief, unhappy marriage, had joined her at the hotel, and I found out they had been ordering one dinner and two forks in the dining room, splitting one sixty-cent meal between the two of them.

"And why not?" Mother demanded indignantly. "Everybody knows we all overeat."

How could I help but worry?

And I worried, too, over my hotel family. They had all been intensely loyal and it had been some time since any of us had had regular money. We managed to pay the hired help, but the executives and their families were all living now in hotels and working for free room and board. Bill Irwin was at Marlin, J. B. Herndon at Dallas, L. M. Drown in Abilene, and his grown son Joe in Plainview. At Abilene a talented bellboy, Spearl "Red" Ellison, had been promoted to assistant manager just in time to share our fate. The depression low had made other new talent available. Robert P. Williford, whose uncle was president of the University of Texas, had joined us as key clerk at the Dallas Hilton—$30 per month, no room or board. Bob, a very polished young man had been a great friend of my brother Boy and frequently my partner at bridge. Over the bridge table we were "Connie" and "Bob," but once we were in the same business it took some months to get my very correct new key clerk to relax the formality of addressing me as "Mr. Hilton."

That was my hotel family—Bob, Red, Bill, J.B., the Drowns. If I lost the hotels where did we go from there?

I, personally, was living out of my suitcase, rushing from one hotel to another, from one town to another, borrowing my fare where I could, always trying to raise a dollar here, a dollar there, and not having much luck.

It was on such a trip in the final grim month of 1931, that I saw in a magazine that picture of the brand new Waldorf-Astoria in New York. Like my depression baby, the El Paso Hilton, here was another, a bigger and finer, hotel flag flown confidently in the face of adversity. It was even more to me than the most beautiful hotel I had then seen. "The greatest of them all" was a brief glimpse again of the high mountains, the wide horizons I had all but forgotten since I had been so long in the valley.

I clipped it and put it in my wallet. My own small hotel world might collapse. My own mountains might come tumbling down. But this was America. I could still hope. I could still dream.

At that very moment the Moodys in Galveston were preparing to foreclose. They considered my position hopeless. I was clearly in default on payments on my $300,000 loan. The Hilton hotels were their collateral.

Within a few weeks they took over my hotels. They now owned the roof over my wife's head, over my mother's head, controlled the fate of my loyal partners.

I had nothing left.

This time I needed to see a jackrabbit jump out of that hat. A cottontail wouldn't do. And the hat seemed to have a hole in it.

Again "something" happened.

What happened next gave me back some faith in myself, proved to me that I was a good hotel man as well as a faithful *pray-er*. For the Moodys invited me to Galveston and offered me back the management of my own hotels together with a flock of very sick ones of their own.

The idea was that we merge the Hilton hotels and the

Conrad N. Hilton on his horse, Chiquita.

Family group (*left to right*): Felice, Mrs. Mary Hilton, Connie, Baby Carl, Gus Hilton, Eva.

Connie's mother,
Mary Laufersweiler Hilton.

Connie's father, Gus Hilton.

Connie's father, Gus Hilton (*at wheel*) driving down Hilton Boulevard in the Ford in which he was killed.

Hillsborough Road parade led by veterans. Col. Gus Hilton, officer of the day, on foot to left of the parade.

Conrad Hilton *(back row, second from left)* on baseball team,
New Mexico School of Mines.

Hilton Trio *(left to right)*:
Viva Head, Eva Hilton, Edith Chapman.

Conrad Hilton, manager of the Hilton Trio, on tour.

Conrad Hilton (arrow, second row) at Officers' Training Camp, Presidio, San Francisco, 1917.

Three Hilton brothers at their mother's home in Socorro, 1921 *(left to right)*: Boy, Carl, Conrad.

Conrad Hilton with his mother, Mrs. Mary Hilton, at Town House, Los Angeles, 1947, shortly before her death.

The first Hilton hotel, the Mobley, in Cisco, Texas.

The Waldorf Astoria, Park Avenue, New York City.

Nick *(left)* and Barron *(right)* with Zsa Zsa Gabor
in Los Angeles, 1944.

Nick Hilton with his bride Elizabeth Taylor, Conrad Hilton,
and Mrs. Mary Saxon (Nick's mother and formerly
Mrs. Conrad Hilton).

(Left to right) Nick, Conrad, Barron at Bel-Air, 1937.
The dog is Torch.

(Left to right) Barron, Nick, Eric, with their father in 1956.

Mr. and Mrs. Barron Hilton
with some of their family.

Conrad Hilton, with Mr. and Mrs. Eric Hilton
and their children.

Conrad Hilton *(center)* with Olive Wakeman and Will Keleher.

Conrad Hilton with Mrs. Alice Statler at the Statler Hilton opening in Dallas, January, 1956.

Hilton Hotels Corporation, top echelon (*left to right, seated*): Conrad N. Hilton, Robert P. Williford; (*standing*): Spearl Ellison, Joseph P. Binns, the late J. B. Herndon.

Conrad Hilton holds checks totaling $111,000,000 used in the purchase of the Statler Hotels system, October 27, 1954.

Conrad Hilton with Col. Henry Crown in Istanbul.

Host at the Congressional Prayer Breakfast,
with President Eisenhower, 1956.

Conrad Hilton's present home, Casa Encantada,
in Bel-Air, Los Angeles.

Moody hotels into the National Hotel Company, I would be one-third owner in the new company and acting general manager at a salary of $18,000 a year. The proposition was put to me by the father. Son Shearn had very little interest in the company which we formed. It was, however, sufficient to put sand in the machinery, as I soon discovered.

The National Hotel Company was the kind of a straw that looks like a raft to a drowning man. I grabbed and hung on. It was the answer to my immediate problem, that of my family, and of the employees who had stood by me. Yet the instinct for preservation did not cloud my common sense.

After a slight brush with Shearn on the second day of my stay in his town I did some thinking. Shearn told me flatly that he liked the Depression and he told me why. "People are down," he said. "They are desperate for money. It's the time to drive a good bargain."

There and then I decided to protect myself so that, should my raft suddenly sink, I would not lose my hide. I went back to talk to the old man.

"What happens," I asked Mr. Moody, "if we disagree some place along the line? What if one of us is dissatisfied and we want to separate? I wouldn't want bad blood between us."

"No need for it," he said. "We'd just separate friendly, that's all."

"I'd like a contract," I said, "stipulating that if we agree to disagree, we would partition the hotels on the same basis we organized. Two-thirds and one-third. You would take two, I would take one, and so on."

I felt a lot better when he promised me that contract, although I didn't have time to wait for it right then. There was some money in my pocket now, and a couple of fellows I had to see. One was the bellboy, Eddie Fowler, in Dallas. Another was a gas station attendant. It was good to arrive in El Paso and be able to reassure Mary and my mother. To tell the boys that Mr. Moody wanted me to bring them down for fishing. To let L. M. Drown know that we were still in business. To phone young Red Ellison at Abilene that he would begin to get paid. To give Bob Williford his $30 per month *with* room and board.

Bill Irwin, who had stayed around until the worst was over, now decided to strike out for California and see if he could find a hotel for himself. "You're going to have to keep to a minimum, Connie, and there may not be enough to go around," he said truthfully. "I'll do some prospecting for us out there."

Like Bill, J. B. Herndon's reaction was not entirely optimistic. I explained that Mr. Moody felt this was the start of a wonderful friendship and a long business association.

"And it could be, J.B.," I said. "He wants me to move to Galveston and there I draw the line. Mary wouldn't like it and neither would I. But Moody and I might do big things together."

Herndon admitted cautiously that it was certainly a nice change of outlook for a man who had been starving a brief few weeks before, "but you've been your own boss too long, Connie," he cautioned.

"I still am. I'm general manager—and one-third owner," I said.

"Shearn's got his finger in this pie," J.B. said slowly. "And I don't think you and he do business the same way."

It didn't take me long to find out that J.B. had a point.

I made a swing of the Moody hotels and discovered that Shearn, a busy man, took the time to go over personally every smallest bill connected with every smallest detail of our operations. For the first time in my experience I had trouble with reluctant managers. In Birmingham I told the manager of the Thomas Jefferson to have the lobby desk repainted.

"Are you authorizing me to hire a painter?" he asked.

"Certainly," I said.

"And pay for the paint?"

"What's the matter with you?" I demanded. "Certainly we'll pay for the paint."

"Shearn Moody won't like it," he predicted. He told me that he had once decided to adorn his lobby with a painting of Thomas Jefferson. When he sent through the bill, Shearn Moody had written: "You have just bought yourself a portrait," and when his next pay check came through he found he had.

"Get the lobby desk re-done," I said. "This is a different kind of painting." And set off for my next stop.

When I got back to Dallas I found a bill for paint sent on to me by the manager at Birmingham. Across it, in Shearn's handwriting, was a note: "I can get paint for thirty cents less a can in Galveston. Next time it will come out of your salary."

To say that I was annoyed would be mild. I got more annoyed when I found that if I ordered a dozen towels for a hotel, Shearn felt we could have gotten along with ten. If we paid x dollars for kitchen supplies, Shearn knew where we could get scouring pads, soap powder, dish towels, for half that price—and considered them a luxury anyway.

I talked it over as tactfully as I could with the senior Moody. But it wasn't easy to tell a partner tactfully that his son, a very small shareholder in our company, was sabotaging my best efforts. I took Nick and Barron with me to Galveston on that trip. It gave Mary a little rest and me a chance to fulfill my promise of taking them fishing. We were trolling in the Gulf off a small boat when I had my talk with Mr. Moody.

The old man shook his head. "Shearn *does* want his pound of flesh," he admitted. "But he's a smart boy, Connie. And I've got to stick by my son."

If I didn't agree as a businessman, at least I respected his honesty and loyalty. These two qualities stood me, as well as Shearn, in good stead. For now, as I plainly saw the handwriting on the wall, I was more than ever determined to get that contract agreeing to the method of our separating.

"Shearn doesn't want you to have it," Mr. Moody said flatly.

"But *you* promised it to me," I pointed out.

For a minute he looked square at me and then said, "Yup, b'gad, I did." Next day the contract was drawn and signed. Throughout the whole dreary business that followed, the senior Moody and I remained friends. He, like Shearn, had his peculiarities, but unlike Shearn's they didn't get in my way. Moody senior was prompt to the point of madness and lived by an absolute routine, as methodical as he was prompt. Every day at four sharp he took his mother, a venerable old lady past ninety, for a drive. Every noon at exactly twelve he ate his lunch. On an exact day each June, year in and year out, he left for his summer camp and on a fixed day in August for his ranch. Although neither he nor Shearn seemed to have any religious convictions, they were both strict about alcohol and tobacco. Not only did they never drink or smoke, but their guests were not permitted a free choice in the matter.

These idiosyncrasies bothered me not one whit. Texas was full of rugged individualists. Even Shearn's overzealousness about my spending had its funny side. Laughs had been few and far between in this tense period and some of our skirmishes were almost welcome.

I recall particularly a drawing of Stephen Austin, the "father of Texas," which I commissioned for the menus in our Austin hotel. Perhaps it wasn't a necessity, but it seemed the right thing to do. We had had a talented but broke artist doing odd jobs at that hotel, painting lavatories, halls and the like, for meals and his room. He did it gratefully and quietly, but there came a time when the holes in his shoes were past the cardboard treatment, and his eyes had that frustrated look that made me expect a landscape might suddenly appear from the end of his brush while he was doing a kitchen wall.

The manager and I talked it over. He wouldn't take charity and we decided to offer him $35 for an "original" of Austin. When Shearn balked at payment, the disgruntled manager wrote that the guests had been very enthusiastic. "They feel he has created a very fine Austin," he advised Shearn. Back came Shearn's answer: "Your artist didn't create Austin. His father did. Your mistake."

But there was nothing funny about the basic disagreement between us on how to run hotels. Nor about the fact that I watched them let my old hotels, Dallas and Abilene, get into more financial trouble. There would be an emergency over the land lease and Shearn would brush it aside, as if the holding of the Hilton hotels in the National chain was of no consequence. For nine months I did my best to hold things together. Then I realized it would never work. I had had no salary. I had had no cooperation. Things had to be brought to a head.

I decided on a simple method of forcing a decision. The next time Shearn returned a legitimate small bill unpaid, I exercised my full authority. I sent it back to him with a penciled notation: "As general manager of this company I order you to pay this bill." If he didn't pay it, he had disobeyed my orders. If he did, he had lost forever his ability to hamper me.

Shearn decided not to pay.

In Galveston, their town, the Moodys sued to end our relationship, to freeze me out entirely.

In Dallas, my town, I brought countersuit, demanding that we separate under the terms of our contract.

It was the end of 1932. Economically the country was still crushed. I was back where I had started from, still broke, still without a hotel to my name. But I had an idea, a direction. It was only a glimmer of light. I thought I saw a way to recover my depression baby, the El Paso Hilton, and make a new start.

The idea was simple. The Moodys were about to abandon the heavily indebted El Paso property. They felt it had so little chance of recovery that when Albert Mathias, owner of the Pioneer Plaza site I had leased so hopefully for ninety-nine years, gave them the choice of paying $30,000 back rent or foreclosure, Shearn refused to "send good money after bad."

"They have the money and they don't want the hotel," I told J. B. Herndon.

"And you have no money, and you do," he replied.

Fortunately Mathias didn't want it either. He was not a hotel man. He gave me an outside chance. "I own the building now," he said, "but you pay up the arrears on the ground rent and we'll make out a new lease."

Once I had cheerfully set out to raise a million dollars— and had done it. It had been an adventure. Now I had only to raise $30,000 and I couldn't seem to get thirty cents. Those next months were not adventure, they were a nightmare.

On the one hand I was fighting the Moodys, trying to negotiate a settlement of the National hotels that would not completely wipe me out. Shearn insisted the contract was no good and they could cancel it. I knew I had a right to a third of the hotels and a third of the stock. Outwardly we kept the semblance of friendship. Negotiations were conducted through their chief counsel, Judge Anderson. But inwardly, I knew it was a bitter battle, that it could drag on for years, and we were not equally armed. I had the contract, true, but they had the money for the long fight. I had no money.

On the other hand, I was crisscrossing Texas on a mad treasure hunt for $30,000 that would put me in business again. It was a battle on two fronts and, as I had done the last time I went to war, I began once more to keep a diary. That record of the year 1933 reads like what it was, the hasty, breathless jottings of a beleaguered fellow, made during odd moments in trains, hotel rooms, nights when I couldn't sleep, days when I couldn't think. It is a travelogue of flying journeys, the minutes of the last meeting, brief family notes . . . a few happy, as for instance, "Mary is expecting a baby," most of them sad.

Glancing through it on my desk today I can almost feel the dreadful urgency I knew then. "*Galveston*: Judge Anderson has threatened to call off negotiations. Mr. Moody has issued an ultimatum. His offer isn't fair. I have countered. Moody says *no*. Very Firm! . . . *New Orleans*: Bondholders' meeting of National hotel in that city. No conclusion reached. . . . *Abilene*: There is an emergency here. They are threatening foreclosure and Shearn says it's not very important. . . . *Dallas*: Saw E. P. Greenwood, president of Great Southern Life Insurance Company of Dallas, and described the deal on the El Paso Hilton to him. He will consider loaning the $30,000! . . . President Roosevelt has closed the banks. This is going to throw everyone for a spell. The boys are trying to get me to worry about the political situation. Like telling a drowning man to worry about the view. . . . *El Paso*: Have decided to move Mary and the boys back to Dallas. Don't know how I'll manage but I must. They need a home *now*. . . . *On Katy en route to Galveston*: Papers are full of news about what repeal of 18th Amendment will mean to business. Employment etc. Will mean a lot to hotels just with 3.2 beer and wines. If I could only *get* a hotel. *Galveston*: Shearn Moody and I are as far apart as ever. Asked him for his interpretation of contract and he said: 'No durn good. You just get out of National Hotels.' They are willing to return a couple of sick properties they don't want. I am demanding return of my hotels plus a $110,000 loan for my interest in the whole thing. . . . *Dallas*: July 1, Eric Michael Hilton born at St. Paul's at ten A.M. . . . *On train to El Paso*: Must get something solid to show Greenwood. I know I can straighten that hotel out if I can only get a *chance*. . . . The CRISIS is coming. Mathias is leaving for California. Has given me six weeks to raise money. . . . *Dallas*: Greenwood has agreed to back me! Said 'I'll give you the money if I have to steal it!' This is *it*. . . . *El Paso*: Meeting with attorneys. Greenwood's, Mathias', mine, to go over deal. We give a little, take a little, barter, bargain. Sure feels good. . . . Greenwood has gone to St. Louis, but called first and said he'd wire the money if necessary. The worst is over!"

Yes, I remember exactly how I felt that day and I remember how I felt two days later when Greenwood called and asked me to fly to St. Louis. "There are a few matters I want to discuss," he said ominously.

"He's going to back out," warned J. B. Herndon who called shortly afterward from Dallas, "told a mutual friend it's too risky."

I was astounded. Immediately I phoned Greenwood. He was, said the operator, too ill to talk to me. This was the first time I had heard of any illness. I flew to St. Louis to lay the matter before him in person.

I gave Greenwood a copy of the agreement, explained in detail that every request his lawyer had made had been incorporated, and asked him to sign. He advised me to come back in fifteen minutes. In less than that the phone rang. "I've decided not to go through with it," he said.

"You're making a mistake," I said as calmly as I could.

"Well, it's not the first one," he retorted.

"I don't suppose I could do anything to change your mind?" I asked.

"No," he said, and there was a finality about it.

Greenwood and I were to do friendly business again, but that night I jotted down bitterly in the diary: "Greenwood reneged on this deal in a cold blooded fashion."

I didn't have time to sit and weep. "*Back in El Paso,*" the diary reports on September 5, "and no time to stop off and see Mary or the baby. What a Labor Day week-end! Called everyone I could think of as a substitute backer. My time's running out. McKee, the contractor who built the El Paso, said he'd consider it. He'll let me know this afternoon. . . . J.B. arrived and talked about possibility of getting guarantors to endorse $30,000 note for Bob Thornton. He called Bob while I called everyone I could imagine who might endorse in an emergency. Herndon reports Bob is sending over Ben Read, a vice-president of his bank, to look into the situation. McKee called and we rehashed the deal. He might, says he, and he might not. Great time to play games! . . . Up at five as usual. Go to church. Come back. Pace. Stew. Make phone calls. Funny thought, three years after opening, after raising $1,750,000 to build this hotel, I can't seem to raise one-fiftieth to keep it. . . . McKee called and said he had decided to decline the deal. Read arrived and looked around, then we all talk on the phone to Bob, in Dallas. This is hard to do since Mathias has put his own manager in here and I'm operating out of my bedroom. Thornton feels endorsers aren't enough. Wants lien on furniture. It isn't mine. He's asking more than I can give. . . . Read left today. Unless something happens right now the situation looks hopeless."

And again something did happen.

Seven people who still believed in me put up $5,000 on my unsecured signature. It is hard to imagine now what $5,000 meant to a private individual in the fall of 1933. Today almost any wage earner can realize a $5,000 mortgage on his house, if he hasn't already got one. Then, only six months after the closing of the banks, it was a very large sum indeed.

As I sat around a table in my lawyer's office and looked at six of those seven friends, I knew this vote of confidence was the reward for refusing to quit, for refusing the easy way out. In my pocket already was a check from my prime backer, Mary Laufersweiler Hilton. It represented all she could borrow on her properties. At one end of the table was Joe Goodell, once a member of the old Thirty Club in Albuquerque, now of the Citizens Finance Company. Around it sat two distant cousins, Bill and Clarence Rank, acting as one backer: Bob Price, who owned an El Paso dairy company: Bill·Tooley, a hotel man; and Frank Fletcher, owner of a large laundry.

All my elevating thoughts, however, were caught up by down-to-earth impatience as they sat there, their checks in their hands, and made polite talk. It wasn't much more than a gesture, but I assured Bill Rank, a representative for Blatz Beer, that the El Paso Hilton would serve his beer exclusively forever. I promised we would drink no milk but Bob Price's, eat no ice cream unless Clarence Rank sold it to us. Frank Fletcher alone would launder Hilton linen. It reminded me of the days when I went around New Mexico in my father's buckboard and did "courtesies" with the Spanish dons before such a vulgar word as "business" could be mentioned.

Finally, I could stand it no longer. "You'll understand, gentlemen," I said soothingly, "if I leave you now and go get me a hotel." With which I gathered up those waving checks, raced across to the bank, and thence to Mathias' office. The following morning at 9:45 the El Paso Hilton was returned to me.

I was back in the hotel business. It felt wonderful.

It would be more wonderful to say that we all "lived happily ever after." But such was not the case.

True, some encouraging things happened shortly thereafter.

Bob Thornton invited me to take a $110,000 gamble, to play double or nothing on my outstanding $55,000 loan at his bank. "We've taken in an oil run as settlement on a loan," he advised me. "It's a good one but banking rules won't let us keep it. How'd you like to buy it from us?"

Now I had a hotel, it was true, but no money. "With what?" I demanded indignantly.

"We'll loan you what you need," Bob said. "You might as well owe us $110,000 as $55,000. As things stand now we've as much chance of getting the one as the other. If the oil run is big you can pay both."

With an inner prayer, an outer flourish, and exactly eighty-seven cents in my pocket, I signed a note for another $55,000. I had never made a penny on oil in my life. But I did now. Over the next three years that oil run paid off my entire loan.

I also got back another hotel, this time at Abilene. Once again the Moodys dropped out and I rushed over to see if there was any way it could be salvaged. I was still dead against bankruptcy, but in perfect accord with the recently adopted law, 77B. It was designed during the extreme distress of the Depression to keep American industry from collapsing. Under its sheltering arm a corporation could go to court, tell its tale of woe, and the judge could keep debtors from foreclosing, wiping it out. He could reduce interest rates. Put creditors in line. We reorganized Abilene under 77B.

Two hotels. No money. It wasn't a good score, but it was an improvement.

I had gained a little on one front. On the Moody line I was holding my own. Now a third front opened up. I should have been prepared for it. I wasn't.

From time to time there had been terse lines in the diary:

"Trouble at home . . . another quarrel, worse than before. . . . Mary was tense and tearful tonight. I was tense and cross. We've been married eight years. What *is* the matter with us?"

More recently when those lines appeared the word "divorce" began cropping up. I couldn't blame Mary. What kind of a life had she led over the past three years? I couldn't honestly blame myself. What else could I have done but what I did?

Yet I resisted the idea strongly. I was a Catholic and divorce spelled long, lonely years. The thought of our sons raised in a broken home made me feel leaden. And then, there was the girl in the red hat. I would miss her. And the laughing eyes. What had happened to them?

Still I had to admit that all semblance of harmony had gone from our relationship. The breach was too wide to heal.

I realize now that there has never been a war without casualties, never a true victory, for something treasured has been lost on both sides. When I had done torturing myself with "might-have-beens," and "might-have-dones," I honestly came to believe that our marriage was a depression casualty and that no blame attached to either side.

Early in 1934 I settled with the Moodys. They gave me back Lubbock, Dallas and Plainview. They loaned me $95,000—$60,000 on El Paso, $35,000 on Dallas.

A few months later Mary and I were divorced.

I had won—and I had lost.

10. PUSHING OUT HORIZONS

The next three years were like the slow recovery from an operation. The patient would live, but the pulse was weak and shaky. My business required careful nursing during its convalescence.

I myself needed time for my wounds to heal. My head-long descent was arrested but I did not instantly regain normal perspective. For the abrupt switch between fighting for life and dreaming again the big dreams necessary to forward motion, I needed a little time.

I needed a rest. I couldn't afford one. But I found a hotel man's makeshift that served.

With Bill Tooley, one of the seven who helped save the El Paso Hilton, I leased a resort at Cloudcroft, nine thousand feet up in the pine-scented mountains of New Mexico. We didn't make a good thing of it. We didn't expect to. The national economy was in the same precarious state as my personal economy. But we did get a retreat that paid for itself.

At Cloudcroft my mother, who hated heat, could escape the oppressive Texas summer, Nick and Barron could hunt and fish, Bill Tooley and I could play golf on the highest golf course in the world. It gave the physical man a needed dose of relaxation, the mental and emotional man time to take stock.

If the Moodys' offer to take me into the National Hotel deal had convinced me I was a sound hotel man, I could see now that over the long pull I had been an equally sound businessman. There had been moments during the Depression when I had wondered. You can't take a beating like that without questioning how you ever got into such a mess. Detached, with the full score in, I realized I had felt personally responsible for what had been a national sickness. If, for short moments, I had doubted myself, my friends and partners had never doubted me.

And in the end I justified their faith.

The moment the Moody check was in my hand, I had been able to pay off those stalwart seven who put up the all-important $30,000, not only what they had loaned me, but a 50 per cent bonus. I handed my mother a check for $7,500 and she almost fainted. Across the nation depression averages on the loss of hotels stood at 81 per cent. Hotel owners generally then had been able to save less than one hotel out of five. I had kept five out of eight. Furthermore, with the blood transfusion of that $95,000 Moody loan, these five were slowly beginning to show signs of health.

I had even managed to remain on friendly terms with my ex-partners over in Galveston. In the case of the senior Moody this was easy. We simply shook hands and allowed as how there were "no hard feelings." Shearn, however, had been a mite careful about committing himself. Finally he offered to sell me a $100 advertising signboard in his baseball park for $175 and when I accepted he gave me his hand.

From the casualty of my home I had also salvaged something. Once Mary and I separated, our relationship was mutually friendly and there was give-and-take on both sides. Mary moved to El Paso with the baby Eric, and a year or so later remarried. The two older boys remained with me.

Having reassured myself as to my fitness as hotel man and businessman, there was yet one department that needed honest evaluation. How did I measure up, not as a father but as that tragic new being evolving from the divorce courts—parent, singular?

The boys were eight and nine now, and I was on solid ground when it came to fishing, hunting, swimming and the like. I was also adequate as an audience of one in our Dallas backyard where Nick, who had the building fever, erected a platform and he and Barron delivered "stirring orations on important subjects." I could recognize my father's persuasiveness in this new generation. When Nick tried to convince me, his lone listener, "Resolved: We Need Better Hospitals," or "Resolved: We Have Too Many Schools," I had visions of Gus with his cowbell storming about New Mexico for better roads.

Nor did I lose caste for lack of gentleness in emergencies when Barron fell out of their homemade tree house and cut his eye severely, or Nick slipped on a diving board and insisted on having seven stitches taken without benefit of Novocain.

But when it came to helping make lemonade for their penny roadside stand, I was a failure. Barron, after a single sample, spat like a veteran and remarked, "Boy, that's lousy." And when I went with them into a child's furnishing store to select, with the help of a very superior sales person, what the well-dressed youngster will wear from the skin out, Nick noted my perspiration. "Gee, Dad, you sure work hard at this," he remarked kindly, patting my arm.

There were also matters at which I was a total loss, such as proper diet, "regularity," and finding them clean shirts (I, who at that time could never seem to find one for myself!). Besides which, I was not on permanent vacation even at Cloudcroft, and a sudden call from a sick hotel might send me off at any hour to Lubbock, El Paso, Abilene or Plainview. Upon my return I would find two grubby sons who had deviled our worthy cook into threats of resignation.

The climax was reached when I came home to find that they had painted half the neighbor's front steps with some bright orange patio paint "and I just can't keep track of what they're up to," the cook wailed.

Into this growing chaos came Mary's mother, known throughout the family, through some quirk of Nick's baby tongue, as "Mamu," desiring, as she put it, "to lend a hand with these little angels."

Now Mamu, breathing gentleness and order into our bachelor existence, was indeed an angel. And such was the delightful bias of her grandmother's love that she continued to find her grandsons flawless whether they painted the front steps or cut holes in the table linen to make sails for their model boats. If there was any discipline in the house I was *it*, but such is a father's fate and I was content.

Between Mamu, Cloudcroft and the National Recovery Act, I was beginning to feel solid ground under my feet again. I was even dreaming tentative dreams. I was ready now to make two small moves in the direction of expansion. One, Bill Tooley and I planned carefully. The other was thrust upon me.

In 1935 I bought the Paso del Norte in El Paso. Two years later I sold it outright to Bill. The importance of this hotel was that it was a minute blueprint of a pattern I was to follow throughout the next phase of my innkeeping.

Up 'til then I had used two forms of operation. First, leasing my Texas dowagers and rejuvenating them, then building from the ground up on leased land, again in Texas.

Now I found that the nation was full of fine hotels, four-fifths of which had been lost by their original owners, had gone into receivership, or 77B, or wound up in the hands of people who knew nothing about hotels and regarded these properties as "depression White Elephants." They were there for the taking and at depression prices. All a man needed was a little capital and a lot of faith.

The Paso del Norte was one of these . . . a small one.

The second hotel I acquired at that time, the Gregg at Longview, was important to me for another reason. Every businessman who had survived the Depression was waiting for a sign, national or personal, that it was time to stop treading water and go ahead.

The Gregg was my green light.

Into my Dallas office one morning, unannounced, walked a gentleman who said he owned the Gregg Hotel. "But I'm a doctor, not a hotel man," he added. "I'm too busy to run it."

I knew the hotel and knew it as a good one. At that precise moment, however, I had nothing with which to buy, so I listened. "Longview is a growing town," the doctor continued in a worried tone, "and not only needs the hotel but needs more rooms."

It was good salesmanship and I knew it was true. But I couldn't make an offer so I just went on listening.

"I will sell it to you," this surprising man continued, "on time. And you can borrow against it to build the addition. Of course, I suppose you should have some money in it—so if you haven't got it, I'll lend it to you."

This was as close as I ever came to being given a hotel.

I took it, too, and renamed it the Longview Hilton. And then gave it away myself—but that comes later in the story. The Longview Hilton was somehow always special to me. Not because it made money. That it did from the start. Not because it was acquired as a gift, without any cash outlay. But because it was my personal sign; as though I had been living in a desert having to wrest each bite of food, each drop of water, from a reluctant earth, and suddenly an oasis appeared and started showering these things effortlessly upon me.

After the desert of the Depression this hotel stood as my symbol that American business was ready to grow again.

On the strength of that deal I now did something I had

never done before and have never done since in my life. I
took a real, true vacation with no business side line.

Friends from El Paso, Mrs. Helen Keller (not *the* Helen
Keller, but another fine woman) and her sister Elizabeth,
had taken a house at Playa del Rey near the ocean in southern California. Their invitation to visit them meant I would
see Bill Irwin again, my cousin Dr. Joe Hilton, who had
gone out there after the war, and my old friends Sam and
Ella Flint, from the Circle Theater days in Dallas.

When I took the train for Los Angeles it was exactly two
years after I had hit rock bottom. True, I wasn't on any
Olympian peaks as yet, but once again I had eight hotels.
Some of them were breaking even. Some of them were making money. I had begun to level off my mountain of debts. I
felt I had earned a holiday.

There are a lot of theories about how tired businessmen
relax. I can't vouch for anyone but myself, but I actually
know how I spent every minute of my only vacation. For
the third time in my life, during that short month I kept a
diary, which proves that leisure time in California seemed to
me personally as momentous as World War I or the Depression. Yet what a tame little record it is: no redheaded
showgirls, no bonded whiskey, no all-night parties. It started
off with my cousin, Dr. Joe, putting me into a hospital:

"Joe says this is the place to rest and maybe he's right.
. . . Glorious 4th of July spent in Hollywood hospital . . .
some more hospital . . . hospital still but feeling good.
. . . Decided I was well so I left today. I wasn't. Feel punk
again. Maybe Joe is a better doctor than I am??? . . . At
the Kellers' in Playa del Rey. Can hear the ocean. Nice and
restful. Had a grand sleep. . . . Helen has gone to town today. Nobody here but Nellie, the cook, and me. Nellie and I
don't bother each other. Spent the morning on the patio
reading *The American Hotelman*. . . . Bill Irwin drove
over today and we took a swim. Bill hasn't been doing so
well with his hotel ventures here. . . . Went up to Los Angeles to get my reservations home. Down beautiful Wilshire Boulevard. Saw the Town House, very elegant, facing
on a green park. There is a *hotel*. Back to del Rey on the
red trolley car and the conductor let me ride past my stop.
Had a nice long walk back."

An uneventful holiday for sure. Yet I had seen the Town House, been dazzled by Wilshire Boulevard, been soothed and blessed by the beauty of a mild climate I had not known since I was a lad in my teens. Once again I was aware of a great, wide world beyond Texas. And stirring within me again were infant dreams of moving outside one single state.

The trip, or rather the diary, served another purpose. Like a giddy schoolgirl I poured some of my pent-up feelings onto paper, feelings a man can only admit to if he is a great artist or completely inured to the accusing finger that shrieks "sentimentality"—"corn." I was neither, yet corn is the common man's poetry and sometimes the "Dear Diary" method serves as an emotional release. When I see now the secret plea I made for a wounded bird I wonder if it was a personal cry, or if I had actually learned during the Depression to possess true compassion. If the latter is true, then I gained more than I lost.

This single burst of emotion amongst all the pages of my diaries started off with a simple invitation from Sam and Ella Flint to spend a week-end at Leo Carrillo's home in Santa Monica Canyon. Here I met Carrillo himself, not only a well-known motion picture figure but an actual descendant of the early Spanish dons who settled California; I met Guy Bates Post, famed New York stage star; and a deer Sequoia from the picture of the same name. As a matter of fact, my host, while a fascinating man, and his human guests, all famous or important and some of them both, distinctly took second billing to the wild life that roamed within Leo's walled garden. It was the garden and the animals that brought forth the lyric outburst in my diary.

"*Sunday*. I go to Mass at the beautiful new Santa Monica church. Back at Carrillo's. . . . I feed Sequoia apples. He doesn't want his mate to have any. Utter peace. The lovebirds enjoy themselves. The peacock struts. The turkeys do their comic walk. The quail give their familiar cry. But I like to talk to Sequoia. He seems understanding. I see a lovebird that is wounded and others pick at it. Could lovebirds, too, pick on the weak and, when defenseless, put it to death? Do birds have no use for the weak? Is there no one lovebird who will come to the injured one and protect it? Who will stand by his side and warn others that only at their peril will they again attack the wounded one?"

I did not try to answer my own questions. The diary closed

abruptly next day. . . . . "*Monday*. On train for El Paso. Not much to talk about." As a matter of fact the whole vacation was nothing much to talk about. But it was food for future dreams. I knew now my next venture lay outside of Texas.

In 1937 I made the big jump out of the Lone Star State and into San Francisco, to me still a jewel among cities. In the interim I stubbornly worked my way out of debt.

During that waiting time my life had three centers: Dallas, where my sons were; El Paso, where my mother lived and where my central business office was now located; and California, which commanded my future.

My sons were manly, intelligent and fairly well behaved. My family folk, with the austerity of the Depression behind them, broke out in a rash of mild frivolity. As if to make up for those skimpy meals shared with two forks, there were now luncheons and teas and dances. Society items always included what my sister Helen wore or what "Mrs. Dean Carpenter, the former Broadway actress, Rosemary Hilton," had to say to the Young Matrons' Club. When there was a costume dance at the Country Club, Mother sent to Socorro for her wedding dress for Helen. She and the girls were rapturous over it but to me, until I read the fine points as described in the newspapers, it just looked like a fifty-year-old gown. It is hard for a man, unaided, to appreciate fully "heavy cream brocade satin made with a very full skirt fancifully cut about the bottom and with basque primly buttoned down the front with pearl buttons and appliquéd crochet."

My brother Carl, now a Lieutenant Commander on the Coast Guard cutter *Northland*, materialized suddenly one day and dizzied the newspapermen as well as Barron and Nick with tales of "ghost" ships he had seen traveling in the great Arctic ice pack and messages picked up in the shadow of the North Pole from Commander Byrd at the South Pole, some 10,000 miles away.

Other Hilton visitors who delighted the press were mother's twin sisters, Aunt Elsie and Aunt Edith. These elderly spinster ladies had just completed the rugged round trip over the Pan-American Highway to Mexico City. Aunt Edith was a rather timid maiden who had spent her life a martyr to following the indomitable Aunt Elsie into and out of adventures. Aunt Edith had never driven. Aunt Elsie was not only one of the first women drivers in the United States but the only one I ever met who could actually change a tire, patch a tube, and take her engine apart and put it together again with the aid of only an old-fashioned hatpin.

My bachelor status which had sometimes had disadvantages, especially when my sister Helen wanted to "double date," became absolutely painless after I learned to hide behind my mother's skirts. Mother, with a fine show of matriarchal bossiness, had taken over my social life and was quite capable of intercepting an invitation beamed at me with a definite "Connie's been out too much lately," quite as if I were just past fourteen instead of forty. It had its advantages, however, for when I didn't wish to be an "extra man" or a "double date," I said quite candidly without any embarrassment that I can recall, "My mother won't let me." To anyone knowing Mother, that was that!

Truthfully, it was a good life. For two summers I rented a house at Malibu Beach, the famous movie colony in southern California, and took the boys out there during their vacations. That first summer the closest I got to Lillian Tashman, Jack Gilbert, Constance and Joan Bennett, Gloria Swanson, or any of the other celebrities with whom I shared this exclusive strip of beach, was when my dog fought with their dogs or when Barron and Nick, who spent most of their days on the fishing barge, peddled fish at their back doors. By the second summer I was completely at home.

That second summer, the summer of '37, was a milestone for me. The day I left Texas I had squared off my last debt. I had money in the bank. My credit was excellent. I could have rested there. But I didn't enjoy resting. I enjoyed buying hotels. The adventure, the challenge. This blessed state meant just one thing to me.

I could afford my dreams again.

So I went to San Francisco and fell in love with the Sir Francis Drake.

Bill Irwin made the trip with me. There we were, exactly twenty years after we met at the Presidio, a couple of raw recruits for officers' training school, and now I had returned, determined to buy for myself a little piece of this sparkling city.

Once again I felt the fog in my face, the crisp autumn sunshine, saw the violet vendors and the lovely ladies. Bill and I went to the Bohemian Club and rode the same fat ferry across the bay. We looked at a couple of small hotels but my heart was set on the Drake.

"If I am big enough to move out of Texas," I told Bill, "then I have to be big enough to do it right."

The Sir Francis Drake was "right." Twenty-two stories at Powell and Sutter Streets, 450 rooms, a $300,000 luxury night club, and a reputation for elegance and taste. While I had loved my dowagers, gotten tremendous satisfaction from building my own dream girls, this was like marrying into the social register. This lady had a family tree.

What would have been a hopeless courtship before the Depression had been turned now into a possibility. As a matter of fact, when I went wooing, the Huckins-Newcomb Hotel Company, which owned the property, treated me as if I had come to take an elder spinster daughter without dowry off their hands.

The Sir Francis Drake had originally cost $4,100,000 to build, and I acquired it for a cash outlay of $275,000. Since this formula was used with variations in much of my post-depression buying, and since it's always interesting to see how you can get a lot for a little, I'll just set down simply the way the financing worked.

The first step was to form a buying group.

In San Francisco at this time I first met William J. Friedman, a Chicago lawyer, who had come west representing Lawrence Stern, Chairman of the Board of the American National Bank and Trust Company of Chicago (later a director of Hilton Hotels Corporations), Stern's brother Harold, and Packey Joseph Dee, who were also interested in the Sir Francis Drake. When Billy Friedman's principals joined in the purchase, Billy assisted me in putting the deal together. It was the beginning of a long association.

In forming my buying groups in those post-depression years when I was traveling outside Texas, I would telephone Sam D. Young, my banker and longtime friend in El Paso, and Sam would get in touch with the folks back home who usually joined in my ventures, telling them what I had in mind, asking how much they wanted to go in for.

We raised $300,000 in the case of the Sir Francis Drake. Of this I took the first $75,000 myself, following my usual rule to take one-fourth personally. I then used $125,000 of the cash on the first mortgage, taking it from $1,625,000 to an even $1,500,000 and getting a reduced interest rate of 3½ per cent for five years. For $50,000 I was able to buy outright $1,800,000 of capital stock and shareholder notes while $75,-000 went to take the second-mortgage note of $500,000. And $25,000 got the third-mortgage note of $175,000. That left me with $25,000 cash for operational expenses and more embossed certificates than I have ever seen at one time in my life.

They poured in to the office J. B. Herndon and I shared in such volume that our desks were stacked high and they spilled over into wastebaskets, cardboard boxes, and on to the floor. These were, of course, to be distributed to our buying group in proportion to their subscription.

J.B. viewed the distribution problem with alarm. "Why don't we just tell them to come get 'em?" he suggested. "If we're going to deliver them we'll have to hire a van."

In January, 1938, we concluded the purchase of the Sir Francis Drake. It was a great way to start the New Year, taking over my first socialite in one of the world's leading cities. This time, I thought, I was in the hotel "blue book" for sure.

And then, of course, I had to buy a house to match my hotel.

The house was in Bel Air, an exclusive residential section just beyond Beverly Hills on the outskirts of Los Angeles. It was, I decided, stretching things quite conveniently, halfway between my Texas hotels and my new San Francisco gem. The boys and I thought the low Spanish stucco and tile residence a palace and Bel Air a promised land. The house adjoined the Bel Air Country Club and I truly thought I should never have anything finer. It astounds me that today we call it the "little" house.

Mamu's "angels" were eleven and twelve, ready for the masculine world of a near-by military school and Mamu, her job well done, returned to Kentucky. When the boys got leave from school and I was not at home they consoled themselves by getting Wilson, a first-rate chauffeur I acquired, who called them "the bosses," to teach them to take apart a car. Later evidence indicated that the lessons ceased before he taught them to put it together again. I myself golfed, commuted to Texas and San Francisco, and dreamed of more hotels.

Once the forward motion was established again I knew no peace.

My next venture was far from a pedigreed hotel, but she certainly had a past. A grim one, and for once the Depression could not be blamed. The Breakers at Long Beach was a hotel with a broken back. Since 1926, when it was built at a cost of $1,500,000, it had never done well, but its meager career was permanently ended when the 1933 earthquake shook the beach city. The Breakers parted at the seams and her carcass had been standing there empty ever since. Here was a new kind of invalid.

"I can't see a durn thing to interest you here," muttered J. B. Herndon when I had sent for my Devil's Advocate to see if he could talk me out of it.

But I saw more than the beautiful view it commanded of San Pedro Bay, a view I remembered as a high school boy. I saw oil wells, not as many as in Texas, but enough. I knew that the city of Long Beach had been forced to turn down several big conventions for lack of hotel accommodations. I saw a hotel with possibilities that could be acquired for a song.

In forming a buying group for the Breakers, I invited in two new backers. Red Ellison, who had graduated from bellboy to assistant manager at Abilene during the Depression, had gone to the Sir Francis Drake in charge of food and beverages. Now, when I asked him if he thought he could manage the Breakers, Red answered, "I don't think. I *know* I can." "Then you ought to own a piece of it," I said. "Borrow a thousand at the bank and I'll go on your note." I made the same proposition to Bob Williford, my bridge-crony-key-clerk in Dallas, who had now become manager at El Paso. From that small original investment these two became, as well as increasingly valuable associates, good solid supporters of our expansion program. I was then, and am now, a firm believer in the mutual advantages of the participating manager.

With our buying group formed I cleared up the Breakers' $280,000 tax debt for $61,038. For $110,000 I bought a million dollars in bonds. Then I ordered in the reconstruction crew. If all went well we would have a whole hotel in a booming city for less than half a million. She was not quite like my dowagers, but there was a familiar feeling to this operation.

While the face lifters and master surgeons went to work in Long Beach, J. B. Herndon and I went on our single building spree. Both of us had long since discussed an inner, quite unbusinesslike desire to make good in Albuquerque. Here, where I had once danced with J.B.'s sister and with Eleanor Vaughey, I had been told I couldn't make the grade with an original capital of $5,011. Here J.B.'s father's bank had failed in the cattle collapse in the '20s. Now with the population fifty thousand, the citizenry once again claimed they had everything they needed.

J.B. and I were looking into the future. We got a site close to the station and practically across from where the old Herndon bank was located. And we began to build.

All this activity, buying the Sir Francis Drake, renovating the Breakers, building in Albuquerque, served to stimulate instead of satisfy my dreams. I remember distinctly it was on the train from Albuquerque where building had just begun that a daring new idea popped into my head.

In my wallet still was the clipping of "the greatest of them all," New York's Waldorf-Astoria. I knew she was way beyond me then. But there was another one, the largest hotel in the world, the Stevens in Chicago. The Stevens had been in trouble during the Depression and been reorganized under 77B. Nobody had said it was for sale. But I could dream, couldn't I? I'd dreamed on my honeymoon when Mary and I were there thirteen years earlier, that one day I'd come back and find me a vacant lot in Chicago. Well, maybe someone had built the Stevens on my vacant lot. I made up my mind to go up there as soon as I could and look around.

My sights had opened from Texas, west. Why not to the big city that guarded the Great Lakes? It was a year before I saw the Stevens and six more before I managed to get it. But to see a seed flower, it has to be planted. If you are content with planting radish seeds you'll get radishes in a few weeks. When you start planting acorns, the full-fledged oak may take years. And I was beginning to learn what all gardeners must know—patience.

We opened the Albuquerque Hilton in the spring of 1939. It was an instant success. J.B. was manager and we both beamed upon the distinguished assembly that gathered to wish us well. The Governor himself was there and made me an honorary Colonel. Afterward I laughed about it to Will Keleher, once "press agent" for my Hilton trio, now one of the state's leading attorneys.

"It was a nice try, that 'honorary Colonel,'" I told Will, "but it won't stick."

"No," Keleher admitted, "in New Mexico they got used to one Colonel Hilton and I guess your dad will be *The* Colonel as long as our memories stretch back to the pioneers."

The title was used only once, when we opened the Long Beach Breakers that June. Mother, who, along with Helen and Rosemary had come to the opening festivities, listened in amused silence to the City Fathers, my old friend Leo Carrillo, the Mayor, and "honored guests" praising "Colonel Hilton." Her Colonel Hilton had been dead just twenty years.

Finally, when an overzealous city official sought to flatter Mrs. Mary L. Hilton by saying he knew now after meeting her where "the Colonel" got "it," whatever "it" was, she flashed back, "You say that because you never knew his father."

Later she reminded me that Dad was the dreamer, the adventurous one. "I'm a conservative," she said. "If you'd taken after me you'd still be sitting down there in Texas collecting on the old Waldorf, and the Mobley, and the Melba. Don't you forget it." Then she looked out over the view of the bay from the magnificent Sky Room I had built atop the Breakers, a room that was to make more money from an outlay of like size than any I ever heard of, and asked, "Now that you have hotels in three states, are you satisfied, Connie?"

"No," I said.

"You see," she laughed, "your father all over again."

I wanted the largest hotel in the world.

So I went to Chicago.

I was discovering something this new type of buying demanded besides the patience of Job. You needed the sleuthing abilities of Sherlock Holmes. I was going to Chicago to stalk the Stevens.

Preliminary investigation revealed that it was indeed the biggest hotel I had imagined possible. It had three thousand guest rooms and three thousand baths, a capacity to hold a population of six thousand guests and employees, just about the population of the entire city of Albuquerque when I was first sent there to school. Joseph P. Binns, the alert young manager, was happy to show me around.

"But if you wanted to see every room," he said cheerfully, "and spend five minutes in each, it would take us eight hours a day for a month to complete the tour."

I was satisfied to canvass the hotel's hospital, containing five private rooms, two wards, an operating room; a dry cleaning department that could handle five hundred suits a day; and banquet facilities that would serve eight thousand at a sitting. Binns impressed me by having some stunning statistics at his finger tips.

"To feed the population of the Stevens on an average good day," he said calmly, "takes one thousand pounds of butter, one thousand dozen eggs, the meat of ten steers, and one thousand pounds of pork. We drink seven hundred gallons of coffee and possess a mechanical dishwasher that will clear the debris at a top speed of one hundred ninety three thousand pieces of silver and china per hour."

Yes, I wanted the Stevens. But I was glad my mother hadn't heard that.

My financial stalking revealed that when the hotel was reorganized under 77B, they wound up with six thousand stockholders and a board of trustees. I called on one of the trustees. Obviously, even with the Stevens in trouble, this huge project was beyond my modest buying groups. You didn't get this much hotel for a cash outlay of $300,000. But what I could do, and what I began to do immediately, was to buy first-mortgage bonds, sometimes for as low as twenty cents on the dollar, once in a while as high as sixty. This again was a technique I was to use in acquiring large hotels, because if I held enough bonds, when the time came to try for the purchase, my foot was already in the door.

Slowly and persistently over the next few years as I could afford it, I accumulated those bonds until I had $400,000 worth of them. I talked my locker room buddies at the Bel Air Country Club, Willard Keith, an insurance wizard, and Bentley Ryan, a prominent attorney, into buying along with me. I have a notion some thought the California sun had gone to my head. I knew these prime security certificates were worthless in securing a loan at the bank. The bank laughed. But in the end we had the last laugh.

So determined was I on expanding that, when the lease on the Dallas Hilton fell due, I didn't renew it. The hotel was booming and Loudermilk was eager to take it over. It was another break with the past, with the memories of raising my first million, my first big adventure. To me it is part of the hotel game, or any business, to let the past go cleanly if you are sacrificing it to an expanding future. But it is impossible to be that practical, that impersonal about memories and Dallas, for me, was full of them—my brother Boy, Major Powers, a girl in a red hat, my first partner, L. M. Drown, now very ill in a sanatorium under a medical prediction that he could not live, a prediction which was to become a reality with his death only a short while later. On the night I let the Dallas Hilton go I spent a quiet evening alone at home with my memories.

On the heels of that I sold the Sir Francis Drake. It is only right to admit your slips along with your victories and, while this sale brought me a half million dollars' profit in a little over two years, it was a mistake. It is consoling that the profits came in handy in acquiring another socialite a few months later—but still that sale took me out of a city I loved, a city that was part of my dreams for the future.

When I returned from San Francisco after closing the deal on the Sir Francis Drake, it looked like those profits were going to come in handy at once. On my desk I found a letter marked "Very Urgent." It read:

Dear Dad:

Ime sorry I don't have any better writing paper than this.

I meant to ask you for a raise in salary this week, but Wilson said you might be going away. I'll give you my expenses at scholl as this

(1) Every day Mildean, a friend of mine who has already met your acquaintance and I and a few other guys at the 10 minute recess go down at 10:30 in the morning and have a glass of milk and a pie which cost 15c altogether. Multiply this by 5 days and you get 75c.

(2) Every night I make one or more telephone calls, like: out to the house 10c. (2) To a certain girl I wont mention 10c. So, we will say, that I tellephone on the average of once a day which gives me 50c the week. (already I owe 20c this week because I had no money to pay for them). I reckon Wilson will have to come after me this week because I don't have any money for bus fare.

As you know I usually go to town on one of the week days from school, than I go back. It costs me 14c down & 14c back which gives me 28c for the trip. Alright, to go home cost me 27c and to come back also cost me 27c so that gives me 54c.

$$\begin{array}{r} 28c \\ \underline{} \\ 82c \end{array}$$

Telephone .... 50c per Week
Transportation .... 82c per Week
Milk and Pies .... 75c per Week

Totaling $2.07 just for week days and not for over the weekends.

So, out of 2.00 allowance I am losing 7c beside for what I do over the weekend and I usually spend about 2.00 for pleasure. So I am really losing $2.07 a week. and when I go hunting I usually spend about 7.50 a trip and ive gon 3 times already.

Heres, what I propose.

If you give me $5.00 a week. I will not have to come to you and say you owe me for bus transportation and for tellephone calls and ects. because I will pay for them all out of the $5.00 and by the time I get finished I will have about $2.50 for pleasures over the weekend.

Sorry this is all business.

> Your loving son,
> Barron Hilton

P.S. I would have brought this up sooner but I had some spending money of my own and I used it, but *now* I don't have any.

Barron, it would appear, had inherited much from his grandfather, including his inability to spell.

December, 1941, brought into my life a Hungarian siren, my first invitation to stalk a New York hotel, my mother's eightieth birthday—and Pearl Harbor.

I met the foreign charmer at a party. She was blonde, witty, vivacious, and just off the boat. This fascinating package, Zsa Zsa Gabor by name, appealed to me as a most amusing young person. Seated next to me at dinner she suddenly did one of those fascinating tricks women do with their eyes and announced: "I theenk I am going to marry you."

And I, the confirmed bachelor, to whom marriage from a

religious standpoint was a forbidden fruit, thought that was a fine joke. "Why don't you do that?" I challenged with a roar of laughter.

Four months later the joke was on me.

I went busily off to El Paso for a surprise party we had planned for Mother's birthday and thought no more of it. Mother, who hated surprises, had with her usual efficiency wormed the secret out of each of her children in turn as they faithfully arrived with all or some of the grandchildren for the celebration. In that way she had the satisfaction of running each detail of her own surprise party. It included, I recall, a three-tiered cake, a double-orchid corsage, and two hundred odd guests.

If the birthday party was no surprise, we had a big one three days later. Herbert Marcus, of the Neiman Marcus clan, burst into our sitting room at the El Paso Hilton with a portable radio shouting that the Japs had attacked Pearl Harbor.

There were no festivities on my birthday that Christmas of 1941. Instead Mother, with her brood behind her, guided us all into church where we knelt to pray for the world.

Three days later I was in New York. Arnold Kirkeby, a prominent hotel man, had telephoned from Chicago asking me to look over the Hotel Pierre on Fifth Avenue with an eye to a joint purchase. Any honest hotel man was walking cautiously at that point. We couldn't tell exactly what war would bring but certain things were sure. We would lose manpower to the service. War industries would force wages up. Food and maintenance materials would be in short supply, and prices would climb. Travel would be restricted. It wasn't an encouraging picture and my inspection of the Pierre was little more than a courtesy.

All I accomplished was to wind up in the biggest city in the United States without a friend or acquaintance on New Year's Eve. It was a lonesome feeling. Oddly enough the bigger the city, the more people are hustling about their personal business, the more of an orphan is the stranger within their gates.

I had no desire to join the strays who huddle over New York's élite bars on festive days and so I bought a ticket for Key West where my brother Carl was. The train was lonesome, too, only a handful of passengers boarding in the huge Pennsylvania Station.

I said goodbye to New York this time with no regret but a good deal of longing.

New York was the center of everything big I now wanted. New York had had no reason to roll out the red carpet for one hotel man from the West. But some day, perhaps, it would. As long ago as when Bill Irwin and I sat in the Astor bar in our natty new lieutenants' uniforms waiting to sail for World War I, I had agreed it would be a "tough city to crack."

But on the train rolling leisurely toward Florida I knew that I would never hit the Big Time until I did it. My little people, my little buying groups could never put together the kind of money I needed to put on the "big shoes." They talked in thousands. I would need millions. New York was where that Wall Street was I'd read about. That's where they talked in millions.

The following year did not take me to New York but it brought me a lot of excitement. I acquired another pedigreed hotel, lost my slight hold on the largest hotel in the world, made my first across-the-border deal, and remarried.

When I met Arnold Kirkeby in Chicago he did not mention the Pierre. Instead he said immediately, "How would you like to buy the Town House?"

How would I like to buy that elegant hotel on beautiful Wilshire Boúlevard in Los Angeles facing that gemlike green park? I would like to first rate. But why would an astute hotel man like Kirkeby want to sell it? My bargaining instinct kept the gleam from my eye and I said it required some thought.

Back in Los Angeles I found the Town House empty of its usual glamorous guests. As a matter of fact I found the natives looking for shelter or deserting the golden land of sunshine. People in the East never realized that Honolulu and Japan had always seemed to be at the back door of the west coast. Now Pearl Harbor had sent many of them into a state of shock. There were searchlights in the sky and patrols along the miles of open beach. I could see why the Town House was empty.

Still, it was a $3,000,000 property, a likely inn. I decided you either had to go ahead with full faith in America—or quit. Quitting had always been hard for me.

Besides, if the Japs landed wouldn't we all be in the same boat anyhow?

I called Kirkeby and settled down for the bargaining. Here again was a worthy opponent.

"Name a figure," he invited. "But make it large enough so I can accept it."

"Well, I've been considering the risk . . ." I said slowly.

"Just say some numbers, Connie," he insisted.

I closed my eyes, took a deep breath and said, "Three-quarters of a million."

Kirkeby howled, which was the thing for him to do! "Nine twenty-five," he countered.

"Your hotel is empty," I said. "I was there today . . ."

"Nine," said Kirkeby.

"Eight," I said.

"And a half," he added.

"Done," I said. "I'll mail you a check today to bind the deal."

It was a good place for the profits from the Sir Francis Drake and I had bought me another gold mine. We installed a few dainties, a tennis court, a swimming pool with white beach sand and, as the U. S. Navy and the U. S. Marines indicated that they intended to stand firmly between the Japanese and our mainland, we got our customers. Kirkeby's gross profits for 1941 had been a weak $33,000. Our first year we took in $198,000 and thereafter never less than a quarter of a million.

I moved my offices into a suite in the Town House and slid my cherished clipping of the Waldorf under the glass on my desk. Among the first people to call on me were the brothers Laguette of Chihuahua, Mexico. Julio and Luis Laguette were persons of importance south of the border, being, as they were, grandsons of that fabulous character, the late General Luis Terrazas. Terrazas had assisted his country in freeing herself from the Emperor Maximilian and wound up with seventeen million acres of land. He had so many cattle that when a buyer once ordered five thousand head, Don Luis waved his hand politely and asked, "What color would you like?"

His grandsons and I did business in the courteous manner of the dons, talking leisurely over luncheon of this and that, exchanging many mutual compliments in their flowery native tongue. Then they got to the point.

Would I be interested in leasing and operating a hotel they were just completing in Chihuahua? If so, we would, of course, call it the Palacio *Hilton*.

On a trip to Chihuahua I decided it was a good, if bold, venture. I felt that by organizing week-end bus excursions with guides, large-scale entertainment at the hotel, an all-expenses-paid holiday, we could make a very good thing of it —which we did.

In drawing the leases I dealt mostly with brother Julio, and Luis was not called in until the contracts were drawn and ready to be signed.

He looked at them suspiciously and demanded, "How much rent do we get?"

I told him.

"Who pays the taxes?" he asked.

"You do," I said. "You own the land."

"Who pays the insurance?"

"You do. It's your property." And then, because he looked so upset, I tried cheering him with the news that the United States government was about to pour a hundred million dollars into his country for war purposes.

"You should do so," he said solemnly. "Didn't you take Texas from us? And New Mexico? And Arizona and California?"

"Luis," his brother Julio intervened sternly, "perhaps you should have negotiated with Don Conrado. Had you done so we would have been able to get back Texas and California in the deal."

In April, just before the opening of the Palacio Hilton, I married Zsa Zsa Sari Gabor.

It is difficult to figure out now how I, a staunch Roman Catholic once divorced, wound up before a judge in Santa Fe, New Mexico, entering into a civil marriage ceremony which my church would not recognize, with a divorced Hungarian glamour girl. I can only say that I was then as incurably romantic as I had been when I languished over the miller's daughter in Socorro, or danced with Jouett Adair Fall at the Governor's ball, or followed a red hat through the crowd at Dallas. I still wanted to sprinkle stars in a lovely lady's lap and I must confess I had never met anyone so willing or qualified to receive them.

When Zsa Zsa's sister Eva married, a conservative elderly

friend wrote the bridegroom: "Dear old fellow, I feel every man should have a Gabor in his life." Perhaps it would be better put if he urged that every woman have a touch of the Gabor in her. Or if his advice could be taken literally, it could be qualified—*if* you can afford it, and *if* your faith permits it.

Our marriage was doomed before it started.

I could afford it, yes. Glamour, I found, is expensive, and Zsa Zsa was glamour raised to the last degree. She also knew more days on which gifts could be given than appear on any holiday calendar. And then, of course, you could always give gifts because it was no special day at all and thereby transform it.

Zsa Zsa was not always on the receiving end by any manner of means. She herself loved to give. She showered presents and attentions on my mother, escaping the heat that summer at the Town House; Zsa Zsa would drive halfway across the city to take her a nosegay. Mother was enraptured and, much as she regretted that our church would not welcome Zsa Zsa, referred to her affectionately as "that dear girl."

Zsa Zsa also bought tennis rackets and fishing poles for Nick and Barron.

The old Spanish house in Bel Air got interior decorated from its tile-topped roof to its lowly lintel.

And for me there were custom shirts and solid gold cuff links, most of which showed up mysteriously on my charge accounts. Now this was strictly against the rules. I had tried to instill sound business principles into my beautiful Circe, but I might as well have practiced on a statue in the park. Zsa Zsa's logic was completely beyond my limited business experience. Directly after our marriage I made my first attempt.

"There's too much trouble," I informed her, "caused by women being foolish with money. We're not going to have that trouble. I will give you a check on the first of every month."

Zsa Zsa beamed.

"And out of that you are to pay for everything you personally want. Clothes. Amusements."

Zsa Zsa nodded solemnly.

"I mean *all* your clothes," I said, feeling this was too easy. "All your luncheons and hair appointments. You are not to use my charge accounts. I, of course, will take care of everything for the house."

"I understand," said my beautiful blonde bride. If she did she had a short memory, for each month little items slipped onto my bills. I confronted her with it. "Look at this bill. You've been charging again. Next time it will come out of your allowance."

"But what could it *be?*" she pouted.

"Housecoats. *Six* chiffon housecoats."

"Aaah." Light dawned. "But you are to take care of everything for the house!" she cried triumphantly.

Being married to Zsa Zsa brought me, in many ways, more laughter and gaiety than I had ever known in my personal life. But it brought headaches and heartaches as well. It was a little like holding on to a Roman candle, beautiful, exciting, but you were never quite sure when it would go off. And it is surprisingly hard to live the Fourth of July every day.

And then there were Sundays when we went to church, for I went as I had always done, and Zsa Zsa went with me. But there was this difference. When the congregation rose and made its way toward the altar rail to receive Holy Communion, I stayed on my knees in the pew, chained as it were, to the side of my beautiful wife.

It made Zsa Zsa sad, but it did more than that to me. To be deprived of the sacraments was a price I had not truly understood. Until a man accustomed to this consolation is without, he cannot know what toll it will take from him. I went on praying as fervently as before but now I felt adrift, cut off, spiritually forlorn.

In the end it was more than I could pay.

Another young woman entered my life three months after my marriage, a woman who was to be Zsa Zsa's friend, a staunch friend and ally to my two sons, a loyal friend and valued associate to me from that day on. Her name was Olive Wakeman.

She came to me as secretary when Father Lorenzo Malone of Loyola College, my frequent companion on the golf course helped me win her away from a prominent downtown club where she had served for eleven years as business and social secretary to the Board of Directors.

"Your need," said Father Malone thoughtfully, "is greater than theirs."

And so it was.

But Mrs. Wakeman had to see it to believe it.

She looked over the converted suite where I had my offices at the Town House and immediately into her eyes came the anguished look of a woman who sees a job that must be done at once. Important papers were at that time lodged in the disconnected refrigerator of the kitchenette. My address files and telephone books were in the oven. Some of my ledgers were not quite up to date.

"I will be here two weeks from Monday," said Mrs. Wakeman, and she was. From that time until she became my administrative assistant a few years ago, those initials O.W. appeared at the bottom left-hand corner on every important paper I wrote. Come to think of it, they still do.

While Olive was carefully reorganizing my office and Zsa Zsa was merrily disorganizing my home, I went on doing business. I sustained a major blow when the United States government took over the Stevens Hotel in Chicago for the Air Force, but they applied quick balm to the wound by paying off one hundred cents on the dollar plus accumulated interest on my first-mortgage bonds. That check for $400,-000 was the largest I had ever had in my hand in my life.

"We'll get it yet," I predicted to Olive Wakeman.

"It'll just take a little longer."

We did, too. Meanwhile, the stage was at last set for that all-important move into the great city of New York.

11. HOW BIG CAN YOU DREAM?

In the spring of 1943 I came into New York, tipped my hat to
the Waldorf—and bought the Roosevelt.

"Why?" demanded J. B. Herndon.

"Because it's a fine hotel," I said. "And because I've got to
practice."

"What for?" J.B. was suspicious.

"For the Waldorf," I said calmly. "I'm not quite ready for
that one yet."

But I thought I was ready for the Roosevelt. I had done my
stalking. I had sent Bob Williford at the El Paso Hilton a
penny post card alerting him to the beauties of this great
hotel adjacent to Grand Central Station, half-luxury, half-
commercial—a socialite, so to speak, with a working husband—twenty-three stories, a thousand seventy-nine rooms,
a lobby that reminded me of the vast open spaces around San
Antonio. I had also alerted Sam Young and my usual backers
and the purchase was smooth and quick.

I phoned Bob Williford down in Texas. "Come on up," I
invited. "This is a great town."

"That would be real nice, Connie," said Bob, "but I've got
an Elks Convention—"

"Well now, Red Ellison is on his way from Long Beach to
take over your convention—and your hotel." There was a
stunned silence on the other end of the line. "And you are
coming to New York to take over the Roosevelt."

"Me!" Bob let out a startled yelp, but I didn't hear any
more. I hung up.

If I had startled Williford, it was as nothing to the shock
sustained by faithful habitués of the Roosevelt Hotel. I was
ready for the Roosevelt, true, but was the Roosevelt ready
for me? It didn't appear to be.

It was scarcely flattering to have everyone assume that I
would ride my horse into the lobby or install spittoons in the
famous Roosevelt Grill, yet on every hand I received communications in various forms begging me to deal gently with

my newest lady. One state assemblyman at Albany took the trouble to couch his fears in verse:

From what we hear it would appear there's been some
    changes made,
That great hotel, the Roos-e-velt, is mixed up in a trade.
Some bird named Connie Hilton from his California nest
Is gonna show New Yorkers how they do it in the west.

The stalker was now being stalked and I was watched warily for signs of sacrilege or vandalism. It didn't take long to prove that this particular bird had no intention of dislodging Guy Lombardo from the Roosevelt Grill or blocking off the subterranean tunnel that connected our hotel with the beehive activities of the Grand Central, and that we are with knives and forks out west just like New York.

While I was concentrating on proving I was no vandal, however, the smart money boys had decided I was something else. I was a sucker. Why? Because I had been buying Waldorf-Astoria bonds at four and one-half cents on the dollar. Jim Blainey, a friend of mine who was a New York real estate broker, broke the news to me simply. "Better look out, Connie. Word's around you are ripe for stock in the Brooklyn Bridge."

"Why, Jim," I said, "I've never gambled on the stock market in my life. I'm not gambling now. I know hotels. They're getting healthy. This is the chance of a lifetime."

"Maybe hotels are getting healthy out west, but not here," he said sadly. "In New York hotels are dead. There are too many of them."

That was the attitude about hotels all over the East. They had watched them go down, and further down, during the Depression. They had seen what the war brought, increased patronage perhaps, but nothing yet to offset the difference between rising costs, wages, shortages and the OPA ceilings. Maintenance was difficult and not only did the financial picture show strain but the physical plants themselves were deteriorating.

These eastern hotel men were a downhearted lot. It seemed to me they were so close to the present picture they couldn't see a future. Even Duncan Harris, president of a big real estate firm and an old acquaintance, thought I was showing poor judgment. Duncan was too polite to call me names to my face, but he wasn't above letting me overhear what his broker said when Duncan called to query him about Waldorf bonds.

"Some wild man from the West has forced them up to 8," the broker chortled over the wire. "We're unloading by the bushel. This is the first time in years that anyone holding hotel paper has believed in Santa Claus."

Yet Harris bought and so, sweating and swearing, did a small faithful group who backed "Connie's hunches." Later hotel securities boomed and the wild man who bought at 4½ was considered an astute fellow when he sold at 85. Santa Claus had planted $22,500 and reaped almost $500,000.

I've been accused more than once of playing hunches. Since I suppose I do and it sounds so mysterious, a little like following a Ouija board or gazing into a crystal ball, and since I further believe most people have them, whether they follow them or not, I've tried to figure out what's in a hunch.

I think the other name for hunch is intuition, and I think intuition can be a form of answered prayer. You do the best you can—thinking, figuring, planning—then you pray. It's no use praying, "God, do this for *me* and let the other fellow hold the bag," but it's perfectly fair to ask: "What will you have me do?" Or, "What is the right answer?" Nor is it selfish. Everyone else has the same right. But the key to intuition is not in the prayer but in listening for a response. If you don't listen you make it a pretty one-sided affair.

This listening can become an intense thing, can even resemble absentmindedness or preoccupation. Olive Wakeman claims she met me at the door of the Town House one morning and politely inquired about a cold I'd had. "How are you today?" she asked. According to Olive we then crossed the lobby in complete silence, rode up on the elevator, entered our offices where I hung up my hat. Then I said: "I'm fine, Olive, how are you? By the way, I have a hunch. . . ."

I have no recollection of such a performance but I admit its possibility. I know when I have a problem and have done all I can to figure it, I keep listening in a sort of inside silence 'til something clicks and I feel a right answer.

A good example of that occurred when the government took over the Stevens Hotel. The Stevens Corporation was then for sale. The Air Force only needed the hotel building but the corporation held miscellaneous assets, accounts receivable, inventories, tax claims. If I couldn't have the hotel, I decided I wanted the corporation. It would give me a finger on the building if and when the government released it, as well as possible profits from the assets.

The trustees asked for sealed bids. Now few businessmen like sealed bids and I'm no exception. My first bid, hastily made, was $165,000. Then somehow that didn't feel right to me. Another figure kept coming, $180,000. It satisfied me. It seemed fair. It felt right. I changed my bid to the larger figure on that hunch. When they were opened the closest bid to mine was $179,800.

I got the Stevens Corporation by a narrow margin of $200. Eventually the assets returned me two million.

"Connie's hunch" on the Waldorf bonds wasn't psychic. Business-wise it was perfectly sound. Those bonds could only go down 4½ points, and look how far up they could travel. But what pushed me into buying them was my feeling, that go-ahead intuition that nudged me into action when the doctor in Texas "gave" me the hotel at Longview, led me to buy the Sir Francis Drake, the Town House, the Breakers, to build in Albuquerque, to go into the Roosevelt in New York.

The hotel business was set to grow again—and grow to greater heights. That was my hunch and I was going to back it to the limit.

The killing on the Waldorf bonds did something much more important than net me a handsome profit. That, coupled with the Roosevelt purchase, brought me to the attention of Wall Street. For the first time the Big Money I'd prayed for, that I needed for expansion, made a move in my direction.

The Atlas Corporation, an investment trust headed by Floyd Odlum, approached me through Boyd Hatch, their executive vice-president. Would I, inquired Mr. Hatch, be interested in joining them in the purchase of the Hotel Plaza?

Would I not?

Atlas wanted to invest some money in this magnificent old New York landmark, but they knew nothing about running hotels. It would be ridiculous to say that such subtle tribute to my talents left me unmoved after my initial welcome to the hotel business in New York. The proposition they made was that they take 40 per cent of the Plaza deal, I take 60 per cent and assume the responsibility of management. It suited me fine.

In October, 1943, we bought the Plaza for $7,400,000.

Originally this hotel cost $17,000,000 to build back in 1907 when I was in high school in Long Beach and my father was a $100,000 millionaire, in the days when the dollar was a dollar plus. Now, once again, we were able to swing a famous hotel for comparatively little cash. Six hundred thousand paid for $3,992,500 worth of notes and preferred stock. The rest was represented by a first mortgage held by the Metropolitan Life Insurance Company. And again I managed to get an extension on the mortgage and a reduced rate of interest.

Then the trouble began.

If I had thought the habitués of the Roosevelt were upset by my advent into their midst, the Plaza dwellers, much more bound up in tradition, much more conservative, truly seemed to think my connection with their hotel might mark the end of their world.

And quite a world it was, too. While the Stevens was the largest, the Waldorf the greatest, the Plaza, facing elegantly on its own small square on the southern edge of Central Park, was considered by the discriminating to be the smartest hotel in America.

Generations of Astors, Vanderbilts, Goulds and the like had made it their playground as well as preferred hostelry. It was the last word in luxury as far back as 1912 when strawberries could be had in the winter for twelve cents each. It had molded the forms of New York society by introducing the *thé dansant*, left its permanent mark on the entertainment world by bringing in the first ball room dancing team as supper entertainment. It was the week-end playground for young bloods from Harvard, Yale and Princeton, and a haven for the wealthy eccentric as well as the socially prominent.

At one time Edward Ellsworth, a real estate broker, had been permitted to fit out a suite in the basement complete with bath for his French poodle. The poodle was attended by a personal maid, tutored by a professional to improve her tricks, and fed from the Plaza cuisine. Nor was Kay Thompson's Eloise the first child to turn the Plaza upside down. Some years before, George A. Fuller, Jr., ten-year-old son of the construction company president, drove his custom-built automobile at the scorching speed of twelve miles an hour around a specially built speedway also in the Plaza basement.

During the Depression this historic hostelry escaped bankruptcy, and I inherited some of the reasons why it escaped—

a number of permanent residents who paid as high as $27,500 a year for their apartments. They loved their Plaza, bless 'em, as it was, and they defied me to so much as buy new silverware.

Yet there was no use mincing matters about the dilapidated condition of New York's dowager duchess. Her paint was peeling, her marble dull and pockmarked by sand blasting. Her tapestries were faded, her plumbing and her elevators misbehaved. The only difference between her and my Texas dowagers was one of degree and pedigree. And like my dowagers she sorely needed a face-lift. The Old Guard might remain blind, yet unless some changes occurred at once, their elegant headquarters were in danger of collapsing around their elegant ears.

The mere mention of touching a sacred pillar and I was once again cast as Genghis Khan or, at the very best, Tom Mix about to shoot his guns off in the lobby. It was a delicate situation. I was on trial as host as well as businessman.

I brought J. B. Herndon on to supervise the renovating of the Plaza. We did not intend to change a thing, only to refurbish what was there. But this would require tact, endless patience, and a great deal of money. In the end it cost us almost $6,000,000.

The first challenge was to break the ice. We decided to show them we would take nothing away, by restoring a tradition as a gesture of good faith.

We gave them back the Oak Bar which had been sacrificed to house a brokerage firm. The brokerage firm was moved to the mezzanine, the Oak Bar polished to its original luster and an Oak Room custom of bygone years resurrected. Ladies were not permitted in the Oak Room until after the stock exchange closed. Not only were the gentlemen pleased to recapture an old sanctuary, but the ladies (such is the way of ladies) delighted to patronize the Oak Room in the late afternoon feeling as they did that they were invading a masculine world.

When these changes were complete J.B. and I were greeted with a firm nod, a direct look, and a grimace approximating a smile by two permanent residents. It was a major victory. Surreptitiously then, at night when our guests were fast asleep, we began restoring the marble, calling experts to clean the magnificent old tapestries, renewing fractious plumbing.

When we took over the Plaza it had 61 per cent occupancy.

Before the redecorating was completed we were filled to capacity. So successful was this initial deal with the Big Money that when I needed to raise $19,000,000 to acquire another magnificent dowager in another city I had less trouble raising it than I had once had raising the $30,000 that saved my skin ten years earlier in El Paso, Texas.

I felt I was ready for anything—almost. I even had a few preliminary talks about the Waldorf. But I wasn't ready for that. Not quite yet.

My inns now stretched from coast to coast, each one the best of its kind in its own city, the personality of each varying with community tastes and needs.

A glance at our house organ, *Minimaxims*, for one month showed how vastly different these personalities were: The chef and auditor of the Abilene Hotel pulled a coup and carried off the Grand Champion Calf from the 4H Club, a likely bit of wartime veal weighing 918 pounds and costing forty cents per pound. At the Town House a tennis exhibition for a war charity drew a gallery of glittering names to watch Sarah Palfrey Cooke, Pauline Betz, Louise Borough, and the boy wonder, Herb Flam, play. A newly decorated suite in the Plaza boasted beige satin sofas, crystal chandeliers and bleached French furniture, while at Albuquerque, the manager, my brother-in-law Dean Carpenter, welcomed the Wool Growers Association and registered the prize sheep in the lobby.

We were professionally and personally very much aware of the war. While Abilene bought veal on the hoof, the manager of the Town House watered his Victory garden of radishes (how popular that good-natured vegetable did become with wartime gardeners!), lettuces, turnips and pole beans. My astute son Barron was keeping chickens in our back yard at Bel Air, supplying the home kitchen (at a reasonable price) and selling his excess to the hotel. When the boys completed their year of sound religious training, so highly recommended by my mother, at Loyola High School, they worked that summer to help fill our manpower shortage. Nick was in the engine room at El Paso and Barron worked in the Town House garage. In the fall they went on to my one-time alma mater, New Mexico Military Academy at Roswell, where I fervently hoped they would learn not only that "a gentleman tells the truth" but also something about soldiering for now, at sixteen and seventeen, they had begun to talk of the day they could enlist.

Unhappily Zsa Zsa and I continued to wage our own private war. It is hard to remember now exactly why, but there were tensions and strains and explosions until I suffered battle fatigue and crept off to Mexico with my cousin, Dr. Joe, to hunt ducks in exclusively masculine company. When I left there was a strained silence between the embattled parties and we were communicating through our neutral mediator, the imperturbable and tactful Olive Wakeman. Eventually a temporary peace was negotiated and the beautiful Zsa Zsa, all soft eyes and new hat, met me in Albuquerque and insisted on helping me carry my trophies, a brace of very dead duck, aboard the New York train.

It was in New York that I had my first glimpse of what my wife did with her time. An attack of flu put me in bed and there was no way to escape a bird's eye view of Zsa Zsa's day.

Frankly, I suppose I knew very little about women. My world was peopled with men, mostly businessmen, at that. Only my mother and Mary had touched my life intimately and they were a particular kind of woman. My mother worked each day from sun to sun and then worked some more. Mary had always been busy with the children and the household. Outside of them all women had been set reverently on pedestals and/or admired as dancing partners. Thus, it took me completely by surprise to discover that beauty can be a full-time affair.

At ten o'clock each morning Zsa Zsa seated herself at her dressing table and began a ritual, with bottles and jars and pots, large and small, which could have been the rite of an ancient Aztec temple. Naïvely, the first time I watched the performance, I asked: "What are you doing?"

"I am dressing for lunch, seely," she replied casually, as if everyone knew that the time to commence dressing for lunch was directly after breakfast. Then she held up a brooch, discarded it, tried another, sniffed this perfume, that perfume, tried on a gay scarf, frowned and tried another. "You like thees?" she demanded.

At twelve o'clock Beauty took itself off to an elegant luncheon club which was, I suppose, its proper setting. It then shopped 'til around three and returned to settle once more before the dressing table. Again the ritual, again the agonizing decisions as hats, furs and jewelry were tried and discarded.

"What are you doing now?" I asked.

"I am dressing for tea." A very surprised voice. Then holding up a wisp of a hat with a lot of veil, "You like thees?"

After tea, this, too, taken in an appropriate show-case, came the main event. "I am dressing for dinner," the solemn voice of a priestess announced, settling once more before Glamour's altar. Again time stood still and the world hung on a choice between "sapphires to match the eyes, yes?" or "something dazzling, no?"

I found myself suddenly wondering if my fever was magnifying this dizzy business of adornment or vice versa. It had been my personal rule since the post-depression period when Dr. Joe found me physically run down, to stop work at six sharp every night and play—preferably dance.

"Those old saws," Joe had said, "got old through hard usage. You know, 'All work and no play.'"

But you could turn it around.

I began to try to picture my wife in San Antonio, New Mexico in 1893 instead of New York and Bel Air in 1943. I didn't succeed. All I succeeded in doing was missing a cue— "You like thees?"—and precipitating a quarrel. Whereupon Zsa Zsa sped back to California; the tabloids picked up the crumbs from our table and made a goodly dish of it; and I spent another birthday in church barred from the sacraments and feeling pretty much alone.

In the next twelve months I had nothing but trouble. There was trouble with Zsa Zsa, trouble with my sons, trouble with the Stevens and, as if this was not enough, my house burned down.

I do not think my guardian angel had gone on vacation. On the contrary I think he was probably very much on the job, making sure I did not confuse financial prosperity with successful living, nor business success with peace of mind, nor feel that the loneliness of separation from my church could be overcome by time.

First the War Department abandoned the Stevens, leaving not so much a hotel as an empty shell and a shell in poor repair at that. The furnishings had been sold, since maintaining a barracks required none of the niceties of hospitality expected by guests who pay money for their lodgings. Although my ownership of the Stevens Corporation together with my new happy connections with Wall Street gave me a kind of priority, I decided not to exercise it.

I figured no sensible hotel man would bid enough to get the hotel (and that far I was right) and that it would probably be waiting there when conditions were normal again. I could afford to bide my time. There I was wrong.

Out of nowhere came a buyer, one Stephen A. Healy, millionaire contractor and ex-bricklayer, who had decided to take a flier with the Stevens.

To Healy it was quite simply a challenge. He got it at a bargain and then before our astonished eyes worked a major hotel miracle and proved that he, with no hotel experience, was probably the only man in America who could put the Stevens back together again.

Healy whistled and out from the gravel pits, the underground tunnels, the cabs of steam shovels came his loyal labor crews. The Stevens was patched and plumbed and painted as if a genie had been called forth from Aladdin's lamp. Materials appeared from thin air. Furniture was unearthed in the most unlikely places and when the man's work was done, including windows washed, rugs shampooed, the vast kitchens scoured and scrubbed, calloused hands hung curtains, made beds, plumped sofa pillows.

Did Healy need elevator boys? The sand hogs and riveters donned monkey suits and piloted this new type skycraft. Did he require bellboys? The cement mixers hopped to the baggage. Telephone operators? The Stevens house phones were answered courteously by suspiciously masculine voices announcing "Evelyn speaking."

Healy had accomplished the impossible and it was thrilling to watch. But once the Stevens was an operating hotel again I wanted it badly, as I always had. Now I made a mistake. My intuition was either not functioning or I wasn't listening. Probably the latter, for I figured that when the spectacular job was done, when the contractor and his boys had to buckle down to innkeeping, catering to the gentleman in 818 who wanted his toast done on one side only, or the lady in 1211 who liked her eggs boiled a minute and one-eighth, he would be only too glad to sell.

I was wrong. Healy was having fun. His boys were having fun. They were making money and getting a lot of attention.

And I had tipped my hand. Healy knew I was eager. I had placed myself in the worst possible position for bargaining. But I went on trying.

"Some day," I said confidently, "he'll want to sell. I'll just keep an eye on things."

It was a fish eye, though, for Healy played me like a well-hooked trout and I didn't like it a bit. It was a disheartening business.

I was disheartened, too, about my sons. Let me admit right now that I took the teenage hard. Late hours, dates on school nights, troubles at school, all the things that most parents go through seemed magnified to me, looking as I must through the prism of accumulating wealth and a broken home.

My boys, I know now, were no better and no worse than other boys. And I was at least a conscientious father. But I was a fusser, a comparer. Once when Nick showed up with a pair of outrageously expensive alligator shoes (charged to my account) I was absolutely shocked.

"Nick," I said sternly, "I have never paid that much for a pair of shoes in my entire life."

"Ah," said Nick, who had a kind of candid humor in which there was no trace of impudence, "but you never had a rich father."

Instead of calmly disillusioning him and returning the shoes forthwith, I cut his allowance and launched into a frustrated diatribe on how hard I'd worked at his age.

"But I thought you wanted us to finish school," said my candid son. "I'd rather work, Dad."

School was a major problem between Barron and myself. When Barron had trouble in high school and he had it practically all the time, I was apt to lose my temper.

"Why can't you be a *man?*" I demanded.

Barron didn't make the obvious answer, which was simply that he *wasn't* a man yet. But I found that age—when the boys appeared perfectly adult and sensible 90 per cent of the time, when we enjoyed each other's company in a comradely way 80 per cent of the time and yet, children in grown bodies, they would suffer a sudden lapse and do incredible or foolish things—the most trying stage of fatherhood. Now I recognize the fact that they were suffering growing pains, that it hurt them quite as much as it did me, but while we were going through it I felt helpless. If I was kind it did no good. If I was strict it did less.

Not once, but several times, we entered into business contracts setting forth our mutual responsibilities, allowances, duties, restrictions, and privileges, duly executed and witnessed—to me a sacred trust—and just that many times some point was violated.

I was heartsick.

It was my mother who forced me to a more objective view, carried me back over the years and reminded me that my father and I had not always seen eye to eye. "Nick and Barron are not businessmen yet, Connie. They're half boy, half man. You weren't so different yourself. Only your temptations were limited."

In honesty I had to confess I had quit school at sixteen, even if I returned a year later. I had to admit further, I had never seen a pair of alligator shoes nor had the opportunity to own a car. I remembered that I had once written home requesting that my mother restrain my father from bothering me. I was beginning to understand my father now in a way my boys would some day understand me—when they had sons of their own.

Mother had a soothing influence on all of us, Zsa Zsa and the boys as well as myself. During that summer Zsa Zsa and Mother and I had one good laugh together in which the boys could join heartily. We had had some informal family pictures made at the Town House, and Olive Wakeman asked the photographer to send one of Nick and Barron and Mrs. Hilton along to *Minimaxims*, our house organ. Then she dropped a note to the editor to expect a picture of the boys with their grandmother.

Back came the editor's reply saying, "The lady in that picture is *no* grandmother" and we all took it as a charming bit of flattery for Mother until the new issue of *Minimaxims* arrived. There on the cover was a photograph of Nick and Barron on either side of a blonde beauty wearing tennis shorts and a big smile. Beneath the caption read: "The Hilton boys with an unidentified lovely. Maybe Hiltonites wouldn't be interested but the editor would like further information including telephone number."

He got it airmail special delivery the following day. "Unidentified lovely is truthfully no grandmother. She is blonde, blue-eyed, Hungarian, and her telephone number is currently the same as my own. Her first name is Zsa Zsa and her last name is Hilton. C.N.H."

The photographer had sent the wrong Mrs. Hilton to fill the grandmother shoes.

That moment of laughter was about the last one we knew, Zsa Zsa and I. In November of 1944 while she and her sister Eva were in Washington seeing to their passports, the Bel Air house was gutted by fire. When she returned I had moved into the Town House and Zsa Zsa took up residence in a separate suite. A few weeks later we left the Town House and went our separate ways permanently.

Like my hotel negotiations at that time, our divorce arrangements were drawn out and difficult. It was almost two years before the suit was filed in September, 1946. When the settlement was made it seemed ironic that it was the exact amount I had once raised to buy the Sir Francis Drake, a large and beautiful hotel. I did not grudge a penny of it. It was true that a Gabor could bring much laughter and gaiety into any man's life—if he could afford it and if his faith permitted.

It was a priceless moment for me, however, when I was able to approach the altar of my church and participate in the sacraments once more.

There were pleasant moments even during that difficult period. Just after Zsa Zsa and I separated I bought the Dayton Biltmore in Dayton, Ohio. I also set up the Conrad Hilton Foundation to receive and distribute a portion of my share of profits from hotel operations. Among my letters now were appeals from old friends and new, as well as many I had never seen: a schoolteacher in the Ozarks whose car had broken down, two elderly ladies running an orphanage in South America whose roof leaked, a boys' club that needed equipment. The very day after I established the fund I got a letter from one of the Sisters of Loretto who had taught me catechism in New Mexico. She was now stationed sixteen miles from Albuquerque in the town of Bernalillo and she wrote: "We have started a campaign to build a gymnasium which is badly needed. We have been praying quite hard for the success of the campaign. I thought perhaps you could afford a small donation."

I remembered sister as small, frail and not young when she taught me. I remembered, too, how very long it took to collect money among the poor people of those outlying districts. I would love to have seen her face when she got my message. "Dear Sister: I received your letter of recent date. I am sure you have been praying extra hard, for your campaign has begun and ended."

It also gave me a great deal of pleasure to give away the Longview Hilton as it had once been given me. All our managers in the servcie "bought" an interest in it without putting up any money and the hotel paid for each one's share out of the profits. In other words, when they returned from the service they were all a little rich. Joe Harper, Fletcher Brumit, Bob Groves, Vernon Herndon, all found themselves as owners of a hotel.

Because I am me and not as yet truly unselfish, I also gave myself a present. I bought Friar Tuck Lodge at Lake Arrowhead, a few hours' drive from Los Angeles. Here, complete with speedboat and fishing tackle, I hoped to establish a thoroughly masculine retreat where the boys and I could be together in the outdoor activities we had always shared; where J. B. Herndon or Red Ellison or Bob Williford and I could sit before a log fire and thrash out business problems. For some months no woman except my mother and Olive Wakeman set foot in the Lodge, and it was remarkably refreshing.

We were there, the three of us, J. B. Herndon, Mother and I, when I decided one night to go to Chicago. "And I'm going to stay there 'til I get the Stevens," I announced firmly.

"Well, goodbye for a long time," said J.B. yawning.

"I've been wondering, Connie," said Mother, "before you go . . . you see I've made a little money on a small investment and I wondered what you'd advise me to do with it."

"I'd advise you to go in on the Stevens deal with me," I said.

"Oh, Connie," she cried, "are you sure that's safe?"

With these words of encouragement ringing in my ears, I took the train to Chicago.

The buying of the Stevens was probably the single most tantalizing affair in my entire career. Not the most complicated, not the most costly, but certainly the most nerve-wracking, frustrating, ulcer-making.

The reasons for this were the positively unpredictable business procedures of Mr. Steve Healy.

Three times I bought Mr. Healy's hotel. Three times we

shook hands on the deal. And three times the two-fisted, dynamic contractor turned pixie and vanished into thin air, each time raising the ante.

It's a funny thing how big events in a man's life can be governed by seeming whimsy. Had Healy been a direct business-man I would simply have bought the Stevens and gone home. As it was, his elusiveness, coupled with my friend Willard Keith's hearty dislike of cold weather, plus the bold sugges-tion of a sand-and-gravel man, combined to send me back to California with not one, but two hotels.

In the beginning it seemed quite possible I would not get even one.

Healy first agreed to sell the Stevens for a profit of $500,-000. Since I wanted the hotel badly, and Healy knew I wanted it, bargaining was out. "Deal," I said and we shook hands. Healy then disappeared from his familiar haunts to reappear shortly thereafter, having, as he said, "thought things over."

"I want a $650,000 profit," he announced.

I stood the raise. Again we shook hands. Again Healy van-ished only to reappear with more expensive ideas.

"A million," he said. "I think I deserve to make a clean mil-lion after what I've done for that hotel." He had obviously spent this interval reading his press clippings. Swallowing a host of indignant words, I stood the second raise. And then a third time Healy vanished.

I couldn't find him. His boys swore they couldn't find him. Even his friend Colonel Henry Crown, millionaire head of Material Service Corporation which had poured sand and gravel into many Healy constructions and had been acting for him in the negotiations, couldn't find the missing owner of the Stevens. I sat around my suite at the Blackstone with Willard Keith, who had made the Chicago trip with me, in a state of helpless fury.

Once before in my life a banker fellow in Kansas City had played games with me about the price of a bank in Cisco, Texas. Unwittingly he brought me good fortune when he forced me into the hotel business. Now Mr. Healy's peculiar conduct brought me more good fortune. I decided that chances of catching this will-o'-the-wisp were dubious, so I began to look around Chicago.

There, in the midst of the Loop, as regal and dignified and sound as the Queen Mother herself, sat the Palmer House.

Now no one seemed to know whether or not it was for sale for the simple reason that nobody had asked.

"Might as well ask the Windsors if Buckingham Palace is on the market," a friend told me.

Nevertheless, I called on Henry Crown and suggested an introduction to Edward Eagle Brown, chairman of the First National Bank of Chicago and a Palmer House director.

"I've lost faith in this Healy deal," I told him. "I think I'd like to look into the Palmer House."

"Why not buy 'em both," Crown suggested with a laugh. At first I laughed, too. Then I stopped laughing. Why not? The hotels were in entirely different social circles, not in direct competition. On the other hand they could happily join hands for the cause of a big convention, and each could keep its distinctive personality while sharing some of the operating costs. Hadn't the Roosevelt and the Plaza managed to get along very well in New York?

I eyed Crown speculatively and found him eyeing me. Crown was my kind of fellow. A bold thinker. A bold actor. He had a long record of grubbing along before the '30s. I knew that from an original stake of $10,000, exactly $4,989 more than I had pinned inside my shirt when I hit Texas, Crown had built up holdings valued at many millions. His sand and gravel delivered by his trucks and barges had been fed into almost every home, hotel, office building, in greater Chicago as his Material Service Corporation literally dug money from the earth. He was a bold dreamer, too, for to him the Empire State Building was what the Waldorf was to me—the greatest of them all. And today Henry Crown owns the Empire State Building.

Yes, my friendship with Colonel Crown was one of the bits of good fortune that Healy's elusiveness brought me. And, before I even had any assurance I could get either hotel, I began to wonder why I shouldn't have both.

I soon found out. The reason was made perfectly plain to me by Mr. Henry L. Hollis, the dignified elderly trustee for the Palmer estate. Mr. Hollis, in his striped trousers, with firm eyes and a "my-word-is-my-bond-sir," manner, was so very different from my erstwhile sparring partner in the Stevens deal.

When I asked him if the Palmer House was for sale he replied courteously: "We are neither making offers nor refusing them."

I took this as an invitation and a few days later, after some careful figuring, offered $18,500,000 for the Palmer House, subject to an examination of the books and obligations.

"It has come to my attention," Mr. Hollis replied rather severely, "that you are negotiating for the Stevens Hotel. I do not need to tell you that we cannot open our records to possible competition."

Promptly and as truthfully as I could I explained that it was my firm conviction that Mr. Healy had no intention of selling me the Stevens. Whereupon Mr. Hollis let it be known that the trustees had no objections to my price but would have to go into my qualifications for taking over their trust very carefully. I gathered I was to be investigated personally as well as having my business methods, reputation, and past management records thoroughly inspected. It took the very finest of all these, I was led to understand, to replace the traditional Palmer management of a Chicago social and cultural institution.

Back I went to the Blackstone feeling I was now in a most peculiar position. The Palmer House was a jewel. I wanted it. The Stevens was the Stevens. I had wanted that for a long time. Ever since I got to Chicago on this buying trip I had badgered Billy Friedman, the lawyer who helped put together the Sir Francis Drake deal (now assisting me again), by dropping into his office daily and leaving insistent instructions. I would look over the agenda on his appointment pad and slip in my own entry for the same hour each day: "Four o'clock: Close Stevens Deal—C.N.H."

Willard Keith, now president of the insurance firm of Marsh & McLennan, Cosgrove & Company of Los Angeles, a civic leader and a man of broad interests in California, had seen unusual situations before. He had, however, watched with fascination this chess game with two great hotels as pawns, and was inclined to agree that I could face stalemate.

"I want them both," I told Willard. "I can only have one. And I may get neither. What do I do?"

"Let's go to California and get warm," he suggested helpfully. "I am frozen to the bone. Snow. Wind. Let's go home and play golf."

"I don't go home 'til I get a hotel," I said firmly.

"If I get you one can I get a reservation on the next train?" Willard asked.

I didn't pay any attention to his question and even less to his bundling himself up and trudging off in the dismal remains of Chicago's last snowfall. In an hour and a half he was back.

"I found Healy," he announced.

"What did he say?" I demanded.

"I told him you'd lost all interest. That you were buying the Palmer House and going home."

My heart absolutely stood still. I didn't know if they'd sell me the Palmer House and now Willard had kissed off the Stevens.

"And Healy said," continued Willard, "that he wants to talk to you right away. I think he's going to make you a proposition."

Healy's proposition was that he now wanted a million and a half profit for his hotel. "How do I know it won't be two million tomorrow?" I asked sourly, visions of the Palmer House dancing before my eyes.

"Nope. This is firm," declared Mr. Healy.

"How firm? Would you care to sign your name to a document right now?" It seemed impossible that the Irish butterfly was really willing to have his wings pinned. But he was.

We closed the deal right there and then. At the last minute I found that by actual count, overlooking closets and such, the Stevens had only 2,673 rooms instead of the advertised three thousand, and that Healy wanted to back a truck around and relieve us of seventy-five cases of scotch and bourbon whiskey. But none of this mattered. What mattered was that, after six long years, the Stevens was mine.

Joseph P. Binns, the amiable young manager who had shown me the glories of this hotel in 1939, was now in the service and I was keeping a sharp eye on him. Meanwhile I put in a call for Bob Williford at the Roosevelt in New York.

"Dean Carpenter," I informed him, "is coming on from Albuquerque to take over your hotel." I listened to the long pause. Bob's silences were so full of feeling. "And you are coming out to Chicago to take over the largest hotel in the world."

By the time Bob arrived, Willard Keith was California-bound. I didn't go with him. "I've got some unfinished business with Mr. Henry Hollis."

It was no easy thing to face those chill blue eyes and try to explain to Mr. Hollis what had happened. "No explanation is necessary," he said coldly.

"It is a question of my integrity, Mr. Hollis," I said. "It is necessary to me. It looks as though I misled you, to say the least. But when I spoke to you about the purchase of the Palmer House it was my honest belief that Mr. Healy had bowed out of the sale of his hotel even though we had shaken hands on it three different times."

As I mentioned "integrity" and "handshake," the extreme frost melted from Mr. Hollis' eye. I decided to plunge right on. "Is the Palmer House still for sale?"

"It is not for sale now any more than it was when I talked to you before," Mr. Hollis said slowly. "I am willing to listen to an offer but I tell you now I will not consider the offer you made before. It is going to cost you more money."

"All right," I replied. "I understand and I am now willing to bid you $19,385,000."

He rose and stretched out his hand. "I accept," he said. That was all there was to it. No pens, pencils, paper, lawyers, witnesses. Within a few weeks he had other offers for the hotel, one of which topped mine by a million dollars. But Mr. Hollis had given his word and he stood calmly and steadfastly by it. I have done business with many men in my time. I do not think I have ever had a greater experience than dealing with this perfect gentleman. I felt throughout that I was watching a master in the greatest traditions of American business.

Actual completion of the business transaction took some weeks. The Atlas people were with me once more, as they had been in the Stevens deal. And Henry Crown. I didn't lack money, but for the first time I had to sell my old backers hard to let them in on a good thing.

Sam Young back in El Paso voiced the typical reaction. Now Sam and I had never minced words. As a matter of fact, once, not too many years before, we stripped off our coats in front of his bank and prepared to settle an issue with bare fists until a friend intervened. Now when I called Sam, he allowed, not too politely, that I was crazy. "When you bought the Stevens," he said, "you became the world's leading hotel operator. Now you're pushing your luck. Two big hotels in the same city won't work. You are your own competition."

"Now you look here, Sam," I said. "Didn't you just build a branch bank at Five Points? Do I come down there and tell you how to run your bargain counter? I've got all the money I need and I was just letting you in on it. To show you how crazy I am: in 1933 when I was breaking my neck to raise $30,000 and you didn't have $10 to help me out, the Palmer House had a gross operating profit of $1,360,531. Do you want in on it or don't you?"

It's harder for a Texan to change his mind than to change the subject, so Sam asked casually after the health of the Stevens. "It's plenty healthy," I said. "We'll net close to $1,750,000 this year and keep climbing (which prophecy proved true) and now I'll tell you a few more facts. The property the Palmer House sits on is appraised at $21,000,000. The loan valuation set by Northwestern Mutual Insurance Company of Milwaukee is $40,000,000. And I'm paying $19,-385,000. I'm about to hang up. You can come in if you want to but I'm not going to beg you."

Of course he came in and so did the rest of my old backers, fuming and fussing but playing along. I had a fine new backer this time, too, in Henry Crown. And a very good thing it was. For after all my boasting, at the very crucial moment I found myself a million dollars short. I called Henry on the phone. "I need a million dollars quick," I said in a flat voice, carefully disguising any tensions.

"I'll let you have it, Connie," he said quietly. "Just tell Hugo Anderson at the First National that I said to let you have the million." That was a great moment.

When it came time to deliver the money I sat down and wrote a check for $7,500,000, payable to "Honore Palmer, sole surviving Trustee under the last will and testament of Bertha Honore Palmer, deceased." I have a picture taken of me writing that check. No one has ever seen it but my family and a few friends. It is locked away in a safe deposit box and will never be printed. This was Mr. Hollis' request. I didn't even ask him why. It was my pleasure to be able to give my word to him—and to keep it.

Sometimes now I felt just like the old lady tossed up in a blanket—seventeen times as high as the moon. I could borrow a million on the phone, write a check for seven and a half million, and when a check of mine, accidentally drawn for $100,000 on the First National Bank of Albuquerque, where

I had no account, was presented for collection, the bank honored it without question.

I was in the barbershop at the Stevens, swathed in towels, when C. W. "Kit" Carson, the bank president, called. "Glad to pay it for you, Connie," Kit said. "But will you send along a note to cover it when you've got time so we can keep the records straight?"

When I really began to think it might be me doing all this, however, my guardian angel was right there ready to pounce. True, I had no money troubles. But taking over the Palmer House and inheriting her traditions wasn't a task designed to allow a westerner to outgrow his hat.

Once again, as it was when I bought the Plaza, so it was with the Palmer House. The lorgnettes of the socially élite made me feel not so much like Genghis Khan as like a large bug under a small diamond microscope. They were waiting for me to violate Tradition, determined that I should. And I was equally determined that I should not.

And of course I immediately did.

It seemed to me that the Palmer House served chocolate ice cream at each and every meal with monotonous regularity. Totally unaware that entire important Chicago families had waxed strong not on just any ice cream, but on the particular brand of chocolate ice cream served by their favorite rendezvous, I committed the gigantic *faux pas* of ordering it replaced on the menu with strawberry and mocha. After an elderly, shocked captain, an elderly, irate customer, and a horde of disappointed children had showed me the error of my way, I retreated as gracefully as I could, renounced variety for tradition and we all went back to eating chocolate ice cream.

I also began studying Palmer House history. Most fortunately, the United States Armed Forces discharged Colonel Joe Binns as the war was ending in 1945, and he had the exact managerial talent needed to guide us through.

My study of the Palmer House revealed that the first edition was raised by one Potter Palmer in 1871. Potter Palmer was something of an eccentric and a thorough business genius. After starting a dry goods store and introducing into merchandising most of the practices used today, he sold out to Marshall Field and Levi Z. Leiter, some years before my father even thought of leaving Fort Dodge to pioneer the Territory of New Mexico.

Potter then turned his magic touch to real estate, put up thirty-two buildings on some business property which promptly became the grandfather of the present Chicago Loop. Restless for new fields to conquer, he next built himself a hotel, the original Palmer House, completing it just in time for Mrs. O'Leary's cow to catch it when she decided to kick over her lantern and burn Chicago down. Undaunted, Palmer built a second Palmer House which served for fifty-two years until the present structure was erected in 1927.

While Potter was busy about his enterprises, his wife became the social dictator of the great city and decreed her husband's hotel as the center of the loftier cultural activities. There has always been some doubt as to how far Mr. Palmer followed Mrs. Palmer into the higher realms of elegance. It is a known fact that he stoutly resisted any attempts to place him in a separate office and always sat at his rolltop desk in the hotel lobby. When he slammed his desk shut, denoting the close of his business day, instead of wending his way directly to the soirées, where his wife held sway, he worked in a businesslike fashion through the Palmer House bar buying a drink for each guest in turn. His personal reward for this hospitality was that he often slept in the carriage house of the enormous castle he built for himself on Lake Shore Drive.

He was a man of mighty moods and once, when several suits of armor he had ordered from Europe to brighten his castle were delivered by mistake to the hotel, two frisky young clerks discovered he was not a fellow to trifle with. They thought Palmer had departed safely homeward and donned the armor for a little light combat when the old man appeared in the doorway. In the ensuing confusion and attempted flight they tripped over each other, fell flat, and struggle as they would, could not rise.

"Get a can opener," bawled the irate Palmer, "and we'll see what the bloody hell they sent along inside those things."

The builder of the Palmer House was also a man of mighty appetite and it was no doubt to satisfy the owner that the early tradition of fine and generous cuisine was established. His forward vision won for his hostelry a bevy of firsts: the first hotel in the country to have electric lights, the first to have a telephone in each room, the first to use display advertising. And this anticipation of his guests' wants enrolled in the Palmer House guest books almost every President who ever traveled west, celebrities, social leaders, the truly discriminating from around the world. After the first Potter Palmer's death the Palmer family carefully nurtured the traditions that he had established and that now fell on my shoulders.

There were a few, of course, which the old man didn't know about. The directors, I was informed, had traditionally developed a taste for the fine whiskey carefully laid down in the Palmer House cellars. Mrs. Potter Palmer II had always gotten her meat from the hotel. "It's the very best, you see."

When I had deferred with two hundred cases of whiskey and a personal message to Mrs. Potter Palmer that I would never fail them, I hazarded a small change. Much to my astonishment the overflow guests cluttered up the lobby daily in a disorderly, restless and very unhappy mob. "Shades of the Mobley," I muttered, wishing L. M. Drown were here to see it. Above their heads was a sign reading boldly: SORRY! NO ROOMS WITHOUT RESERVATIONS. And this in the most elegant hotel in Chicago! "Take it down," I ordered.

Then Joe Binns and I devised an Interim Club where the orphans and strays could rest, bathe, telephone, and generally keep themselves out of our beautiful lobby while our accommodations clerk worked to place them elsewhere. It brought great good will on all sides, from competition, residents, and transients alike.

I also knew the old thrill of sniffing out waste space, a storeroom in the arcade that, converted into a cocktail lounge, brought in $200,000 in five months. By judicious rearrangement we added sixty guest rooms. As a matter of fact, Joe Binns increased the revenue of the Palmer House $1,724,250 in the first year without sacrificing a single tradition.

I had gone to Chicago hoping to buy one gold mine and come home with two.

Between the completion of the Stevens deal and the day the Palmer House was officially ours, my sons had both joined the U. S. Navy. Nick was a Seaman First Class, radarman on a super-dreadnought, the *North Carolina*, and advised us by V-mail that he was "plenty busy." Later we were to discover that the business consisted of shelling the coast of Japan.

Barron likewise made Seaman First Class and became an official photographer U.S.N. He was stationed in Honolulu and I was deeply touched when his letters admitted he was "lonesome."

The service wrought amazing changes in my teenagers. The reasons Nick carefully explained in a letter: "You have to learn to take it and like it over here. It doesn't matter in the service how much money your dad has because you're in exactly the same boat with everyone else. If I was ever a smart Alec, or Barron either, and I guess we were, this is a fine place to get it kicked out of you."

It was a funny feeling for us parents. Pride, mixed maybe with a little fear and a touch of awe that they were out there doing a job that we, the efficient ones, the omniscient "elders," were unable to do.

"We're about thirty years too late for this one," complained Bill Irwin. His son had been discharged and gone to work at the Roosevelt at the time Nick, aged nineteen, went in. And that same month Olive Wakeman's boy Bob, a radio gunner on a B-24 with the Eighth Air Force, was decorated.

Olive put into words what we were all thinking. "We've been doing things for them for years. Now they've got to do it for us. I only hope we taught them what they need to know."

Yes, they were men now—or they never would be!

On August 14, 1945, the Town House was filled to capacity with three thousand women of the Assistance League holding a charity affair all over the public rooms, spilling into the gardens and onto the tennis courts. At three o'clock manager Frank Wangeman stepped to the microphone and announced that Japan had surrendered. From our offices we heard the announcement, the moment of deathly stillness, and then a chorus of three thousand women's voices, some brimming with tears, as they rose and spontaneously sang the national anthem.

We closed the office for the rest of the day. Temporarily the world was safe. It was a moment for sober rejoicing. Most of the staff went home.

"Where are you going to celebrate?" someone asked Olive.

"I think I'd like to go to church," she said in a very small voice.

"I'll go along," I volunteered.

Our sons had fought the war. Our part would be to fight for the peace. And I know I prayed most earnestly that we be given the light we needed so we would not fail them.

When the boys finally came home, at my earnest insistence they went back to school. It was an anticlimax. Nick dilly-dallied at Loyola College wishing to get on with the grown-up business of living. After a few months he went on to Chicago where he worked in the Stevens under Bob Williford, taking one job after another.

Both of the boys had taken up flying to try to hold onto a trace of the excitement that had recently spiced their living. Barron, in fact, flew back and forth to college at Santa Maria. It struck me forcibly that my father walked to school, I rode a horse, and my son casually used an airplane.

This, I suppose, is progress.

We felt another kind of progress in our hotels. In May of 1946 the Hilton Hotels Corporation was organized. A year later our common stock was listed on the New York Stock Exchange, the first hotel stock in history to be thus accredited.

The incorporation did several things for us. First it made the operation easier. Nine hotel properties, excluding the Roosevelt and the Palacio in Chihuahua which would not fit into the structure, and the Hilton at Longview, which now belonged to the managers, were welded together. Until then we had operated each hotel as a separate entity with different stockholding interests and no unifying overall plan to coordinate the activities. As we added more hotels this method became unwieldy. To security holders in the original separate companies we issued common stock and convertible preference stock in the corporation and in each case they were able to see their original investment make substantial gains.

Personally I found myself the largest stockholder with the $2,238,456 I had originally invested in the different hotels valued in the corporation at $9,193,096. Looking back at the displaced ex-soldier who had hit Texas with a hatful of dreams and $5,011, I wondered ungrammatically, but with awe and humility, "Can this be me?"

I was proud of the corporation and proud of the men who were its elected officers. Bob Williford, once key clerk at the

Dallas Hilton, now executive vice-president of the corporation and vice-president in charge of the Central Division; Red Ellison, bellboy, Abilene, vice-president in charge of the Western Division; Joe Binns, ex-Colonel in World War II, once manager of the Stevens, vice-president in charge of the Eastern Division. J. B. Herndon, Jr., the man who dug dollar for dollar with me throughout the Depression, was vice-president and treasurer; Billy Friedman, secretary and general counsel.

I must confess I was pleased, too, to find that I now rated *two* secretaries. My faithful Olive Wakeman became executive secretary and Ruth Hinman, a lively, efficient girl, became my secretary. I'm afraid I bragged about it.

"You are looking," I told my mother, "at a very important man with hotels valued at $41,000,000. I now also have two very lovely secretaries."

"You don't look a bit different to me," she retorted, "except that you have a spot on your tie." Later when I had some new very "president of the corporation" portraits made, she looked them over and said, "Very pretty. But you have too many pictures of yourself already."

"Very well," I said, "you shan't have one of these 'til you take that back."

She wouldn't take it back, either. But she wanted one of the pictures. While I couldn't yield, I did let my sister Felice, who had never learned to lie, take two, "one for a very close friend."

In December of 1946, without any struggle, our corporation acquired the Mayflower, dean of the diplomatic hotels in Washington, D. C., and we changed our slogan from "Minimax" to "Across the Nation." But the really important event was the gathering of the clan in El Paso to celebrate Mother's eighty-fifth birthday.

All her children and sixteen of her grandchildren, including Nick and Barron came to pay her honor and she took that, along with the affection of the entire population of El Paso and much of Texas and New Mexico, as her just due. She was frailer, smaller, but very much the matriarch and she gallantly helped us hide from the fact that she was approaching the end of her life by displaying more spunk and sparkle than usual. One afternoon she took a fall, cutting her knee and injuring her arm. When I dashed to her side, breathless and badly frightened, she waved me away, saying casually, "Don't fuss, Connie, I'm all right. I wasn't wearing my best nylons."

The following summer, however, things were not "all right," and we all fussed a good deal. While spending the hot months at the Hilton in Long Beach with my sister Helen, Mother suffered a coronary attack. The prognosis wasn't good and Rosemary, Eva and Carl hastily flew out to be with her.

Two weeks later she rallied sufficiently to be match-making between Helen and the doctor and a few days after that the doctor pronounced her out of danger. "Amazing woman," he said. "When I made my call this morning she greeted me with 'Do you have to come and see me every day? How much is it costing me? No! Don't tell me. I'll have another heart attack.' "

The crisis over, everyone went home. Forty-eight hours after they left, Mother slipped away quite painlessly in her sleep, her old rosary in her hand, a look of satisfaction on her face.

I took my mother home to Socorro to rest beside Gus in the cemetery in the shadow of the blue Magdalena Mountains, probably the first thing she saw in the distance when she approached the Territory sixty-two years before. In California the cemeteries are gardens of love, with velvet grass, colorful flowers, soft music. My mother and father are buried on a sandy bit of high ground behind Socorro, only the tall spires of San Miguel rising to break the long view over the adobe town to the untamed spaces of New Mexico where the tiny green thread marks the passage of the Rio Grande.

Perhaps it is not elegant, but I knew my mother would want to go home.

On the train that carried us back to New Mexico, Mother and I together for the last time, I looked through the small cedar box she had always carried with her from Socorro to El Paso, to California, to Massachusetts, wherever she went.

In it were her marriage certificate, a picture of baby Julian who died so long ago, a post card from Boy when he was in South America, the itinerary of her trip around the world. There were ill-spelled letters from her grandchildren, a telegram jointly sent by Rosemary and Carl and me on Mother's Day, 1923, a newspaper clipping giving the rules laid down by a champion son-in-law (who had gotten along with his mother-in-law for fifty-one years) on how he did it: "Have but one mother-in-law: Never criticize her because she always means well: Always take her advice if you can: Show an interest in her stories of the 'good old days': Always let her have her own way." The last was underlined.

She had clipped "Niemoeller's Best Sermon" from *The New York Times* which maintained that the Prelate's silence in a concentration camp, when requested by the Nazis to reverse his edict that "We must serve God rather than man," was the most eloquent of living sermons.

There were two other newspaper clippings she had cherished; one a column written by Elsie Robinson called "Ask —and It Shall Be Given You!" "Faith," the columnist had written, "is the greatest force in human life. [Underlined.] It is greater than intelligence, charm, physical beauty or strength, political power, money, or social position. There is practically nothing a man can't do for or with himself if he has faith." My heart jumped when I saw that she had written, in her firm, old-fashioned script, the name "Connie" beside that statement.

The second clip was a poem dedicated to Schumann-Heink, the great leider singer, by Nat Campbell. I like to think that this one was saved through the years in order that, at that exact moment, she could reach out and comfort me. It read:

> There's a password to Heaven, and it is this:
> (I'm sure she needed no other
> When she stood at the gate of Eternal Bliss)
> "Saint Peter, I'm a mother."

That cedar box—I have it still—was a sort of last conversation with her as if before she went, she decided to leave a message, the things she treasured, the things she thought, the things she might have said if she had been sitting on the train beside me.

When we arrived in Socorro a host of friends from all over the southwest came to pay tributes of love and affection to Mary Laufersweiler Hilton. The newspapers wrote glowing editorials. One of these I clipped and placed in her cedar chest because I knew she would have treasured it: "Salt of the earth were Mrs. Hilton's kind, and as they yield to the inexorable march of years, the earth loses something of its savor. It is fortunate such women as Mary Hilton passed by here, and sad that her kind will never come again."

12. THE SKY IS THE LIMIT

In one of the last talks I had with Mother she issued again her laughing challenge. "Now you've got hotels across the nation," she said, "are you satisfied, Connie?"

"Nope," I said. "I haven't got the 'greatest of them all.' But I'll get it. Wait and see."

Now that she was gone I filled the sudden emptiness in my life by concentrating on the purchase of the Waldorf-Astoria. For two years I had believed I was finally ready. Ever since the bond purchases in 1942 I had been flirting with the Queen. Now I buckled down in earnest.

One did not, however, simply walk in and buy the Waldorf any more than one casually acquired the Territory of Alaska or called a real estate man and negotiated the Louisiana Purchase. She had two royal parents, both of whom had to approve any change of status. First there was the Hotel Waldorf-Astoria Corporation, organized to build the hotel, owner of the proud name and governor of her operation. Then there was the New York State Realty and Terminal Company. It was from them that the site on which the Waldorf stood was leased. This company also had advanced $10,000,000 toward the cost of the building and held a veto power over who operated the Waldorf. It was thus necessary to purchase control of the corporation and win the approval of the company as well.

Finesse, diplomacy, patience, time were required—not to mention money—and every trick I had learned about negotiating since I struck my first bargain over a pair of shoes with the volatile Spanish señora in Gus Hilton's San Antonio store.

It was the same old game in full dress. A group of Wall Street fellows who had gained control of the stock at low depression prices were holding it for a profit, but they wanted to sell. I wanted to buy. The buyer was entitled to a bargain, if he could get it. The sellers were entitled to their profit. Somewhere there existed that fine margin where the price was right. We had to find it. I had come around full circle into the deal I had dreamed of so long and found the rules exactly the same, only now the settings were very plush and I had graduated to blue chips.

But why should a man get a bargain when buying the greatest of them all?

The "new" Waldorf, as the tall edifice on Park Avenue was still sometimes called, was an enigma, a riddle as tantalizing to the hotel man as the sphinx with its mysterious smile is to the archeologist. How could a hotel that was not a profitable hotel be the greatest in the world?

Both could be truthfully said of the "new" Waldorf.

She had opened her doors to greet a depression, fallen into 77B, struggled back to make a little money, but it was only pennies compared to the debts that clung to her. There was no way on paper, using cold figures, to justify the Waldorf purchase, no way to back up my certain feeling that she had the potential to be as successful as she was great.

My Board of Directors, on the one hand, took a dim view of my courtship. Twice during the period of delicate negotiations when it looked as though the deal would close, when my associates were secretly alerted to fever pitch for the great acquisition, I met rugged opposition. Y. Frank Freeman, a Board member and executive vice-president of Paramount Pictures, even called me from Los Angeles to tell me of a long-distance warning he'd received. Ned Brown, president of the First National Bank in Chicago who had helped us out with the Palmer House, had called him in California. "Ned says," Frank Freeman reported, " 'For God's sake don't let Connie buy the Waldorf.' "

The gentlemen who were in a position to sell me the necessary control, however, took the reverse view. The Waldorf's elegant rooms might be almost entirely empty, but the few that were used housed the VIPs of the world. They could point out that during World War II, when a telephone call came in asking to be connected with the King, the Waldorf operator asked casually, "Which King, please?" It would have been a breach of delicate Waldorf diplomacy to give by mistake the calls of Peter of Yugoslavia to George of Greece.

They were selling, and they knew they were selling, a unique commodity. Successful or unsuccessful, the Waldorf was the Waldorf, and a valuable property.

Why?

Because James Thurber could report in *Thurber's Album* that on a visit to Columbus, Ohio, his mother asked, "Would it be possible for you to take me to lunch at the Waldorf-Astoria next time I am in New York?" "And," remarked Thurber, "from the tentative way she put it, I could see why she never asked before. She was afraid I couldn't swing it and hadn't wanted to embarrass me." The name was magic, a promise of luxury, the very best. Every honeymoon couple dreamed of a week-end at the Waldorf.

Because a hard-boiled magazine editor, approached by a staff writer who wanted to do an article on the growth of our hotels, dished out a tidy rebuff. "Hilton?" he said. "Sure I've heard of him. I read the *Wall Street Journal* and the *Hotel Monthly*. But what does he mean in Oshkosh? If you want to do a story on him, tell him to buy the Waldorf."

What had made it, despite debts, depressions, empty rooms, such a symbol?

In the first place the "new" Waldorf was one of a kind. There never has been and there never will be another building in a comparable location to equal it. The cost of such a property today—the real estate, craftsmanship, materials, luxury of furnishings, elegance of design—would be so great that only a very solvent government could afford to raise it. No hotel man could fail to recognize this, any more than an engineer could brush off the Hoover Dam.

In the second place it bore the imprint of some of the ablest men the hotel business has ever known. The "old" Waldorf, a stout success, had been the world's first great hotel; unofficial palace for the world's notables, the last word in luxury, service, hospitality. European hotels, and there had been many fine and famous ones, were mostly devoted to travelers, tourists, transients in one way or another, and as such the people of Europe regarded them, and they were small compared to the Waldorf. It was the All-American dream of the Waldorf's first manager, George Boldt, to make his hotel a social center as well as a superior lodging—a luxurious clubhouse, an integral part of his city's life and history.

His chances of making anything of it when he opened the doors of the Waldorf were less than average.

Built in 1893 on Fifth Avenue, in the most elegant residential section of New York, among the handsome mansions of the socially élite, it was not a welcome innovation and the owner hadn't meant it to be. For many years two Astor families, William Waldorf Astor and his aunt and uncle, William and Caroline Schermerhorn Astor, had lived in twin edifices side by side, one on the corner of Thirty-third, the other on the corner of Thirty-fourth, facing Fifth Avenue. There had been no love lost, so rumor had it, between William Waldorf and his Aunt Caroline. When young William, a man who took his politics seriously, was christened "Wealthy Willie" by the press and defeated for the United States Congress, he retaliated in a fit of pique by ordering his mansion destroyed and a commercial hotel raised on his corner. This could be counted on to annoy his aunt as well as other influential neighbors who had failed to support him. He then renounced his American citizenship and prepared to move abroad. His uncle William announced that if Wealthy Willie committed this sacrilege next door, he would tear down his own house and build a large livery stable. William Waldorf, on his way to England (where he became a viscount and later the father-in-law of Lady Nancy Astor, M.P.), didn't care a fig what his uncle did, and up went the first Waldorf.

George Boldt, a German emigrant who had been successfully managing the Bellevue in Philadelphia, had the vision and the courage to take on this stepchild of society. His first move was to hire as head waiter one Oscar Tschirky, a young Swiss, away from Delmonico's for the munificent sum of $2.50 per month. This was the self-same Oscar who became maître d'hôtel, Oscar of the Waldorf, and probably the richest and most famous maître d' in history.

In the midst of a depression following a panic, among distinctly hostile natives, the Waldorf opened its doors. It was promptly christened Boldt's Folly.

Boldt reversed this decision inside a few weeks with a single bold gesture. He offered his hotel rooms and an eight-course champagne dinner for a benefit concert, the recipient to be the Saint Mary's Free Hospital for Children, pet charity of Mrs. William Kissam Vanderbilt, undisputed social arbiter of New York's Four Hundred. Its chief patron was none other than Mrs. Caroline Schermerhorn Astor.

The tickets were set at the exorbitant price of $5.00 per person, a young conductor named Walter Damrosch was engaged to lead the orchestra, and everyone who was anyone pressed into the thronged hotel.

New York's Four Hundred was there—and its equivalent number from Boston, Philadelphia, Washington, Baltimore and Chicago. There were Mrs. Potter Palmer and the Stuyvesant Fishes. Lippincotts and Lowells and Averys mingled with Biddles, Belmonts and Goelets. "All Swelldom," as one newspaper reported, graced Mr. Boldt's soirée. The society editor of the *Herald*, with a happy turn of phrase, christened the wide corridor connecting the Empire Room and the Palm Room, a parade of fashion and beauty; "Peacock Alley," he called it. The name stuck, proved irresistible, and soon thousands of people would wander each day over the plush carpets, pause in the gilt chairs, to see and be seen.

Within a few years America's fabulous hotel gained fame around the world. The King of Siam, Prince Henry of Prussia, Indian maharajahs, crown princes, prime ministers, African diamond kings, Admiral Dewey, on his return from Manila, all flocked to the Waldorf.

Wealthy Willie's cousin, John Jacob Astor IV, occupying the mansion next door, could not overlook the dazzling parade. Not even a livery stable would stop it, and so Jack Astor decided to join in instead. A second hotel rose on the other corner—the Astoria—and was wedded to the Waldorf by means of a hyphen and the joint management of George Boldt.

Boldt continued to add to the prestige of the Waldorf-Astoria. Here for the first time room service was introduced to the United States, gifts were sent to prominent guests with the compliments of the management, name orchestras played behind the potted palms. As times changed, Boldt changed with them. When new fortunes fell into inexperienced, calloused hands in the coal fields, the oil fields, Oscar and George Boldt graciously undertook to educate the nouveau riche in the art of spending, of ordering from a French menu, or selecting proper wines.

Originally the Waldorf was said to purvey exclusively to the exclusive. Later Oliver Herford announced that it "brought exclusiveness to the masses." But the exclusiveness remained whether the hotel catered to a convention of three thousand or a tête-à-tête between crowned heads.

In 1916 George Boldt died and two years later another great hotel personality took over the Waldorf-Astoria. Lucius Boomer was reportedly approached at the McAlpin Hotel, which he had long managed, by General T. Coleman DuPont. "I'll buy the Waldorf if you'll run it," proposed the General. Mr. Boomer was the first hotelier to send greeters to the railway station, to pay foreign visitors the courtesy of bilingual staff members who could speak their language. When he took over the Waldorf, Oscar was still with him, and another able hotel man, Frank A. Ready. But for all his ingeniousness, Boomer was taking on a losing fight. The income tax law of 1913 had taken its toll. The residential élite were moving uptown, leaving the 30s to commerce. The crowning blow fell when prohibition padlocked the famed Waldorf cellars, closed the bars, and then the Claridge dining room. As another hotel man said at the time, "Our patrons do not want a dry supper and a dry dance afterward. This is altogether too dry a time."

At the end of 1928 while I was still building a hotel a year in Texas, Boomer threw in a very dry sponge. The site of the Waldorf-Astoria was sold and the historic pair of buildings torn down to make way for the Empire State Building. A grateful Board of Directors, as a tribute to Boomer, sold him the million-dollar name, Waldorf-Astoria, for $1.00.

Nothing then remained of the famous hotel but that name. Gone were the canopied beds, the famous four-sided bar which had been polished by the elbows of "Bet a Million" Gates, Diamond Jim Brady, Andrew Carneigie, J. P. Morgan. There was no Peacock Alley to shelter ghostly memories of Lillian Russell, Buffalo Bill, Li Hung Chang, Viceroy of China, or heavyweight champion Bob Fitzsimmons.

Frank Ready, who is still at the Waldorf today as vice-president, watched the last canopied bed disappear at auction and pronounced a fitting epitaph: "It was a magnificent old hotel. It had the daintiest china cuspidors I ever saw. But it didn't have enough bathrooms."

A year later, Boomer was ready to start all over again and remedy that situation. In 1929, just a few days after I had announced the building of the El Paso Hilton, Boomer dusted off his magical name and found backing for a new Walorf-Astoria. When the stock market crashed a few days later, Lucius Boomer did just what I did. He went ahead and finished his hotel.

Hotel history repeated itself. Once again, in 1931, the Waldorf opened in the face of a depression. This time it wasn't called Boldt's Folly. It was called Boomer's Folly.

But the President of the United States saw in it exactly what I saw in it when I found that clipping, riding across Texas on a train . . . a brave flag, a vote of confidence, flown in the face of adversity.

On the "new" Waldorf's opening night, over a newly installed radio system, the voice of Herbert Hoover from the White House spoke to the thousands crowding the hotel, and to Oscar as he stood at the portal just as he had stood at another opening thirty-eight years before, and to Lucius Boomer who had had the faith and courage to follow his dreams: "The erection of this great structure at this time," said the President, "has been a contribution to the maintenance of employment and an exhibition of courage and confidence to the whole nation."

Once again Society moved through Peacock Alley and the Waldorf was a mecca for the world's élite.

At one time or another everyone of any note seemed to arrive at the Waldorf. James Thurber's mother. Albert Einstein. The Prince of Wales had been to the Waldorf. He returned as the Duke of Windsor with his American duchess. Queen Wilhelmina of the Netherlands was a guest at one time and then her daughter, Queen Juliana. There were the Crown Princes and Princesses of Norway, Sweden, Denmark, the King of Siam.

Glittering parties filled her magnificent new public rooms; the Birthday Balls for President Roosevelt, Cobina Wright's Circus Balls for the Boy Scout Foundation. Amelia Earhart was awarded the Zonta trophy. Italo Balbo and the Royal Italian Fliers were honored. Yet every small detail and tradition that had made her famous was maintained as of yore, including the Men's Bar—"Haven," as Irvin Cobb expressed it, "of the Male's occasional emancipation from the emancipated Female."

History, too, left fingerprints on the "new" Waldorf. Here 2,500 leading Americans marked this country's recognition of the Soviet Union by a dinner in honor of Maxim Litvinov. And later, when Molotov arrived for a high-level conference, Frank Ready reported the proletariat more demanding and less gracious than crowned heads. Or, to change the flavor entirely, the Waldorf would serve Winston Churchill, Pandit Nehru, and His Holiness Pope Pius XII, then Cardinal Pacelli.

This, then, was the hotel I wanted. It was indeed the host

to kings. It made history. It made news. It made everything but money.

Some day, perhaps, they would call it Hilton's Folly, as it had been called Boldt's Folly and Boomer's Folly. But I had a hunch I could prove, as both of them had done, that "they" were wrong. Boldt had given the Waldorf a personality, a tradition. Boomer had given it the most beautiful building in the world. I felt that I, without changing either of these things, could give it present-day business success as well.

And so, while my directors looked at the books and groaned, "Get away from that White Elephant," I went on with the delicate negotiations. It was a Royal Elephant, a Sacred Elephant, and I meant to get it if I could. Every few months either I, myself, or my suave ambassador, Joe Binns, then managing the Plaza, met with the Wall Street men who controlled the Hotel Waldorf-Astoria Corporation. They wanted this. They wanted that. How much would I give? It was never enough.

Or we met with the railroad magnates or their representatives whose veto power was dangling over us on the grounds that the Waldorf had always been the shadow of one man's personality, and perhaps she would not fare so well if she didn't stand alone as Queen. We talked of the Plaza, of the Palmer House, two other great ladies who had not suffered any loss of attention or tradition by becoming one of the Hilton hotels.

Thus it went, this dignified fencing, feint, parry, attack, parry, riposte. We could not agree. We did not disagree. We went on trying.

I could not honestly deny that I had other things on my mind. I had a hotel family. I had a personal family. I did not propose to neglect them. But over the years, at the back of my consciousness, like the beat of a drum beneath the melody of events and ever growing, was my awareness of the Waldorf, my realization that having the Waldorf would be my own measure of my stature as a hotel man.

So important was this hotel to me in my career that now, in retrospect, it is the central point around which I focus my life. Events happened "before the Waldorf." "After the Waldorf." Or "during the Waldorf negotiations."

It was during the Waldorf negotiations that I became a grandfather for the first time. Here was a main event in the life of my second son—and my own. For Barron it also precipitated a crisis.

In June of 1947, shortly before my mother's passing, Barron married a lovely girl from Los Angeles, Marilyn Hawley. The gentle Marilyn, a graduate of Marymount and a close neighbor of ours at Arrowhead, had done for her young man what neither I nor a number of schools nor the United States Navy had been able to do. Overnight Barron acquired a sense of responsibility. The teen-age trials and temptations ended abruptly at the altar. Later, with a baby on the way, he took life even more seriously.

"Dad," he announced, walking into my office one morning, "I have been thinking about my future."

"I am glad to hear it," I said.

"I am a family man," said Barron, "and I need steady employment."

"I agree," I said, knowing full well he had been using some of the capital I had invested for both boys in our hotel ventures over a period of years. "Now I myself have found the hotel business both interesting and profitable. I could start you at $150 a month."

At this Barron, the very same Barron who only yesterday, as it seemed to me, had been pleased with a raise in allowance to $5.00 per week, was aghast.

"Why, Dad, I couldn't work for any man for that," he said. "I've got it all figured out. As head of a family of five—a wife, myself, a baby, a nurse, a cook—I'll need at least $1,000 a month."

"You certainly will," I agreed. "And I can't use you at that price. I myself got $5.00 a month when I started and I'm not sure you're worth a penny more. Currently we're paying a little better than that to learn the business but the figure I gave you is top."

"Then that's out," said Barron, preparing to leave.

"If you think you can make $1,000 a month you go right ahead," I said firmly. "If you come down to earth we can always talk again."

"Sure," said he without any enthusiasm. And out he went. I expected him back before the baby was born. Instead, by the time young Barron made his entrance, his father was making better than $1,000 a month. He was partner and sales promotion manager in a business he and a friend started, the Vita Pack Company, in which they concentrated, froze and sold the juice of, and generally squeezed every dollar possible from, the handy California orange.

Quite honestly I was half proud, half annoyed, to find that $1,000 coming to him so easily. But as five other little Hiltons arrived in happy if rapid sequence at the home of Marilyn and Barron Hilton, I was pleased to think that if he and his wife had set out to better my own mother's and father's record, he had at least inherited some of Gus's ingenuity and business sense.

If my personal family was enlarging during the Waldorf negotiations, my hotel family was growing as well. We began to have offspring outside the United States and a whole new vista was opening up.

This was to be the fourth and, in many ways, most satisfying phase of my innkeeping.

Once I had leased dowdy dowagers in Texas. Then I had built a hotel a year, still in Texas, the grandest costing less than $2,000,000. Following that I had bought cheaply, great established hotels across the nation and doctored the financial wounds left on them by the Depression. Only once, in Chihuahua, Mexico, and that in a very small way, had I ventured across a border.

Now the opportunity came to assume a position on a world-wide stage.

Dimly, when we opened the Palacio Hilton in 1942, I had dreamed that some day this might be possible. I had thought then of a quotation I'd read stating that if business didn't cross frontiers, armies would. But it was an unreal, impractical time to pursue such dreams, with frontiers already topsy-turvy and flying armies crossing borders until they hardly seemed to exist at all.

Again, on V-J Day, after I had prayed that my generation would be given light and courage to help confirm the peace our sons had won, my mind had toyed with a vision of hotels, the only thing I knew anything about really, being used to draw the peoples of the world into closer understanding. I knew that people who had exchanged ideas, done business together, laughed and relaxed at play side by side, tended to lose their fears and suspicions, their hostilities. Hotels were ideal for just that. It was not a profound theory, not a new one, but it had given me a momentary happiness to feel that some day possibly I might have something to contribute in some small way to the peace of the world.

The dreaming and praying led to opportunity. A chance now came along to work toward it.

Both the State Department and the Department of Commerce suggested that the Hilton organization could make a substantial contribution to the government program of Foreign Aid by establishing American-operated hotels in important world cities. These hotels could stimulate trade and travel, bringing American dollars into the economies of the countries needing help. Besides, and this pleased me most especially, they felt that such hotels would create international good will.

Providentially a chance presented itself almost at once for testing the idea and laying out a blueprint which, when it proved itself, we could follow in subsequent operations. The Puerto Rico Industrial Company, a government agency, wrote letters to six or seven American hotel men stating the desire of Puerto Ricans to build a hotel in San Juan with their own capital, providing they could interest an American hotel man in furnishing and operating it.

I replied at once in their own graceful Spanish tongue and with all the enthusiasm I felt. However, I expressed my sincere belief that providing the building was not enough. They must also furnish and equip it. Then it would be their hotel. We in turn would provide consultants on architectural design and, during building, furnishing and equipping. We would then come in with operating capital, managerial controls and techniques, extensive worldwide advertising, sales promotion and publicity programs, to insure that any hotel in a given area would produce the highest volume of profit. We would operate their hotel under a long-term percentage rental agreement with renewal options, two-thirds of the gross operating profits to go to the owners and one-third to us. We would also hire Puerto Ricans for a large percentage of our staff and work out a program of on-the-job training in our United States hotels where their own people could learn the best we knew in techniques of modern hotel management.

It seemed a very good basic plan to me. I was immensely pleased with it. I was even more pleased when they wrote back at once accepting my terms.

"I don't think those others had a chance," said Olive Wakeman. "Anyone who could write so flatteringly in their native tongue and call them 'My Esteemed Friends' had the inside track."

J. B. Herndon overheard her. "You think he got it because he called them 'Estimados Amigos'?" he growled. "I think he got it because no one else had the nerve to tackle it."

My Board of Directors agreed with J.B. Once more they wanted none of the stuff dreams are made of. When they weren't pleading with me to stay away from the Waldorf, they were begging me to stay within the continental United States.

They muttered about "wars," "revolutions" and "inflation." "You can't tell what's going to happen," said one. "We're perfectly safe and happy just as we are," said another. Then I was called an idealist.

Now I take that for a compliment. And I also believe that idealism can be practical, as I explained. "I work for our stockholders," I said. "I am in business to make money for them. All right, here's the way I see it as a hotel man. The world is shrinking. What used to be a month-long vacation trip is now almost a week-end possibility. Businessmen can cover far-off territories. The airplane is here to stay. Americans not only can but want to travel farther, see more, do more, in less time. This is progress and the hotel business must progress right with it. Father Junipero Serra set his California missions a day's journey apart. Today you can fly over the whole string in a few hours. If we were to set our hotels a day's journey apart, we'd be around the world in no time. So perfectly sound business is in line with national idealism."

"All right," said the Board reluctantly. "Go ahead if you're determined. But set up your own corporation, elect your own Board of Directors, and paddle your own canoe. We are willing to provide limited amounts of money."

Thus Hilton Hotels International, Inc., a wholly owned subsidiary of Hilton Hotels Corporation, came into being. Our goal was "World Peace Through International Trade and Travel." And we made an immediate impression on our parent corporation by changing its slogan from "Across the Nation" to "Around the World." I had my own Board and a new vice-president who shared my enthusiasm. His name was John W. Houser and I had been keeping an eye on him for quite some time, waiting for the right spot. John had no hotel experience but he had what seemed to me a most valuable asset, a great belief in our future. "I want to get with a company that's going places," he said the first time he came to see me. "I think you are."

Bill Irwin, with me still thirty years after World War I, now also joined Hilton Hotels International and was dispatched to Puerto Rico to keep an eye on the Caribe Hilton as our pilot project rose in San Juan.

I made a flying trip to Florida to track down one of my Wall Street fellows and make another pass at the Waldorf. There was still that discrepancy between us, the difference between what they wanted and what I'd give. So I plunged back into rearing my infant international family.

I made my first trip to Europe since World War I in the company of my son Nick, my brother Carl, USN Retired, and Joe Binns. Once I had looked at it through the eyes of a soldier. Now I saw it strictly as a hotel man, a man stalking cities and countries to find out where an American-operated hotel was both needed and wanted.

It made a world of difference in what I saw.

Like every other American in London I wanted to see Buckingham Palace—and I wanted to see King George VI and his Queen, Elizabeth. I got to do both.

I think much of America had been impressed during the war, not by their royalty but by their gallantry. I know I had. I was lucky enough to be a guest in the box of the owner of the Dorchester, Malcolm McAlpin, on Derby Day. And our box was right next to the Royal Box.

When I wasn't sightseeing I was looking at hotels. I couldn't help it. But I wasn't buying what was there. I was anxious to see them built where they were needed instead.

To operate a hotel in postwar England would have turned an American innkeeper gray. Here a people who had taken all kinds of wartime punishment were now absorbing an equally stringent peace. The hotels were in poor condition, not from bombing but lack of maintenance. No repairs were allowed. Government permission to do a small job of painting was almost impossible to get. They had had no new linen for years. Still they put up a gallant show wherever it was possible. The service was exceptional. The quality of the food was good, considering they were allowed to charge only five shillings per meal regardless of what was served.

It was in England, however, that the fact was brought home to me that American business methods are uniquely American. This is not to say that other methods are better or worse. But I do mean to say they are different. All over Europe I found that the time sense varied most definitely. Ours is a new land. Theirs is very old. It makes for a variance in perspective.

Looking at available property in London I met an old Scotsman who owned a desirable site. He was eighty-five at the time, shrewd, spry and very much the businessman. He gave me to understand in no uncertain terms that, if he leased that land, in five years' time, I would have to do certain things. In ten years the conditions would be so and so. In fifteen years they would be different again. "And I want you to know," he concluded, "that I'm in no hurry to do business, either."

At a later date I found that, although the British and the Americans share a common language, it is subject to vastly different interpretation. Through a firm of architects which designs hospitals for the Crown, we learned that a certain central piece of property, in the heart of the city had become unsuitable for a hospital and the hospital was anxious to move. It was an ideal location for a hotel.

"It could be bought," said our informant, "if someone were ready to buy it now."

"How soon could we get it?" I asked.

"Oh, immediately, I should say," was the answer.

Quickly I figured how long it would take, in all probability, for the hospital to find a new location and move. "Roughly six months or a year, then?"

"Oh, no." The poor man was horrified. "But very quickly. Perhaps five to ten years."

And I had thought a six-year wait for a chance at the Waldorf an eternity.

In France there wasn't any soap. But there had been no soap when I was there before. Deprived of imports, France does not have the necessary ingredients for soap manufacture, but so far as I could see this was the only thing she was lacking. Paris was Paris, and the French hotels were going very well. The black market of France was in definite contrast to the deprivations we had seen in England.

Rome and Madrid interested me mightily from the standpoint of building hotels. An integral part of my dream was to show the countries most exposed to Communism the other side of the coin—the fruits of the free world. In Rome I found Christian Italy most anxious for a hotel, for friendly exchanges with Americans. And Communist Italy most anxious to stave it off. A private tussle developed between these factions which, even later, after a contract had been drawn, money raised, the location selected, and the Cavalieri Hilton opening date set, continually prevented the first spade of earth from being turned to commence building.

Seven years after my first visit to Rome, seven years after those preliminary talks, I picked up a paper on my arrival in Chicago and read a headline: REDS BLOCK HILTON. How and where, I wondered? A filibuster, the story announced, by Communist members of the City Council in Rome had prevented the Italian company from getting the license to build the hotel.

That the Communists are aware of the danger to them of having the fruits of democracy displayed in their own backyard was very evident recently. In reporting the groundbreaking ceremonies for the Berlin Hilton now being erected in free Germany, the Communist press headlined: LOOK HERE—WHAT A HELL OF A BUSINESS and HOTEL KING ON PLUNDER CAMPAIGN.

These international babies have required much nursing, much diplomacy and patience. If they are to serve as ambassadors of good will, they must be successful and forced in no way, including the matter of time. Over and over I have had to remind myself that, when you consider how long the catacombs have existed in Rome, how long the Colosseum has been standing there, and what a comparatively recent event was the arrival of the Pilgrims at Plymouth Rock, perhaps time for them has a longer lens than it has for us.

In Madrid we ran into something that brought the immediate feeling of success to our trip. Here there was a hotel already started with private capital, but progressing slowly after three long years. There was a lively interest in negotiating a deal along the lines of the one laid down in Puerto Rico. I left Madrid with the firm conviction that we had just seen the foundations for Hilton Hotels International's first European hotel, the Castellana Hilton.

A part of my personal family I left in Europe when Nick

decided to attend the École Hotelière at Lausanne, Switzerland, the most famous hotel school of them all. Personally I was ready to go home. John Houser could return to Europe to follow the leads in Rome and Madrid and prospect new territory. As for me, I felt it was time to get back to the Waldorf.

The first thing I heard when I reached New York was that the Queen had, in my absence, acquired a second suitor, a wealthy fellow who had no other lady on his mind. With another buyer in the offing it was, I knew, now or never. The chance to buy the Waldorf, if it slipped away from me, would not come again in my lifetime.

My Board of Directors still could not share my sense of urgency or enthusiasm. And I, as president, could not buy or sell real estate for the Hilton Hotels Corporation without their consent. But as Connie Hilton I could do exactly what I had done in Cisco, Texas, thirty years before. I could buy me a hotel. I could put up my personal money, for there was no one to tell me what to do with that, and I could form a buying group to raise the rest as I had learned to do long before I had a corporation.

I set the wheels in motion along the old familiar pattern.

I called the man I considered to be the leader in the Wall Street crowd and announced: "I am ready to make you an offer today. What time shall I come down?"

"One-thirty this afternoon," he replied.

At precisely one-thirty I walked into his office, offered to buy 249,024 shares of stock in the Waldorf Corporation at $12 a share. There were 366,040.75 shares outstanding so my offer, if accepted, would give me control. "The offer is good for twenty-four hours," I said, and fished out my personal check for $100,000.

"Give me forty-eight hours to submit it to the others," he said. I agreed.

In forty-eight hours the offer was accepted with a time limit to turn over the cash, and nothing stood between me and the Waldorf except about $3,000,000. There were rumors that I played golf every afternoon and did the rumba every evening during that crucial period. It is true that I adhered to my rule of stopping work at six and that I danced every evening that I could. But the final negotiations temporarily put an end to my golf game and eventually cut into my evening recreations.

The one thing I didn't miss was attending Mass each morning at St. Patrick's Cathedral. I still knew a visit with God in prayer was the best investment a man could make—and the one thing I couldn't do without.

My Board of Directors, now that the chips were down, showed enough confidence in me to allow the Hilton Hotels Corporation to participate in the syndicate formed to buy the hotel. Charles Deere Wiman, president of Deere & Company, Moline, Illinois, said, "I'll take a chance with you for $250,000." And so it went. We lacked $500,000 but Joe Binns had a candidate in Philadelphia who was scheduled to take up that slack. Joe, who had gone down to get the money, called and said the fellow was asking questions. I answered them. On Saturday morning Joe arrived back in New York empty handed.

"Where is the money?" I asked.

"He has some more questions," Joe said. "He'll meet you at the Plaza at ten o'clock Monday morning to ask them."

"I hope he isn't looking forward to a long powwow," I said. "We've only got 'til Tuesday."

At ten o'clock Monday morning the gentleman from Philadelphia postponed our meeting until six o'clock that night. It was against my principles to do business after six and I wasn't pleased. But I wanted the Waldorf and I needed that money. I wasn't pleased either when he kept me waiting for an hour. And I was even less pleased when he sailed in accompanied by two lawyers.

Before I had finished saying good evening, he started. "I am in the insurance business," he said. "I would like the Waldorf business if I go into this deal."

"That will be considered," I said.

"That's not satisfactory," he stated. "I want to know now. I am also connected with a firm that deals in stores and supplies. If the price is right I want the Waldorf patronage."

"That will be considered," I said again, restraining myself.

Again, "That is not satisfactory. I want to know now."

I checked that one. He called it. "If I had known then what I know now about the Waldorf deal I wouldn't have committed myself—"

Getting up from my chair I said, "You are hereby relieved

of your commitment" and stalked from the room. Never before had I talked myself out of half a million in as short a time nor in as few words, nor with such a complete sense of satisfaction. Joe Binns followed me to my room. "We're all proud of you," he said happily. And then his eyes shadowed and he asked aloud the question I had been asking myself. "But what are you going to do about the money?"

"I don't know. But I'll get it."

The next morning at eight, Henry Crown arrived in New York. Over coffee I told him what had happened. We sat silently mulling over the problem for a minute or two, and then I said: "Henry, let's you and me put up that extra $500,000."

Once before at the crucial moment, with the Palmer House in the balance, Henry Crown came through. He didn't hesitate this time. "Okay," said Henry.

That day, October 12, 1949, I became "the Man Who Bought the Waldorf."

The Man Who Bought the Waldorf!
I couldn't get used to it.

The night after the hotel was transferred to us I stood under her elegant canopy lost in admiration as, with the rain pouring down on both sides, her resplendent doorman whisked guest after guest into a waiting taxi and sped them on their way. With me was Arthur Foristall, a valued public relations counsellor, and Arthur was growing restless for we were almost overdue at a dinner arranged to celebrate the purchase. "We've missed our turn several times," he muttered.

Finally Arthur's Bostonian sense of fitness drove him to speak to the offending doorman. "Do you know whom you are keeping waiting?" he demanded so witheringly I looked around quickly expecting to find myself a "host to kings." "Your employer," Arthur said with a flourish. "This gentleman, Mr. Hilton, now owns the Waldorf-Astoria."

It sounded fine! It felt good, too. And it felt better and better as we saw our tried and true methods justifying my faith in the Waldorf's potential. That first year it made a million dollar profit. My Board of Directors worked now to bring the Queen into the Hilton Hotels Corporation fold. Gradually we paid off our debts at one hundred cents on the dollar, acquired the balance of the stock. We, too, made our

contribution to the greatest of them all. The very one I had
foreseen. Sacrificing none of her beauty, her prestige, her tradition, we still put her where she belonged, on a pedestal of
solid earnings.

Acquiring the Waldorf seemed to those around me not
only the climax but the fitting end to my career. Very few
things in life have surprised me—this did. Olive Wakeman
shocked me one morning after our return to California by
mentioning her own plans "after you retire."

"Retire?" I said. "Who said anything about retiring?"

Arthur Foristall accused me of being a "man without a
future."

"How can you say that?" I demanded sourly. "The sky is
the limit."

"Yes," said Arthur speculatively. "I suppose there's always
Buckingham Palace or the Vatican."

But I knew full well that my horizons would continue to
expand as long as I had the capacity to work, to pray, and
to dream. There were great things yet to come "after the
Waldorf," as there had been "before the Waldorf" and "during the Waldorf purchase."

There were countries the world over where we could
open hotels. I was about to find a home for myself that was
the equal of a palace. My oldest son would marry one of the
most beautiful women in the world. And I would once more
try my long-suffering Board of Directors by attempting the
biggest real estate deal in history, a deal involving seven
times as much money as the Louisiana Purchase.

Nick's romance was on stage, front and center, from the
beginning.

This was as inevitable as it was tragic—for he fell in love
with a motion picture star or, rather, with her photograph.
When he burst into my office insisting that he simply had to
know Elizabeth Taylor, I thought he was joking.

"You can't get to meet her," I said. "I'll bet you."

I lost. Nick bombarded friends at her studio until he was
invited to take her to lunch. A short time after that there
were two young people very much in love. I realized how
serious it was when, a few months after the Waldorf, we flew
down to open the Caribe Hilton and Nick, who loves a
party, didn't want to go.

This opening was quite a party. We had planned to set a

precedent with the debut of our first International Hotel. Two plane loads of notables from the United States would arrive for gala festivities centering around the new hotel, giving prominent Puerto Ricans a chance to play host and their countrymen an opportunity to get acquainted with some of our representative people.

No hotel, as I had discovered, is ever quite ready to open. Thus it becomes necessary at the psychological moment to force it into business. Sometimes this means novel deviations in the most carefully prepared plans. Even with painstaking preparation neither the human element nor the elements of nature can be brought under full control. At the Caribe opening, manager Frank Wangeman had rehearsed his staff thoroughly, going so far as to have the waiters practice serving the formal dinner to empty seats. He had also arranged for hand painted individual place cards. As the Puerto Rican artist who had labored over them for weeks approached the banquet room on *the* night, his masterpieces in his hand, he tripped at the door, sending over a hundred place cards flying in every direction. With true Latin emotion he burst into tears and vanished under the cloud of the confusion which ensued to nurse his hurt feelings. Two hours later Frank had not succeeded in rounding up all the place cards. The puzzled guests were restless.

"Let's eat," I told Frank. "We'll just sit where we please."

But the excitement wasn't over for the evening. Our most dramatic moment occurred when Dame Nature got out of hand. Actor Leo Carillo was on the stage when a crackling thunderstorm caused a power failure. As if it had been a rehearsed part of his act Carrillo stood a moment in the pitch darkness and then a single match flame blossomed. In the words of Father Keller he announced: "It is better to light one candle than to curse the darkness." Slowly, as if by magic, several hundred other tiny, warm lights glowed like fireflies as cigarette lighters, candles, more matches flared until the light from so many small flames fully illuminated the room.

Each of our openings has generally had a little unrehearsed excitement and over-all has proven a most satisfactory method of accomplishing the trick of forcing the hotel open plus promoting good will and, most important to the guests, giving everyone a good time.

I noticed at the Caribe that Nick was suddenly incapable

of good times that didn't center around his startlingly lovely young star. His thoughts, plans, his present and future, were centered in Hollywood.

They were married in the spring. The wedding was large, formal, beautiful; the kind, said Elizabeth, of which she had always dreamed. And as Nick's mother, Mary, now a widow, and I stood side by side in the receiving line, I found myself thinking that even without prejudice, to my romantic eye they were the handsomest young couple I had ever seen.

"They have everything, haven't they?" I said to Mary. "Youth, looks, position, no need to worry about where their next meal is coming from."

"Maybe they have too much," replied Mary thoughtfully. "I don't think it's going to be easy for them."

"Nonsense," I said. I said the same thing to Olive Wakeman later when she reported a wistful Elizabeth, shortly before the wedding, saying, "I want my marriage to work. It must work. We love each other—but, oh, everything is against us."

"You women and your intuitions, your emotions," I snorted. "What could possibly be against them?"

Elizabeth, as it turned out, knew far better than I, far better than Nick, what she was talking about. For they never had a chance.

If Elizabeth had been just a shade less beautiful—

If she had been a counter girl at Macy's instead of a movie star—

If Nick had been older, wiser, less headstrong—

These two had dreamed of a normal life. Their aims were not much different from those of that old married couple, Mr. and Mrs. Barron Hilton. Yet one thing Elizabeth's extraordinary beauty barred them from forever was anything approaching the ordinary. This is what Elizabeth knew. Already she had had an unusual career, an unusual amount of fame and success. They had even had a most unusual courtship, for these modern times. For Mrs. Taylor, who had guarded the youthful star through thick and thin, guarded her right up to the altar.

The young couple had a most unusual honeymoon. In my home state we would have called it a farce, something you only saw on the stage or in the movies. When they sailed for Europe I could just imagine Nick with that wonderful feeling that comes to every bridegroom that now, for perhaps the only time in his life, he would have his bride all to himself. Nick was in for a rude shock. Elizabeth was news and, by becoming her husband, he found that he was news too. There were reporters, photographers, fans, wherever they went. Sometimes the photographers arrived before their breakfast coffee and made pictures of a happy bride and an unhappy groom with the sulks. Nick was resentful, hot-tempered, and handled himself accordingly.

Sometimes his temper really flared and he stalked out. "He leaves her alone," said the gossips. Or worse, he stayed and was openly antagonistic. Then he was "unpleasant, uncouth, uncooperative."

"Poor Liz," sighed the gossips.

"Poor Nick," said Elizabeth. But she could do little about it.

By the time they came home on the *Queen Elizabeth* the papers were printing tall tales of a separation. Stalking into my office, his hands thrust deep in his pockets, looking absurdly young, Nick said, "It's life in a goldfish bowl. They'll print anything whether it's so or not. They've had us on the ship-to-shore phone all the way across so we could hardly finish a dance. When I said we wouldn't talk to them Elizabeth said we must. But when we deny it they print it anyhow. I don't get it. Why can't they let us alone?"

He was angry, hurt, bewildered and defiant. I did the best I could.

"They're doing their job, Nick," I said. "It's the price you pay for marrying a famous woman. Whatever you both do is news. They can't ignore you. You'll have to learn to keep yourself in hand, to cooperate cheerfully. You know what's true and what isn't. If someone prints a rumor, rise above it. Let it run off you. Be big."

This was sage advice but there are few people with twice Nick's years and experience who could have taken it. It served to calm him temporarily but I didn't help matters when, a few days later, I had a brush with the press myself. I personally like the press, collectively and individually. They have been kind to me, and I have tried to be honest with them. There are, however, always exceptions and each man has his Achilles' heel, his small vanity.

Mine, of course, is my dancing.

At the Persian Room one evening the orchestra played the

varsoviana, the dance I had learned in my youth, now reborn to a new spell of popularity. Ann Miller was in our party and she and I took the floor. No one else did. It turned out to be an exhibition. The following morning I got a first class roasting from a columnist under the title of "The Caterer's Waltz."

I was incensed. He hadn't even gotten the name of the dance right. I spent the better part of an hour dictating irate letters to the columnist. Olive Wakeman, wise woman, dutifully took them word for word, with a perfectly straight face, then filed them in a bottom drawer.

But it was Nick who brought me sharply to my senses. "It's the price you pay for being a famous man," quoth he. "You'll have to learn to keep your temper. Rise above it. Let it run off you. Be big!"

There is nothing like a good laugh as an antidote for resentment. One of Nick's charms has always been his knack for nonsense, gaiety, his ability to make most people feel that the sun is shining. Olive and Ruth Hinman have claimed that they can tell from the other side of a closed door which of my sons is in my office. If the conversation is deep, centered around millions of dollars, it is Barron. If peals of laughter float through the door, they know it is Nick.

Nick and Elizabeth had recovered their optimism after their European trip and planned to stop in El Paso on their way home. Here, in this Between-Town, U.S.A., they hoped to find the quiet wherein they could finally have their honeymoon. But Elizabeth's glamour, which followed her willy-nilly wherever she was, went right along to the great southwest.

They never did get their honeymoon, those youngsters, for before they were mature enough to handle the difficulties that beset them, they were divorced. Their marriage had lasted seven months.

I bought Casa Encantada at Christmas in 1950. That wasn't its name then. It was referred to quite unromantically as "Mrs. Weber's House." But that was the name that occurred to me when I first saw it.

The House of Enchantment!

I resisted seeing it for quite a while. Bill Irwin brought it to my attention as a bargain—"a house that cost $2,500,000 to build," he said, "and, like the Waldorf, no one would be wealthy enough to duplicate it today. It's on the market at $400,000."

That was a bargain right enough. If we'd been talking about hotels I'd have been on my way. But we were talking about a home in which I was to live. This one had, according to Bill, nine acres adjoining the Bél Air Country Club, a swimming pool and giant recreation house, thirty-five thousand feet in the main dwelling, a private elevator, five kitchens, laundry facilities that could handle the daily washing of twenty-five families, twelve rooms reserved for servants, each with its own marbled bath and me, one man from San Antonio, rattling around in it.

What would Mary Laufersweiler Hilton have said!

"Bill," I told my friend, "it sounds like a wonderful buy. But the home I have now is adequate. I'm not sure I'd be happy in a house like that."

It had been designed for Mrs. Hilda Boldt Weber, the widow of glass millionaire George Boldt of the Owens-Illinois Glass Company, after she remarried. J. E. Dolena, one of California's famous architects, did it. It was, so I was informed, "Modern Georgian with clearly discernible Greek influences." It certainly sounded very elegant. When I heard of private steam rooms, a valet shop, glass houses, badminton and tennis courts, upholstered walls in the ladies' lounge off the pool-side recreation house, enough electric power to handle a thirteen-story building, not to mention a "spice" kitchen designed to consume the evil odors of garlic and onion, a "cool" room in the interests of happy salads and firm desserts, and a master bath in green marble with gold fittings, I began mentally to call it "Mrs. Boldt Weber's Folly."

"Why, a few years back," the enraptured Irwin told me, "the Prince of Iran saw it and said he would move to California if he could find a house like that. Of course he couldn't and it wasn't for sale. You'd never find another like it. There isn't one."

"Look, Bill, the Prince of Iran is used to palaces. I started out in an adobe room back of a store."

Bill didn't give up easily. "It's a bargain, Connie. You can't turn down a bargain like this," he insisted. "Maybe you *were* born behind a store, but look at your position today. You're host to the world. You've acquired social and business obligations. You need a place to entertain properly, a place for your grandchildren. Why, you haven't even got a swimming pool!"

"That's right," I said. "I haven't. And I've managed to get along pretty well without one for a good many years. It all sounds too pretentious." Then, when I saw how crestfallen he looked, I made a proposition. "If it ever gets down to $250,000, I'll take a look at it."

That seemed pretty safe to me: one-tenth its building cost. And then there I was, a few months later, looking at Mrs. Weber's house offered at that price. I had asked to spend the morning there alone. It is one thing to stalk hotel property, another to stalk a home. I had to know if the house and I would suit each other.

It was a case of love at first sight.

From the moment I stood alone in the first floor gallery I knew it was, for me, Casa Encantada.

This huge house was completely warm and livable, entirely without ostentation. It was big, yes, but with a bigness that felt good to a man from New Mexico. The furniture was beautiful and comfortable, meant to sit in. The fireplaces in each room were meant to burn fires in. The carpets were thick but resilient, like the pine needles that blanketed the forests around Cloudcroft, New Mexico. Each window in each room extended from floor to ceiling, making the loveliness of the garden an integral part of indoor living and broad terraces extended under the California sun brought outdoor living just beyond each door. I have never seen such green lawns this side of England, nor such choice pieces of statuary displayed with more subtle dignity and beauty. And a private walk and tunnel connected the property with the Bel Air golf links.

I bought Casa Encantada furnished and complete. I never rattled once. From the day I moved in I felt at home and I knew that Mary Laufersweiler Hilton, too, would have loved it. She had a great eye for beauty, did my mother, and in my new home *objets d'art* had been placed again with restraint and dignity.

For a while I was constantly discovering things. The panels in the living room painted by Jean Baptiste. In the drawing room an eighteenth century Viennese clock. Bronze figures of Devi and Siva done in India in the fourteenth century stood in the entrance hall. The beauty belonged to all times and all countries. A pair of genuine Mings, gods sitting in contemplation, had been in existence in China when Europe was barely

an infant and the New World still savage. There was a china
set executed for a Russian Czar and Blanc de Chine vases
from Denmark.

The instincts of a host were stimulated to share this wonderful house and I was always as awed as my guests when we
made a tour. I quite understood one who remarked, "I
shouldn't know whom to call if anything went wrong, a
plumber or a jeweler."

Fortunately I didn't have to worry if anything went wrong.
Mrs. Wakeman, the indispensable Olive, had taken it as
calmly under her wing as if she had run palaces all her life.
Outside I had seven gardeners and inside I had seven house
servants: a head butler and valet, a second butler, a cook, an
assistant cook, and three maids. There were also the maintenance man and assistant maintenance man who knew all the
arts of elevators and the like. If the second butler threw cans
at the cook, and he did once, I called Olive and she dealt
with it. If I came home unexpectedly to find the maids giving
a swimming party, Olive was unperturbed. If I wanted to
give a party myself I simply told her when and for whom.
She made up a guest list, submitted it to me, the cook submitted a menu to Olive who didn't have to consult me any
more because she knew what I liked, just what you'd expect
Mary Hilton's son to like. And then, when the time rolled
around, I went to my party.

It is a very nice plan. It made entertaining a pleasure.

Socially, for me personally, for my children and grandchildren, for my friends, I think Casa Encantada has been as
great a success as any I have made. I love my home. But I have
not retired there. It is my base of operations but I am still in
the hotel business.

I began to find, however, that a business meeting by the pool
could be much pleasanter sometimes than one in a smoke-
filled office. Since I gave up smoking myself I have lost my
taste for smoke-filled rooms.

And so, it was by the pool at Casa Encantada in 1954 that
I got the go-ahead to negotiate the largest real estate deal in
history.

For some little time, in the early '50s, J. B. Herndon and I
had had our eye on the Statler hotel system. Eight established
hotels, two under construction. It had been noised abroad in
the hotel world that these fine properties with their fine repu-

tation and sound management were going to come on the market. And, through friends, we kept our finger on the Statler pulse.

"One day we'll get it," I told J.B.

And for once my Devil's Advocate didn't argue. "I'm for it, Connie," he said. "But the time isn't ripe." J.B. didn't live to see the time come ripe. After a six-month illness he died on January 4, 1953, and left an empty spot in my business and personal life that no one can fill.

J.B. was gone when "Hap" Flanigan, Chairman of the Board of the Manufacturers Trust Company of New York, offered to sell me the Hotel New Yorker for Hilton stock instead of cash. That was the first time I knew our stock was now better than money and could be used for various purposes, such as the purchase of hotels.

Since we had passed through the nightmare of the Depression together, J.B. would have regarded it as a major victory when, in December of 1953, the purchase price of this hotel, approximately $12,500,000, was paid by the issuance of the corporation's securities and Mr. Horace C. Flanigan was elected a member of our Board of Directors. Later, after we sold the New Yorker, I offered to buy back the stock. "No, thanks, Connie," Hap said. "We'll hang onto it." He still preferred it to cash.

J.B. and I liked the victories but it was the Depression that had bound us together with iron-strong memories that neither of us would forget. The last time I saw him in the hospital we reminisced. "Remember those days when we had to borrow carfare?" I said. "They were pretty exciting when you look back."

"You can have 'em," said J.B. "I like things the way they are now."

And just as I was going out the door he called out, "Keep after the Statlers, Connie." It was good to know, when I went in there to fight for them, that J.B. had been on my side. Because, once again, my Board of Directors was not.

The news that suddenly made the Statler an urgent project came out of New York. The Statler Board of Directors announced that Webb & Knapp, a New York realty firm, had bought the Statler hotels. My first reaction was one of sick disappointment. J.B. had warned me to keep after them, but this surprise sale was unforeseeable. Now it was too late.

Then I noted that the New York announcement didn't give

the closing time. The Statler assets were valued at $111,000,-000 and I had an idea it would take a lot of money to swing the deal. William Zeckendorf, president of Webb & Knapp, must need time to look for the money.

If that was so the Statler deal wasn't closed and we still had a chance—an outside chance. True, the Statler Board of Directors had accepted Zeckendorf's offer but I didn't know how the owners would feel. Webb & Knapp were not hotel people. Their purchase apparently meant the famed Statler chain could be broken up, perhaps sold for real estate speculation.

How would I feel if that were to happen to my own hotels? I wouldn't like it. And Mrs. Alice Statler, the widow of the great hotel man who put those hotels together, how did she feel? Mrs. Statler was trustee for the stock held by Cornell University, for that of a stepson and other family members. She had stood beside her husband throughout many years. I had a hunch she might feel exactly as I would have felt.

I thought I had time to find out.

A hurried call to Joe Binns gave me the information that Mrs. Statler was just leaving New York City. "Hold her there for twenty-four hours 'til I can get there," I said, and I dashed for the airport.

Mrs. Statler was a hotel man's wife, a fine lady and a straight-talking one. "Yes," she admitted quite openly, "I would like to see our hotels in the hands of hotel people. A great deal of my life as well as my husband's is wrapped up in those hotels."

I told her honestly that I admired their hotels, their methods of operation, their fine reputation. "Our idea," I said, "would be to change nothing, to perpetuate what you have built up, including the name."

"I would like that," she said simply.

This then was the will of the trustee for a large block of Statler stock, the will of the owners, and I acted on it. It was now up to me to get the money together and for this I had to sell my own Board of Directors.

We met beside the pool at Casa Encantada. I knew it wasn't going to be easy, for even Henry Crown was not entirely behind me. "I'll go along with you, Connie," he said. "But you're paying too much."

"I didn't set the price," I reminded him. "Zeckendorf did. We have to meet this offer. We are in no position to deal. If they agreed to take less, somebody'd have the right to sue 'em."

Everyone tried to talk me out of it. I wished J.B. had been there. "You're taking chances," I was told. Willard Keith said quite firmly that we already had a very good thing. "Why jeopardize it, Connie, by this huge expansion? Why do you want ten more hotels?"

"Because there'll never be another opportunity like this, Willard," I told him. "We have a chance to buy eight fine hotels, proven hotels, in top cities. They're already staffed, have reputations, clientele. They're seasoned and running. One thing we wouldn't be doing is taking chances. We don't have to guess or forecast. And they're building in Dallas and Hartford, two more top cities. We'd better jump at it, not miss the boat."

Willard sighed. They were weakening. Somebody else said: "I wish you wouldn't do it."

"I've got to do it. There'll never be another chance like it."

Then I got the most reluctant vote of confidence, the faintest green light of my entire career. It came from Y. Frank Freeman. "I move," he said, "that we let Connie go ahead and try to make the deal—and pray that he doesn't."

Frank has since admitted that he is glad my prayers were the answered ones in this instance. On October 27, 1954, the Hilton Hotels Corporation officially acquired control of the Statler hotel system. It consummated the greatest merger in hotel history, the largest real estate transaction the world has ever known. It brought the number of Hilton-operated hotels in the United States and abroad to twenty-eight. And there were more in the building.

I put in a phone call for Arthur Foristall at that point. "Would you say," I asked him, "that I am a 'man without a future'?"

For once Arthur didn't have an answer.

13. HORIZONS UNLIMITED

I suppose I have been asked a hundred times how it feels to reach a high spot on one's chosen mountain. Each time I have to pause and think, savor some of the pleasures and some of the responsibilities.

How does it feel?

Well, for myself, I am sometimes completely surprised. At others I am tickled. And then I find that under it all, and constantly, I am deeply humble and tremendously grateful.

The surprised feeling can catch me completely off guard over odd, small things—like the episode of the parking spaces behind the small Beverly Hills building we occupied a year ago while our new offices were under construction.

There were a limited number of stalls for parking and we played a sort of musical chairs with them. Each of us gravitated to a slot we thought of as our personal property—and the early birds got these spaces—if someone else didn't get there first—a patient in the doctor's office a block away, an early morning shopper, a lady who had a hairdresser's appointment over the way. Olive and Ruth were all for painting our names on our stalls.

"We're entitled to it," said Olive. "You own the building."

"Too ostentatious," I decided. And so we went on playing games while the girls looked glum. I made a flying trip to New York and on my return found the game further complicated, for one of the spaces, my favorite, had been marked RESERVED. I'd been back a few days when Olive said accusingly, "You took my parking place this morning. Why don't you use your own?"

"I can't," I said. "Somebody's got it staked out—marked RESERVED."

Olive has no capacity for surprise any more. "I don't suppose you even suspect for whom it might be reserved?"

Then I did. And grinned sheepishly. And that's how it feels. You keep forgetting, and then something happens to remind you. And you are surprised, then tickled, then humbly grateful. Not by the acquisition of hotels, you understand. That you feel you work for, earn. But by the added things, the by-products, as it were.

Why, I have even become a success in the entertainment field. I, Connie Hilton, the frustrated impresario who shepherded the Hilton Trio about New Mexico, failed at the Circle and Hippodrome theaters in Dallas, by the simple means of acquiring hotels find myself the largest single employer of supper club talent in the world.

I can admit I enjoy it, too, since very little credit is due me personally. My chief boast is that my past experience is close enough to my surface memory so that I do not put my eager fingers in the smoothly running machinery of our hotel supper clubs and dining rooms.

Since the death of vaudeville and stage shows, these spots have given opportunity to the very best in name bands, artists and acts, and been a fertile field for developing new talent as well. I can remember when Liberace and Victor Borge performed (separately) at the Palmer House, they were so eager to show what they could do that they were always out there twice as long as they were paid to be. I remember too that Marge and Gower Champion owed us an appearance at the Waldorf when Gower got out of the service. At that time they were not too well known. Gower had a chance to make a motion picture and I okayed a release for him from his Waldorf contract. Later, when he was a big name, Gower insisted on paying off that suspended engagement.

I discovered that show business requires a seventh sense, that particular feeling I have for hotels plus experience, and that you cannot acquire either out of thin air. The trick seems to be to know exactly when a talent is ripe and grab it. George Gobel and Harry Belafonte both appeared for us just as they were ready to take that tiny step that carries a performer from being good to being great.

I even had a few firsts to my credit, insofar as I okayed the building of the largest ice stage ever in a hotel, a $125,-000 sheet of mirrored glass at the Stevens. And we were the first to overcome the language barrier and bring unusual talent from all over Europe, from Cuba, from all over the world.

Oh, I liked that fine. And I liked, too, feeling a part of the traditions of show business. Time was, when I was proprietor of unsuccessful ventures, that the mere idea that "the show must go on" whether we sold only six tickets or the violinist broke her arm was more than a headache, it was a tragedy. Now I saw it work in the big time with never a worry as to whether we'd have to give notice tomorrow.

In the very best tradition and with all the elements of a melodrama, I watched Eddie Duchin risk his neck to arrive at the Palmer House in time for an opening night. Eddie had flown to Palm Springs, California, to visit his small son, with the promise, "I'll be back for the opening; count on me!" He had scheduled a last-minute departure from Palm Springs on a commercial airline when suddenly the weather folded and the plane was grounded.

Frantically Duchin called the Palmer House. "I'll be there," he promised again, "but I may cut it a bit fine. Have my valet meet me at the airport with my clothes." He chartered a private plane for which he personally paid $2,000, and a breathless audience in the Empire Room got the lastest bulletins as the plane battled storms and winds winging its way into Chicago. Precisely five minutes after the hour scheduled for his appearance there was the usual dramatic blackout and then the spot picked up Eddie Duchin at the piano, calm, unruffled, debonair, looking in no wise as if he had changed for the performance in an icy hangar by the light of a mechanic's lamp. I remember, too, another fine artist, Hildegarde, at that piano after she had lost a very valuable diamond from her ring. She noticed it as she sat down to sing for the supper show. A portly general in full uniform injected drama and then comedy into the act by springing to his feet and shouting, "Don't anybody leave the room." Then, while Hildegarde carried on with her song, he crawled awkwardly about on all fours in the semi-dark, looking for the missing jewel. In the midst of a number he let out another shout: "I've found it," he cried. And Hildegarde was so overcome that she promptly lost it again by dropping it into the complicated insides of the piano. But the show went on.

We were hard-pressed to remain loyal to the old tradition just once, when the musicians' union struck. I had not realized until we were deprived of it how greatly every sort of act depends on music. But at last we found an art that can be conducted without any trimmings—Mind Reading. Dunninger kept the show going and the patrons more than happy by reading minds, sans music, until the musicians unwound their difficulties.

Besides absorbing the tradition, I couldn't help but be tickled when the great bands in our hotels, Guy Lombardo, Xavier Cugat, Tommy Dorsey, Glenn Miller, Benny Goodman and the others, played the music to my favorite dance, the varsoviana, commonly called "Put Your Little Foot," whenever I came in. I never dared dream that big when I was learning the camel-walk in Santa Fe from that pert little thing from Chicago. Nor had I ever dared to dream, while I romantically transformed each partner in those days of my youth—whether Jouett Fall in Santa Fe or the miller's daughter Estelle Greenwalk, from Socorro—into princesses, that I would one day dance with women who needed no transformation to make them the loveliest ladies in the land. Among them Grace Kelly and Dawn Addams who both became real princesses. Irene Dunne, who has a regal beauty I have never seen equaled. Virginia Warren, daughter of the Chief Justice of the United States. Jinx Falkenberg, Merle Oberon, Mary Martin, not to mention those three accomplished ladies who could join me in the intricacies of the varsoviana—my sister Rosemary, her daughter and my namesake, Connie Ann, and Olive Wakeman.

And my other favorite sport, golf, how could I help but be tickled when I could play with, and occasionally, with the help of a few strokes, win small sums from, such men as Denny Shute and Ben Hogan? I could even expose a White House secret, for the fact is that I used to play with Dwight Eisenhower, then president of Columbia University. He confided to me that there was a certain hole at Deepdale, Long Island, that always gave him trouble; he was a man to prove himself even then, for he took a thirteen on it that day.

There was, too, the satisfaction of seeing my sons moving into the hotel business without any assist from Dad. First Nick, who had his debut in the engine room in El Paso, was given his first try at negotiating. He knew Glenn McCarthy and, when we bought Glenn's glittering Shamrock Hotel, the show place of Houston and playground for Texas, Nick handled his part of the deal so well that he was elected to the vice-presidency of that hotel.

Shortly thereafter I heard Willard Keith in a Board of Directors' meeting stand up and propose a new officer for the Hilton Hotels Corporation. "He would be a valuable asset to any business," Willard said, "and we would be very fortunate to have Barron Hilton with us."

My third son, Eric, would have to wait a while for business

honors. He was still in school, studying the theories of hotel management against the time when he would actually enter the industry. I was sure he would prove himself as his brothers had.

I was not present on the day the Board met to pay me a personal tribute. It is probably a good thing, for when I am pleased I show it all over, and that day I might have burst with pride. I have loved all my ladies from that first dowager, the Mobley, to the Queen herself, the Waldorf. But for one I have always had a special affection. In the case of the Palmer House, the Plaza, the Waldorf, the Statlers, my duty was to guard their already established charm. One hotel had nothing when I got it but the factual asset of being the largest hotel in the world and having a reputation for conventions. I worked hard to buy the Stevens, I worked even harder to give her a personality, a position in the life of her city, to change her from simply the largest hotel to the largest and friendliest. The Board, at any rate, felt I had succeeded.

I knew a very warm sense of gratitude when they moved to change the name of the largest and friendliest hotel in the world from the Stevens to The Conrad Hilton.

These then—and my beautiful Casa Encantada—were some of the pleasures success brought me. There were also the responsibilities.

These began to come to my attention gradually "after the Waldorf." At first I tried to duck. I like to think my reluctance was born of modesty. Twice I was asked to address the graduating class of the hotel school at Michigan State College. Twice I remembered my past speaking experiences, first with full oratory to the jackrabbits and prairie dogs around Socorro, and then to my young brother Boy and my mother, and finally thirty-eight years before during one brief session in the New Mexico State Legislature when I managed to follow Mother's advice and "be myself"—to say swiftly what I had to say and sit down.

Then I asked myself: "Who are you to go about making speeches?"

The answer came directly from the Dean of the school when he made a third request. "You can't be the head of a great hotel organization," he wrote, "and refuse to address a graduating class of young hotel men."

So I went. I had discovered I had to take a public stand on hotels. That was my first speech.

In the fall, the National Conference of Christians and Jews honored me with their Brotherhood Award. Charley Wilson, co-chairman and once head of General Electric, asked me to make the main address.

"Some other time, Charley," I wrote back.

"No other time, Connie," was his reply. "Now!"

And so, since hotels were not pertinent and my feeling for the Conference was deep and strong, I talked on something very close to my heart: Peace, Prayer and America. I called the talk "The Battle for Freedom." It made its way into *Vital Speeches of the Day*. It also led, step by step, to the single thing that I've been able to do that I'm willing to stand up and say: "I'm proud of that!"

Again I had been led to take a stand.

A little later we opened our first European International Hotel, the Castellana Hilton, in Spain, whose foundations I had seen on that first trip to Madrid. Here for the first time there was an opportunity to make plain what our international plans stood for to us and, we hoped, to our country and the world at large.

From then on, one way and another, I found myself doing a powerful lot of talking. I can trace the important events of my life after 1950 and the growth of my philosophy, through my speeches. At first I found it hard, the wilting collar, perspiring hands. That wore off. But the strain of having to be in a certain place at a certain time never ended. Once I know I almost broke my neck getting from Mexico City to Fort Dodge, Iowa, my mother's home town, where the Chamber of Commerce had asked me to take a public stand of some description on their anniversary. I felt quite as dashing as Eddie Duchin when Olive and I flew through storms and high winds to get from Mexico City to Brownsville. I felt like nothing at all during a long wait at that airport when neither commercial nor private plane would leave the ground and no trains were going our way. Eventually we got to Chicago, then sat up all night on a milk train, Olive trying to take dictation on the speech, and arrived for a last-minute entrance with me looking not at all like the debonair Duchin as I raced for the speakers' platform.

But these things, said from Michigan to Istanbul, from Ma-

drid to Fort Dodge, have been the carefully thought out con-
clusions of these three phases based on my life's experience.

First then, there is a responsibility to the hotel world—and
to everyone who has ever stayed in or worked in a Hilton
hotel in the past or will do so in the future. We have no se-
crets, nothing up our sleeves as to how we run our hotels.

My hotel philosophy agrees with that of Boswell as expressed in his *Life of Dr. Johnson:* "There is nothing which
has yet been contrived by man by which so much happiness
is produced as by a good tavern or inn."

The innkeeper, as I told the students at Michigan State,
evolved into the hotelkeeper. I was a hotelkeeper myself in
Texas. And from this evolved the hotel man. The proprietor
had moved from the kitchen to the office but the key to success lies still in Boswell's single word "good." It must be a
good inn or tavern or hotel.

Today's hotel industry is the seventh largest in the nation.
That puts our responsibility to the public at a high level.
We know that the inn of the past is obsolete. So is the hotel
of yesterday. The Motels are here to stay, designed to fit a
positive need, and as it develops it may complete the cycle
from country inn back to country inn. But there will always
be hotels and the young men looked to me to predict the hotel of the future.

All right. Here it is for the record!

I do not believe that huge hotels comparable to the Waldorf and the Conrad Hilton will ever again be built in any
country. Construction costs have altered. So have the needs
of the people. Instead, there will be great hotels of smaller
size, a thousand rooms or less, of a new design that will help
bridge the gap between luxurious personal service and the
necessity of keeping the price within reasonable limits. Materials that require a minimum of repair and maintenance—
for instance, carpets, upholstery fabrics that can be easily
cleaned—wear forever and are fireproof. Rooms should be
designed so that space is conserved and comfort and warmth
are not sacrificed.

Any new hotel of the future should include the following:
television, portable libraries, sun lamps, portable beauty parlors, small freezers for ice cubes in each room, automatic tele-
phones that record all calls, improved air conditioning and
ventilation equipment, and other innovations.

Given these things there are still five basic ingredients that the hotel of the future shares with the inn of the past: need for a hotel, proper location, conservative financing, proper design, good management.

The methods we have evolved in the Hilton system for good management include seven points, three of which are unique to group hotels, four of which apply to all.

First: In any system of hotels we have found that each must be an individual personality, geared to the demands of its particular city and country. To ensure this means, among other things, to select good managers, and then entrust to them the authority they need.

Second: Forecasting. The average housewife will appreciate more than the average guest the need for this step. The hotel failures of the '20s and '30s demonstrated that a hotel man had to be a good businessman in precisely the way a good housewife has to budget time and materials effectively. No one whose talents do not exceed the genial *mein host* of the old inn will survive in today's hotel business. A manager must be able to make an accurate forecast. By the first of each month every hotel in our system has forecast the day-to-day business for that month based on reservations on hand and the experience of the same month in previous years. A good hotel manager knows exactly how many maids, bellmen, elevator operators, culinary experts and waiters he requires for each and every day of the year. If he does not, he either wastes money by being overstaffed or provides poor service by being understaffed. Similarly with food supplies which are perishable. Except for some entirely unpredictable "act of God" condition, our actual performance and forecasts are remarkably close together.

Third: Mass Purchasing. This is a decided advantage to the system with several hotels. Certain purchasing, of course, must be done at the local level, but there are twenty-one items such as matches, china, bar soap, carpets, to mention a few, where direct purchasing in large quantities from the manufacturers results in substantial savings—and the willingness of the manufacturer to test and develop products to meet exact standards.

Fourth: "Digging for Gold." This is the term we use for the procedure that came to me in a nightmare at the old Mobley in Cisco and resulted in our making the dining room into bedrooms and cutting the main desk in half to make room for a newsstand. It means ultilization of every possible foot of space for the production of maximum income. At The Conrad Hilton, for example, we created a room out of thin air. We needed space for functions not large enough to justify the use of the grand ballroom and yet too large to be accommodated in the Waldorf Room. We solved this by dividing the Boulevard Room in half—horizontally—thus creating the Williford Room in the top half.

Fifth: Training good men, a common requirement in any industry if it is to keep its standards and progress. In our business, there are hotel schools such as those at Cornell and Michigan State, plus on-the-job training experience.

Sixth: Sales efforts, a point which needs absolutely no explanation to the average American. It includes good advertising, promotion, publicity and the intelligent booking of parties, conventions and the like.

Seventh: Inter-hotel reservations are an advantage which grows along with the number of hotels in a system. We handle thirty-five thousand inter-hotel reservations per month whereby guests leave one Hilton hotel to book into another in a different city or country. We can, we hope, one day book our guests around the world, always under a Hilton roof.

Put all these things together and you have the "hotel of the future," just as easy as that! Actually it is the hotel of the present, too, and proving itself highly successful. These plans more or less describe the last three hotels we have opened in the United States, the Statler in Hartford, Connecticut, The Beverly Hilton, Beverly Hills, California, and the Statler Hilton in Dallas, Texas.

The Dallas opening meant a great deal more to me than merely opening a hotel of the future. It was my return to the city where I climbed my first mountain, raised my first million, built my first hotel, thirty years before. Over the way, in Cisco, I found the Mobley had become a Golden Age Hotel for Retired People or, as the slogan read, a "Shady Spot for Senior Citizens." My first Waldorf, the dowdy dowager, was now the "Blue Bonnet." Bob Thornton, my banking pal, was the Mayor of Dallas. Among the guests were my son Eric, who would serve his hotel apprenticeship in the new hotel, and Eddie Fowler, the bellboy who had once lent me $300 for "eating money" during the darkest days of the Depression. Eddie was an "owner" now; I had arranged for a hundred shares of stock to be put in his name.

Eric, my youngest son, was an eager fledgling and a hard worker. He had had hotels on his mind since his early teens and, whenever he visited me, had tagged happily in my wake absorbing what he could about the business. His attendance at Cornell's hotel school was interrupted by a call into the Armed Forces and his time of service in Japan. When the Dallas Hilton opened he and his pretty young wife had one child, Eric, Jr., and another on the way. They named the second Beverly Hilton—"so we can have a Beverly Hilton in Texas too," said Eric. I was proud of Eric's hotel aptitude, proud to see him beginning to work his way up in Texas as I had done.

It was a great occasion for me, too, because Mrs. Alice Statler was there, and because for the first time the names of Statler and Hilton would be joined in one hotel. My faith in the Statler purchase had been more than justified. The net earnings of Hilton Hotels Corporation from operations increased from $1.26 a common share in 1953 to $2.20 a share in 1955. The prime reason for this increase was the acquisition of the Statler Hotels. Our joint future was still expanding.

The greatest thing of all was to be able to tell them of the world map in my office with the flags of Hilton National and International flying gaily across the world. The red flags for hotels in operation. Blue for those under construction and already contracted for. Green for hotels projected for the next five years.

This dream tied Dallas, Texas, to Istanbul, Madrid, Puerto Rico, with an invisible bond of hospitality. This dream was an infinitely bigger dream than I could have conceived when I first put my country boots in Texas, determined to see the Lone Star State wearing a chain of Hilton hotels.

Lenin, the high priest of Communism, had once declared: "We are fighting capitalism, the free, republican democratic capitalism included, and we realize, of course, that in this fight the flag of freedom will be waved defiantly against us."

"We humbly believe," I was able to report to my friends, old and new, in Dallas—to Bob Thornton who had helped back my early hotel ventures; to Eddie Fowler who had financed my very existence with his savings; to Eric who belonged to the future; to Mrs. Alice Statler who had entrusted the famous hotels bearing her name to our care—

"that our Hilton house flag is one small flag of freedom which is being waved defiantly against Communism exactly as Lenin predicted. With humility we submit this international effort of ours as a contribution to world peace."

The Hilton Hotels International were also justifying my faith in them, both practically and idealistically.

The Puerto Rican government today gives the Caribe Hilton in San Juan, our pilot project, much of the credit for boosting tourism from forty thousand vistors who spent $4,000,000 in 1947, to one hundred sixty thousand visitors who spent $25,000,000 in 1956. The government estimates that the hotel has brought an additional $20,000,000 annually in business to the island. The 350-room Caribe Hilton, built at a cost of $7,300,000 has already netted the Puerto Rican government over $6,000,000 and has been so successful that a hundred room addition is under construction. Our stockholders, of course, came in for their share of the profits.

In 1953 we opened the Castellana Hilton in Madrid, again with much fanfare. Our two plane loads of distinguished guests from the United States were enchanted by the native gypsy dancers who entertained at the hotel and the Spaniards, who dearly love our stars, were thoroughly thrilled when Mary Martin graciously sang for them.

Another first-rate ambassador of good will was Gary Cooper, who is extremely popular in Spain. In fact, Gary's popularity proved to be that unforeseeable element that crops up at the best-rehearsed opening.

During the four days of our stay it was practically impossible to get telephone calls into or out of the hotel despite the fact that the best switchboard operators available had been trained for many months. What tangled up the lines and swamped the board were the numberless calls from Spanish ladies willing to wait and wait and wait to give their personal greeting to Señor Cooper. The minute we took Gary home normal, smooth service was immediately established.

An unscheduled entertainment occurred when some of our guests made their debut in the bullfight arena.

Pedro Gandarias, a wealthy Spanish banker, gave a large party for us at his historic ranch, originally the gift of Queen Isabella of Spain to Christopher Columbus. Señor Gandarias breeds bulls on the ranch, destined for the arenas of Madrid.

An important factor in breeding fighting bulls, it seems, is that they be born of a talented mother, thus the cows are tried out in a small ring to decide if they are worthy material for so great an honor.

We, on the other hand, had among our party several members who thought they might have the matador talent; Gary Cooper, Jinx Falkenberg, Mary Martin, and Dawn Addams, with borrowed capes and Pedro dancing attendance, experimented with the intricacies of the bullfight in the cow ring.

So successful was Pedro's party and so sincere was the interest in Madrid in the good will aims of the hotel that Señor Gandarias frequently now plays host to guests from the hotel at his famed rancho. The guests are not all Americans. At the last Open House I attended there were Greeks, Italians, Americans and Englishmen, among the latter a prominent newspaperman, publisher of forty provincial papers.

At the opening of the Castellana we tried to let the Spaniards who had never visited America know what ancient and strong ties exist between us through the imprint left by their explorers and missionaries of three hundred years ago in our country. I could tell them that in some parts of the United States our cities read like a litany of saints because of them: San Diego, San Francisco, Los Angeles, San Carlos, San Mateo, San José, Santa Monica, San Fernando, San Bernardino, San Luis Obispo. That my own birthplace was San Antonio and my county Socorro, so named in honor of Our Lady of Help.

I told them of the great bluff or mountain of red and white sandstone that rises 250 feet above the valley floor in Valencia County, New Mexico, which has been known for hundreds of years as El Morro (The Rock). Here on the north face, protected from wind and weather by recesses and chiseled out of the rock with swords and daggers, are still messages written by the Spanish explorers for those who came after them. Pasaron Por Aqui, says the handwriting on the wall. (They Passed By Here!)

Now we had come to Spain to return the compliment. First, to admit the great cultural debt the western peoples owe to the Spain of the past; second, to pause in admiration before a nation which had so thoroughly defeated Communism in our own twentieth century. And last, to offer our hotel in the hopes that, years hence, it may be said that those who "passed by here" as our guests at the hotel will have been treated with the courtesy, respect and dignity that is due to people of good will in all parts of the world.

As with the Caribe Hilton we could see the result of dollar flow in our first International Hotel in Europe. The Castellana Hilton brought more than $1,000,000 in dollar exchange to Spain in its first year, not to mention pounds, francs and lira.

Two years after the Castellana Hilton opening, we opened another hotel at the opposite end of Europe, the crossroads of the world, Istanbul, Turkey.

The Istanbul Hilton stands thirty miles from the Iron Curtain.

Five years earlier I had first visited this Republic which so eagerly desired to join hands with us in a hotel venture. Here, with the Iron Curtain veritably before our eyes, we found a people who had fought the Russians for the past three hundred years and were entirely unafraid of them. They went right on doing exactly as they pleased in their own highly democratic way.

I was mightily impressed, on my arrival at the airport for that initial visit, to be greeted by sixteen Turkish reporters, each of whom spoke excellent English. "I only hope we can return the compliment when you come to visit us!" I said, smiling.

I was also impressed to find that here in a Moslem country, one of its most respected citizens was His Holiness, Ecumenical Patriarch Athenagoras A., spiritual head of the Greek Orthodox Church, while directly across from the site we selected for our hotel, a Roman Catholic convent stood in safety and dignity.

We did not share a common language but we did share a common interpretation of words. For instance when a Turk used the Turkish word for "immediate" he meant, as we do, "right now." When their government offered us "full cooperation" they gave us exactly that.

As the construction and furnishing of the hotel opened the way to new industries created to produce the many and varied materials which go into a new hotel, it was interesting to see the Turks grasp and expand the possibilities. For instance, generations ago the Turks had been famous tile-makers but the art had largely died out. Evidence of their handiwork, however, abounded in the old Sultan's Palace. When we decided we wanted to use similar tiles, a local architect searched out a few old men who could teach the younger ones and to-day, long after the completion of the hotel, tile-making is again quite a thriving business.

When we flew into Istanbul for the opening with our guests from America, Carol Channing, Irene Dunne and her husband Dr. Francis Griffin, Mona Freeman, Sonja Henie, Diana Lynn, Merle Oberon, Ann Miller, representatives of the American press, John Cameron Swazey, Bob Considine, Horace Sutton, Louella Parsons, Hedda Hopper, and Cobina Wright, not to mention my very old friend, Leo Carrillo, who once owned a deer named Sequoia, there is no question but that we all felt the antiquity, romance and mystery of this ancient city. It was founded as Byzantium in 658 b.c., then became Constantinople and today enjoys still the great port, the Golden Horn (the great trading center of Turkey), and the Bosporus, where Europe and Asia are less than a half mile apart, which has made it the crossroads of the world for centuries.

Standing before the assembled guests at the opening ceremonies, I felt this "City of the Golden Horn" was a tremendous place to plant a little bit of America. Here was the site that had known the Persian hordes, become Constantine's capital, seen the invading Crusaders, been the center of the old Ottoman Empire, and where in 1923 Mustafa Kemal Ataturk had fostered a young Republic.

"Each of our hotels," I said, "is a 'little America,' not as a symbol of bristling power, but as a friendly center where men of many nations and of good will may speak the language of peace."

The short history of the Istanbul Hilton shows that it has been doing just that.

First, it has been a sound business investment. In the first year of its operation it realized a gross operating profit of $1,629,000 and played an important part in the 60 per cent increase in tourism in Turkey for the year. As with the other International Hotels, it was from the start the social and diplomatic focal point for local residents and distinguished visitors.

Truly men of many nations have gathered there under one roof to break their bread together. On my desk at this moment is the foreign report for the Istanbul Hilton for April, 1957. In that single month, men from thirty-eight countries, three behind the Iron Curtain, had been guests there. Thirty-five per cent came from the United States but there were visitors from Bulgaria, China, Pakistan, all over Europe, Thailand, Trinidad, India. And I found myself hoping that they had found time at least to drink a cup of coffee together.

Drinking a cup of coffee in Turkey has a very special significance. It was explained to me the first time I was offered a demitasse of the strong local brew. "After you drink a cup of coffee with me," said my host, "that commits you to friendship for thirty years."

Imagine what would happen if everyone in that hotel (from thirty-eight different countries) were to drink coffee together in the Turkish tradition!

Imagine, for that matter, what would happen if that much good came out of every cup of coffee we drink at home!

In 1956 we were back on the American continent opening the Continental Hilton in Mexico City. Again there were distinguished guests, among them a familiar and trusted face beaming over a brand new title: Olive Wakeman, administrative assistant to the president, Hilton Hotels Corporation. After fourteen years during which time she had kept the hotel business constantly at her fingertips and learned to dance the varsoviana besides, Olive was a full-fledged executive; Ruth Hinman was executive secretary.

Executive or no, Olive still took my dictation and suffered with me over my speeches. The talk made at the opening of the Continental Hilton was very important to me because I was speaking to our next door neighbor. "Mexico and the United States must and shall go forward together in a spirit of mutual trust and cooperation. With far horizons in mind, the leaders of both nations, today and tomorrow, must continue to adopt ways and means beneficial to the people of both nations, all in a spirit of harmony and cooperation. It is with the spirit outlined here present in my mind and heart, that I dedicate this hotel to you, the people of Mexico."

This, then, was the total score for the red flags on my world map, four Hilton International Hotels operating on three continents. And the blue and green flags, what of them? The minutes of the last meeting of the Board of Hilton Hotels International sound more like a travelogue, the flight of a magic carpet, then a meeting of businessmen. There is first a report on the blue flags, the countries where hotels are under construction: Havana, Cuba; West Berlin, Germany; Montreal, Canada; Cairo, Egypt—then the green flags, projected for the next five years and already contracted for: London, Vienna, Tokyo, Rome, Trinidad, Baghdad, Bangkok, Athens.

After these come reports on places which, as yet, have no flags at all, reports on preliminary agreements in other parts of the world, seeds being sown, dreams in the making: in Caracas, Sydney, Beirut, Panama, Amsterdam, Brussels, and the Hawaiian Islands.

Hilton hotels around the world, in every continent except Antarctica!

And more and more a variety of folk in other lands are anxious to join hands with us in these ventures. The Habana Hilton, for example, is being financed and constructed by the Retirement Fund of the Cuban Culinary Workers, many of whom will be employees in their own hotel. And in Bangkok, Thialand, the new Hilton hotel will be sponsored by Her Majesty Queen Rambhai Barni, the Dowager Queen of Thailand who will participate as a major shareholder.

In taking a stand here in America to explain what we are trying to do I spoke on "Hotels and International Statesmanship" before the Commonwealth Club of San Francisco last year.

"The operation of Hilton Hotels International has evolved from a unique philosophy. Rather than assume the role of invaders intent upon siphoning back all profits to the United States, we have joined hands in a business fellowship with foreign entrepreneurs.

"Let me say right here, that we operate hotels abroad for the same reason we operate them in this country—to make money for our stockholders. That is a fact for which we need not apologize. Indeed, it is a prime motivating force in this as in any other free economy. But if money were all we were after, we could make it right here in this country with a few less headaches.

"However, we feel that if we really believe in what we are all saying about liberty, about Communism, about happiness, that we, as a nation, must exercise our great strength and power for good against evil. If we really believe this, it is up to each of us, our organizations and our industries, to contribute to this objective with all the resources at our command."

In addressing the National Conference of Christians and Jews at the Waldorf-Astoria in the fall of 1950, I took my stand as a veteran of World War I, as the father of two boys who fought in World War II, and as an American. That talk, "The Battle for Freedom," came from a heart filled with a deep and abiding love for and faith in our country and our way of life.

Since in it was contained the seed, the dream which fulfilled itself in the proudest moment of my life, I must recall here in substance what I said.

There was no sense in glossing over existing conditions. We were, if not technically at war, still a long way from peace in Korea. We were failing our sons for we had not secured the peace they had fought and died to win. This had to be admitted. Here is the stand I took:

"We are compelled to face the awful prospect of another war.

"We are losing the battle for peace, for we have neglected, abandoned and betrayed those great principles to which we dedicated ourselves for the establishment of peace.

"We have broken faith with those who fought and died for freedom. Why? Because when the boys had won their victories at arms we permitted the forces of hate, injustice and appeasement to take the victories from them.

"Freedom, my fellow Americans—Protestant, Catholic, and Jew—is foremost in our minds and hearts this evening. It is in the minds and hearts of all the world who look to us as the last sanctuary, the last bastion of free men.

"But what is this freedom? What right have we to it? This is why; because we possess an intrinsic human dignity, an inner majesty, which gives us an appetite, a passion for freedom. Man possesses human dignity because he is made in the image and likeness of God. This image is found personally in every man; each one possesses it entirely and undividedly.

"To many youngsters of today this does not mean too much, but if they only knew, as we know, it is the basis of everything they fight and die for: the privilege to remain free men.

"Peace is more than the absence of war. It is a tranquility of order, it is security, liberty—religious, political and economic freedom. It is life with honor, life with the dignity of the children of God.

"It was for that freedom and that peace we fought in 1917,

and we did not get it. For that freedom and peace we fought in 1941, and we did not get it. For that freedom and peace we are fighting now.

"Are we at war with Russia? Are we at peace with Russia? Are we at war with China, with East Germany? Are we at peace with those nations? No. The old concept of 'War' and 'Peace' belongs to a world which the Communists have destroyed.

"The essence of Communism is the death of the individual and the burial of his remains in a collective mass. And the insidious thing, the frightening thing is this: It can win even when it is losing. They want us to live more and more on a constant war footing without being at war, without being at peace.

"This is a crucial time in the destiny of our nation, in the destiny of mankind. The remaining free peoples of the world must be strengthened and defended. Should there come a time when the Communist flood overwhelms those free nations we must be prepared to stand alone. There must be no more appeasement, no more sacrifice of principle for expediency, and never shall we abandon a free nation that stands with us against the common enemy.

"In this struggle for freedom, at home and abroad, our greatest weapon, both a sword and a shield, will be our love of, and faith in, God. To open the hearts and minds of men to this truth will require a mighty river of faith and effort. Each one of us is a drop to swell that river and augment its force.

"The destiny of our people is to hold high the banner of freedom for all men everywhere."

As I sat down after making my first major speech I had that damp hands, damp brow, wilted collar feeling. If there were applause I scarcely heard it. Never again! Somehow I felt I had lacked persuasion, the professional polish to put it across.

Four months later I was on my feet again.

"The Battle for Freedom" had been printed and reprinted. I told the Midwest Hotel Show in Chicago how bewildered I felt before the overwhelming response.

"Thousands of letters have come in from every corner of the land and from people in all walks of life," I reported. "The receipt of these letters was one of the great inspirational experiences of my life. I was profoundly impressed with the depth of feeling which they expressed. They made me realize the responsibility for care and caution one assumes when one seeks to persuade his fellow countrymen to a course of conduct. And they made me realize the capacity of the people to make correct decisions when permitted to do so.

"Uniformly, they spoke for a love of God and country!

"They expressed a deep attachment to the principles of liberty and freedom for the individual which I feared were losing out in the scramble for promises of a socialistic security.

"They were proof to me that a veritable tower of strength is yet in the heart of America, which bodes no good for the Communist slavemasters, or the despoilers of freedom wherever they are. Here are excerpts from a few of those letters:

"From a young corporal: 'I am on the verge of going over —again. This time, the "why" has been inconclusive, and one of doubt and confusion. One needs a cause. Particularly if one has been uprooted from job, family, community, and a peaceful future. I found it in your idea that we are going out to defend the image of God in ourselves, in our families, in our countrymen, and to preserve it for unborn generations. I'll do my part "over there" again. Will you, and men such as yourself, do your part to insure a lasting, just peace? I have two children. If my efforts will enable them to live a peaceful life, this second interruption in my own life will not have been in vain.'

"There was one from General George Marshall, Secretary of Defense: 'Your definition of why a man goes to war is an excellent one. I am bringing it to the attention of the Secretary of the Army.'

"A salesman wrote: 'Had I known what freedom meant, I do not believe I would have regretted one minute of the years I spent in the Navy, fighting World War II.'

"From a mother: 'My only son was lost in the South Pacific in 1943. I have never known where he sleeps. I pray your words will reach the hearts and minds of all who are in doubt as to their duty in this fateful hour.'

"A young man in Minnesota said: 'I am one of those boys who served in the late misadventure, World War II. I now face the imminent prospect of recall to indefinite active duty to labor a second time in the vineyard of war's desolation. Are you aware how splendid it is to find unashamed reference to God in the public print?'

"A German, a former enemy, wrote this: 'Your ideas of real freedom are the same in the hearts of thousands of Germans. I fully agree with your words that our love of, and faith in, God is our greatest weapon, and that each of us is a drop to swell that river and augment its force. Such a drop I should like to be.'"

There was one letter, too, out of all those thousands that bothered me. It came, a small grimy envelope postmarked New York, nearly lost in a stack of important mail, yet to me it was as important as any letter I have received in my life.

"Dear Mr. Hilton:

I have read your talk in the *Herald Tribune*, and I think it was wonderful. Especially that our faith in God was our only hope. You are very right, and I think if everyone would fall down and pray we would have real peace.

Sincerely yours,
Daniel Paolucci

P.S. I am a boy of 12. May I please have an answer?"

Automatically I did the conventional thing. It looked like I had been wrong about today's youngsters. I wrote Daniel a grateful reply, enclosing an autographed copy of the address he liked. But I couldn't shake off his "P.S. May I please have an answer?"

I reread the clipping in the *Herald Tribune*. . . . "in our struggle for freedom our greatest weapon will be our love of, and our faith in, God." It dawned on me that something had been left out of that speech. Something that had been in Daniel's letter. Funny that I, who have known prayer and trusted the power of prayer all my life, should not have mentioned it.

Prayer was the answer!

It was on a train to Chicago, thinking about Daniel's letter and the answer he wanted, that I first saw a mental image of Uncle Sam on his knees, praying. Praying for what? Certainly not that "God be on my side." Through two ghastly wars both sides made that prayer and it didn't get much peace even for the victor. Obviously that hadn't worked. Daniel himself must have learned how foolish it would be to explain to his algebra teacher how *he'd* like mathematics to work.

"That I be on God's side." That would be Uncle Sam's peace prayer.

Still fired with this concept when the train pulled into Chicago, I was amazed when I bought a daily paper. The first thing that caught my eye was a cartoon entitled "When Problems Overwhelm." Before a littered desk sat the figure of Uncle Sam harassed by troubles. But he didn't look like the Uncle Sam I had visualized on the train: strong, earnest, grounded on a rock of faith. Here sat a harassed old fellow. And from the wall opposite him an infinitely compassionate portrait of Abraham Lincoln spoke: "Have you tried prayer, Sam?"

To me that was confirmation of my vision. I went on to New York where I talked my growing idea over with Dr. Norman Vincent Peale and my good friend, the late Fulton Oursler, both of whom encouraged me to proceed.

In the spirit of humility and with loving advice, a prayer took form.

OUR FATHER IN HEAVEN:

We pray that You save us from ourselves.

The world that You have made for us, to live in peace we have made into an armed camp. We live in fear of war to come.

We are afraid of "the terror that flies by night and the arrow that flies by day, the pestilence that walks in darkness and the destruction that wastes at noon-day."

We have turned from You to go our selfish way. We have broken Your commandments and denied Your truth.

We have left Your altars to serve the false gods of money and pleasure and power. Forgive us and help us.

Now, darkness gathers around us and we are confused in all our counsels. Losing faith in You, we lose faith in our selves.

Inspire us with wisdom, all of us, of every color, race and creed, to use our wealth, our strength, to help our brother, instead of destroying him.

Help us to do Your will as it is done in Heaven and to be worthy of Your promise of peace on earth.

Fill us with new faith, new strength, and new courage, that we may win the battle for peace.

Be swift to save us, dear God, before the darkness falls.

I visualized the portrait of Uncle Sam as I had seen him on the train, not weak, not knocked to his knees, but freely and confidently kneeling, knowing how to do battle for peace, and by his side this prayer.

Because I felt the need of re-expressing the belief of America's founders in prayer as a vital force in national life, on July 4, 1952, I published in some magazines a full color pictorial presentation of "America on Its Knees," the portrait and the prayer. It was my present to Daniel Paolucci and my fellow Americans on Uncle Sam's birthday.

Within twenty-four hours after this was in print I was deluged with letters and requests for copies of this pictorial message. From almost every country in the world, from every state in the Union, from the old and the young, from rich and poor, from military and civilian, the cynical and the naïve, philosophers and advertising men, rabbis, ministers, from wise men and crackpots from every level of society, from schoolteachers and Sunday school teachers, from children of eight to oldsters of ninety-two, came requests for over three hundred thousand reprints and messages that sometimes brought tears to my eyes.

Today, five years later, they are still coming. Never a week goes by without a request for more copies.

As I told a meeting of the American Hotel Association in St. Louis, Missouri, this was the voice of the free world.

From every state in the Union, and all of its possessions. From thirty-one free countries throughout the world. One mother wrote, "We read your prayer as part of our after-supper devotion." Humbling things like that. And one from Austria, "The most noble page ever printed in the *Saturday Evening Post*." . . . A few of them were not complimentary; one said, "This Hilton is a Communist." From Portland, Maine, came this letter: "I am only a crippled wreck in a nursing home; and it is possible that I shall not see the conclusion of our present troubles. I wish I knew how the people of America could be stirred to patriotic feeling and action." And the letter from a New Jersey war widow said, "My little girl's daddy was killed in Korea and perhaps this will help her understand better when she grows up why her daddy died." Then there was a letter from a soldier stationed in Germany that said, "I have just finished reading the prayer. I was almost fed up with being over here, but since I have read your wonderful prayer, it has been an inspiration to me, and I need no other explanation for why I am here." Even one from the niece of the original Uncle Sam, and one from an American of ten generations heritage whose colonial ancestor was Colonel Henry Lee, who was also the grandfather of Robert E. Lee.

I was awed when ministers said they read it from the pulpit and on religious radio programs. And the girls in the office wanted a holiday when several letters came in nominating us for President! From Canada came the most articulate message and the one which best proved to us that we had achieved our objective. It read in part ". . . you have hereby fostered more good will, sold more free enterprise, created more desire for democracy than all the billions spent so extravagantly by the United States government since the present crisis began."

From the *Sunday Express* in Glasgow came the following . . . "*Life* has published a remarkable prayer which might be described as the twentieth century equivalent of Kipling's Recessional. No one has the right to scoff or attribute any motive save that of sincerity, but it does reveal the emotional temperature of the United States at this time."

From Madrid, Spain: "Unquestionably, the unprecedented prayers of thanks of the Moslems toward the United States, particularly coming at this time during the political impasse, because of the oil situation, is tangible confirmation of what a spiritual movement can accomplish, when all other measures fail, notwithstanding the combined efforts of power-nation diplomatic-military forces."

One old priest gave me the greatest thrill ". . . God read it too—with pleasure."

I hoped that Mary Laufersweiler Hilton had read it as well.

My fellow Americans' response to my humble offering was the proudest experience of my life. Once, so many years before, when I sat reading Elbert Hubbard's *Little Journeys*, I had dreamed of doing something some day, however small, for the country I loved.

In the hour when so many thousands made me feel that dream had come true I could only feel very humble and deeply grateful.

Early one Thursday morning in February, 1953, a car pulled away from the White House and the President of the

United States directed the driver to take him to a prayer meeting.

This was the first annual Prayer Breakfast at the Mayflower Hotel in Washington, D. C., where I was privileged to play host to five hundred men who directly or indirectly guide the destiny of our nation at home and abroad.

It was a fitting climax for "America on Its Knees," to see an enlargement of the pictorial presentation dominate the huge ballroom, hushed now as President Dwight Eisenhower, Vice-President Nixon, the Chief Justice of the Supreme Court, Senators, Congressmen and diplomats bowed their heads together in prayer.

I knew, too, that I was committed from now on, regardless of wilted collars and damp hands, regardless of mad dashes to arrive in a certain place at a certain time, to continue to take a public stand on what I believed.

Had I not promised that young corporal, about to go "over there" for the second time, that I would "do my part to insure a lasting, just peace?"

It was a long jump from the adobe store on the Rio Grande to the flower-decked speakers' platforms of the country. It required a willingness to grow on the part of the young soldier who once kept a diary in France concerned with American singers and tennis-playing mademoiselles, who later talked compassion in a Santa Monica garden to a silent, sympathetic deer.

Seven years after the first address to the National Council of Christians and Jews I was asked again to be their chief speaker, this time on familiar ground, in El Paso, Texas. That first time I had spoken on "The Battle for Freedom." How was the battle going?

I asked myself: What is the particular significance of the Judaeo-Christian tradition at this moment in our world history?

The answer was this: That the world does not belong to the Christians and Jews in the fashion we once thought! I couldn't guarantee this conclusion's universal popularity. But it was my honest opinion and I was committed to stand on it.

"Today's world," I told them, "is divided into three parts: the free world, the Communist world, and the uncommitted world of Asia and Africa. In population the Afro-Asian group is the largest, a billion souls. Second in number, with eight hundred million, is the Communist and Communist-dominated world. Trailing them is ourselves, the free world of three-quarters of a billion.

"So let us not talk about Jews and Christians this evening. Let us for once not talk about Communism. Instead let us talk about this Uncommitted Third who, if they do not join us in freedom, will so weigh the scales as to destroy us.

"First we must realize that up 'til fairly recent times it was the Oriental cultures which dominated the world politically, economically and even religiously. Buddha and Confucius were much better known than anyone in Christendom.

"A factor which we must not forget in our association with this Uncommitted Third of the human race is that the Moslems, the Chinese, and the high-caste Indians have always possessed a sense of cultural superiority to the Europeans and the Americans. It is for this reason that the arrogance, bad manners, and tactlessness of our politicians, businessmen, and colonists in these countries have been so thoroughly resented.

"With its long tradition religion among the eastern peoples is not a private matter as it has become among too many of ourselves; for them it is a part of their liturgical culture in which every detail of behavior has some religious significance.

"In every department their lives are traditionally steeped in a religious background. The Moslems believe, as we do, that the purpose of human life is to serve God. The problem then is to achieve a spiritual sympathy between us all. Not tolerance, a mean word used by the superior—but true understanding.

"As religious men and women, Christians and Jews alike believe that the hand of God is at work in history. But we must not leave the entire activity to God. He can only do for us, in this instance, what He can do through us. He gave us heads and hearts and we are supposed to use them under His guidance.

"If we can reach out and assist in raising these billion people, the Uncommitted Third, from the shadow of economic and political want; if we can take their spiritual riches and blend them with ours; if we can take their cultures and ours and fashion them into one great splendid human family; if we collectively and individually will help little by little to make this dream come true, men will say, with Churchill, 'This was their finest hour.' "

This then is the dream that haunts me now, as an individual, as an American, as a businessman—the magnificent dream of one world, a free world, of all men able to look with us into the face of God as brothers of one Father.

If each of us dreams—and works—and prays for that day surely the battle for freedom, the battle for peace will be won.

14. THERE IS AN ART TO LIVING

Each of us strives for success. The housewife, the statesman, the carpenter, saint or businessman, for each forward momentum is established by the desire to accomplish, prosper, grow in his chosen field.

What is this thing—success?

It cannot be measured by the accumulation of money. Too many rich men are failures and too many poor men masters at the art of living to make this the criterion.

The workman is worthy of his hire, yes, but you cannot reckon his achievements by his bank account. Mahatma Gandhi, one of the most successful statesmen of our time, left upon his death as his entire worldly estate: two rice bowls, one spoon, two pairs of sandals, his copy of the *Bhagavad-Gita*, his spectacles and an old-fashioned turnip watch. Helen Keller, another outstanding success, overcame tremendous handicaps to prove that the blind deaf-mute was not mentally retarded, unteachable, thus setting free hundreds of her fellow sufferers. She has succeeded in raising many, many thousands of dollars to benefit her fellows. Yet Miss Keller herself has had only the most ordinary personal comforts. Saint Francis of Assisi during his lifetime affected his entire world, rulers and princes, prelates, artists, businessmen, farmers and housewives. Seven hundred years after his death he continues to affect people in all walks of life in many countries. Yet his very influence was based on maintaining absolute poverty. He was, perhaps, the most successful poor man who ever lived.

The yardstick for measuring success would seem to be not how much a man gets as how much he has to give away.

What do we know of a successful man? The size of his bank account? Never! In my own county of Socorro they have finally adjudged me a success, not because I bought the Waldorf, but because I was able to give as a memorial to Gus and Mary Hilton a new school and convent to the Sisters of Loretto—the Hilton Mount Carmel School and Convent. Albert Schweitzer is known because he gives his services in a far-off hospital in Africa; Arturo Rubinstein because the beauty of his music gives inspiration and joy; Bob Hope because he knows the spiritual value of laughter.

The true fruits of successful living are not material. They are contentment, the joy of usefulness, growth through the fulfillment of our particular talent. Viewed this way God is always on the side of success for the objective is fulfilling a talent He gave, and which He will support and maintain.

To me there are ten ingredients which must be blended in each and every one of us if we are to live successfully. The first is:

Find Your Own Particular Talent: As surely as none of us was given the same thumb print, so surely none of us possesses the exact same talent. This does not mean there will not be two housewives, two carpenters, two artists or two hotel men. We each have two thumbs. But the individual print is uniquely our own.

Emerson says, "Each man has his own vocation. The talent is the call . . . He inclines to do something which is easy for him, and good when it is done, but which no other man can do . . . His ambition is exactly proportioned to his powers. The height of the pinnacle is determined by the breadth of the base."

Finding this particular talent or vocation is the first step in the art of successful living. Great frustration and the *feel* of failure can be present in the face of material success if we follow someone else's footsteps rather than our own.

Don't worry if it takes a little time to find your own niche!

It took me thirty-two years and I started out to be a banker. History proves that this isn't shameful. George Washington began as a surveyor. Somerset Maugham graduated in medicine before he took up the pen. Norman Vincent Peale was a newspaperman for some years. Albert Schweitzer was a theologian, a musician until he was thirty, when he resigned as principal of the Theological College of St. Thomas to become a medical student and devote the rest of his life to healing the sick and suffering African natives. St. Peter, the Rock, was first a fisherman.

This is no invitation to become a drifter, a professional malcontent. But every man has a right, a duty I would say, to search humbly and prayerfully for the place where he fits into the Divine pattern. I am encouraging boldness because the danger of our seniority and pension plans tempt a young man to settle in a rut named Security rather than find his own rainbow.

Don't worry about what you haven't got in the way of talent. Find out what you *have!*

A very poor Greek once applied for a job as janitor in a bank in Athens. "Can you write?" demanded the discriminating head of employment. "Only my name," said the fellow. He didn't get the job—so he borrowed the money to travel steerage to the United States, the Land of Opportunity. Many years later an important Greek businessman held a press conference in his beautiful Wall Street offices. At the conclusion an enterprising reporter said, "You should write your memoirs." The gentleman smiled. "Impossible," he said, "I cannot write." The reporter was astounded. "Just think," he remarked, "how much further you would have gone if you could." The Greek shook his head. "If I could write," he said, "I'd be a janitor."

Be Big: Think Big. Act Big. Dream Big.

Your value is determined by the mold you yourself make. It doesn't take any more energy to expect to be the best housewife, the finest cook, the most capable carpenter.

It has been my experience that the way most people court failure is by misjudging their abilities, belittling their worth and value. Did you ever think what can happen to a plain bar of iron, worth about $5.00? The same iron when made into horseshoes is worth $10.50. If made into needles, it is worth $3,250.85, and if turned into balance springs for watches its value jumps to $250,000.

The same is true of another kind of material—You!

Here is another example. Millet, the French painter, paid twenty-five cents for a yard of canvas. He paid fifty more for a brush and some paints. Onto this quarter's worth of canvas he put all the glory of his biggest visions, his biggest dreams, and gave us a painting called "The Angelus," which brought $105,000.

I recall an occasion not long ago when the temptation to limited thinking had me convinced a certain project was beyond me. The goal was to raise $400,000 for St. John's Hospital. Irene Dunne, Willard Keith and Louis B. Mayer, members of the committee, thought I might undertake to raise that amount. I thought differently. Interested as I was and eager to contribute personally, raising such a large sum, a few hundred dollars here, a few hundred there, even with an occasional thousand thrown in, was a full-time job—a tremendous, long task—and I felt if they pinned their hopes on me, I might very well disappoint them. Better to admit I wasn't big enough and let them find someone who was.

When I sat down with the lovely Irene, I was all ready to say, "I can't do it," when suddenly I realized instead that I could do it. Instead of attempting it the little way, trying to get $200 from two thousand people, I would go at it the big way. I would write a sort of chain letter to a selected number of men who could afford large donations. Hopefully I would assign enough to each one to cover the entire amount. In reserve I held a substitute list of men who could afford to contribute half the assigned amount—and so on. If a man on the first team turned me down, I put in two substitutes. If the two substitutes failed me, I sent out four letters. It was simple—and it worked. I had done what I figured I couldn't do by raising my sights.

Be Honest: What I have in mind is something more than the negative virtues of not cheating, not lying, not stealing. It is a bold, direct, open stand for the truth as we know it, both to ourselves and others. My mother had two old-fashioned quotations she dished out with our oatmeal. The first was Shakespeare: "To thine own self be true, and it must follow as the night the day, Thou canst not then be false to any man." The second was Sir Walter Scott: "Oh, what a tangled web we weave, when first we practice to deceive!"

Once you start it, there's no place that deception can stop —and of course it has to start with self-deception, even if it's only the self-deception of believing we can get away with it. True, sometimes we are not "discovered." But all of modern psychology and psychiatry is based on the belief that our self-deceptions drive things into our subconscious where they make all kinds of trouble.

Myself, I believe if my mother's two bromides from ancient authors were something more than words to cross-stitch on a sampler they would work better than tranquility pills.

I have never in my whole life found anything to fear from telling the full, direct truth. And that includes instances when "a little judicious evasion" was recommended.

Particularly I remember an important court case in El Paso during the Depression which meant a great deal in my "personal recovery act." The opposing attorney asked me where certain records were kept, and I replied they were in a certain minute book of meetings held.

"Where is that minute book?" he asked.

"In my office in Dallas," I said.

"Could you get it before court convenes tomorrow?" he asked.

Now that was a specific question calling for a specific answer. Could I? I could. "Someone from my office," I said, "could take it to the airport and give it to the pilot and the pilot could bring it in."

My lawyer, Thornton Hardie, was furious. "I know, I know," he said testily. "You only told the truth. But did you have to *volunteer?* I've a feeling there could be some things in that minute book very damaging to our case."

At five minutes of ten the next morning, however, it was in our hands. "Well," said Hardie, holding it as though it was a hot potato, "if you can be rash, I'll go you one better."

Without looking inside he strode in and placed it on opposing counsel's table. The opposing counsel was so sure that, had there been anything to our disadvantage in the minute book we wouldn't have been willing to let him see it, that he never opened it. It lay on his table from ten until the noon recess at which time my attorney picked it up and it was never mentioned again.

Live with Enthusiasm: It has been my experience that there is nothing worth doing that can be done without it. Ability you must have, but ability sparked with enthusiasm. Enthusiasm is an inexhaustible force, so mighty that you must ever tame and temper it with wisdom. Use it and you will find yourself constantly moving forward to new forms of expression.

If you have enthusiasm for life you cannot ever know an inactive time of life. Sir Christopher Wren, the famed architect who built fifty-two churches in London, retired from public life at eighty-six. After that he spent five years in literary, astronomical and religious pursuits. Cato, at eighty, studied Greek; and Plutarch, almost as old, Latin. Titian painted a masterpiece at ninety-eight. Verdi wrote his great opera, *Othello*, at seventy-four, and *Falstaff* at eighty. What is that but continued enthusiasm for life?

Everyone faces hardships along their chosen path. What carries them through? Makes them work and pray with no thought of quitting? Enthusiasm! After working long and hard to accumulate his first $50, Frank Woolworth saw three of his first five chain stores fail. The *Saturday Evening Post* lost $800,000 for Cyrus H. K. Curtis before a single dollar of profit came in. Twenty-seven million dollars and eleven years of-work were behind the first pound of Nylon sold by Du-Pont.

There is no such thing as being "a little bit enthusiastic." You either are or aren't. If you aren't you face failure and boredom. You can't take it by the spoonful.

After World War I, a great cholera epidemic struck the Orient. Periodically it has swept through India, the Malay Peninsula, Burma—but never China. The cholera germ cannot survive boiling water and the Chinese drink tea almost exclusively. The American doctors knew this and, when the epidemic threatened to run wild in the Philippines, they ordered the people to boil their water. But cholera continued and, when health inspectors investigated, they found the people were taking three or four teaspoons of boiled water daily, like medicine—and drinking ordinary water.

It cannot be done that way. Enthusiasm, to be effective, cannot be taken by the spoonful. It must sweep into every department of your life—your religion, your chosen job, your home, your recreation. Only this way can the inexhaustible force be released in your life and carry you forward, protect you, inspire you, in the art of living.

Don't Let Your Possessions Possess You: I have in my lifetime had everything—and nothing. In my Bible it doesn't say that *money* is the root of all evil, but the "*love of*" money. I believe that to be true and I believe the exact same to be true about possessions.

They are very nice to have, to enjoy, to share. But if you find even one that you can't live without—hasten to give it away. Your very freedom depends on it.

We have all heard of the lack of sense of the monkey who will put his paw into the narrow mouth of a bottle, grasp a desired nut or bit of food, and refuse to let it go even though the fist he has made makes his hand too large to draw it from the bottle again. "Silly thing," we say, "he hasn't really got the food—and he's attached to the bottle. All he has to do is open his hand and let go."

We laugh. But is it so funny? The monkey has lost his freedom. Do we guard ourselves from falling into the same trap?

Don't Worry about Your Problems: The successful life is a balanced life and includes thought, action, rest, recreation. The artist in living will neither work himself to death nor play until he reaches satiety. Now the chronic worrier is all out of balance. He is like a dog with a bone. Problems, and we all have them, are puzzles offered us for solution and we solve them by keeping in balance, alert mentally and well physically, or we handicap ourselves. To worry your difficulties after the sun is set and you have done all you can for the day is useless—and an act of distrust.

A minister once found himself so beset by the problems of his parish that he could not sleep. Daily he worked amongst his flock and then, after his evening devotions, after everyone else had retired, he paced restlessly about his room. Mrs. Stone's son was in jail. He must visit him tomorrow. The Lewis family was to be evicted. He would see their landlord. And so on. Suddenly a compassionate voice penetrated his consciousness— "You go to sleep, my dear man, and let Me sit up the rest of the night."

Of course we are all concerned that everything be solved immediately and exactly to our liking. Patience in the face of difficulties is one of our biggest hurdles. As one man phrased it: "God is in no hurry and I am!"

But worrying has never solved anything yet. Prayer, thought, action—yes. Just worrying, no! Instead it magnifies, creates apprehension, breeds resentment and self-pity. The other fellow's lot seems easier than our own.

A wise King once, concerned about the unrest and discontent among his people, invited them all to bring their "crosses" to him where he would listen to each and try to help. They came from near and far, each carrying his cross, which they laid at the feet of the King. Then one after another, each rose and told his story.

When the tales of woe were finished, the King spoke: "You have each heard your neighbor's story. If anyone wishes he may now exchange his cross for another's." Silently his subjects looked around, then silently each picked up his particular cross and quietly walked away.

Don't Cling to the Past: Not through regret. Not through longing. To do so is to tie yourself to a memory, for yesterday is gone. It is wisdom to profit by yesterday's mistakes. It is fatal to hang onto yesterday's victories. You limit yourself. The future should be expanding. Yesterday's experiences are the foundation on which you build today.

A man walking with his eyes turned backward is very apt to fall into a ditch. It has been said that I would never part with certain hotels. This is not true. If I have had to let go of a success (and I have had to many times) to build an expanding future, then I've released yesterday. We can only act *now* and then look forward to more activity, greater fulfillment.

To be haunted by past failures or satisfied with past successes is to arrest forward motion.

We should be just starting each day. In 325 B.C., a famous Athenian general, Iphicrates, was twitted by Harmodius, descendant of a long line of illustrious forebears, for being the son of a shoemaker. The general replied: "My family history begins with me, but yours ends with you." To cling to the past in any way is the beginning of the end.

Look Up to People When You Can—Down to No One: Who and what is your neighbor? Do you know him?

Let's take a man standing at 50th Street and Park Avenue in New York City; he is waiting for the light to turn. Who is he? To the statistician standing at the window high above, he is one unit in a crowd. To the biologist he is a specimen; to the physicist a formula of mass and energy; to the chemist a compound of substances. He is of interest to the historian as one of the billions of beings who have inhabited this planet of ours; to the politician as a vote; to the merchandiser as a customer; to the mailman as an address. The behaviorist sees him from his office across the street and tags him as an animal modified by conditioned reflexes; and the psychiatrist in the next suite as a particular mental type deviating in one way or another from the alleged normal.

Each science pinpoints the poor fellow from some particular angle and makes him look foolish, like the candid camera shot that catches you in the middle of a yawn. Let any one of these specialists pigeonhole you and get you to look at yourself through his single eye and what you will see will not be a man, but a fragment of a man. You will be like the elephant examined by the five blind men. One felt his ear and said: "An elephant is like a blanket." Another his tail and said, "No, a rope." The third felt his leg and insisted, "Like a tree." The fourth bumped into his side and said, "A wall." The last grasped his trunk and said authoritatively, "The elephant is like a snake."

We are all looking at each other from outside . . . partially blinded. We do not know intimately a man's splendors, his dreams, his crosses, his weaknesses or strengths. Even our enemies betray us by acts of kindness.

The only thing we are absolutely sure about, the common denominator, is that within each is that Divine Spark called Life. That each was born in the image and likeness of God.

The solitary Robinson Crusoe, in order to know the benighted savage who inhabited his island, Friday, had to adventure in trust, confidence, reliance, and growing insight until loyalty and faith, friendship in fact, welded the unlikely two together.

As we strive to know more about people, to understand rather than to be understood, we are in a better position to fulfill the commandment to "love our neighbor as ourselves."

Assume Your Full Share of Responsibility for the World in Which You Live: Develop your own policy, domestic and foreign. Give it thought. And then effort. Stand on it! Stand for it! Live it!

The whole purpose of democracy is for the participation of the individual. The will of the people. You cannot have "government of the people, by the people, for the people" without the active participation of those people.

Nor can your life be a personal success unless, as a citizen, tourist, voter, you share in shaping your own world. The usual answer to that one is: What can a mere individual do?

I heard Dr. Harry Emerson Fosdick answer that. He said:

"Look what mere individuals *are* doing now. Who elect our public officials? Individuals.

"Who stand aside and let rotten conditions in our slums beget the tragic shame of dope peddling? Individuals.

"Believe me, in our present situation, personal character

counts. As another put it 'No rearrangement of bad eggs can make a good omelet.' "

Our International Hotels well know the value of each individual tourist, whether as an ambassador of good will, a fine testimonial for our way of life—or the reverse.

We are a nation in its youth.

We are the "early Americans."

What do I mean by that? I mean that from 1776 to 1957 is 181 years. When France was that old Charlemagne was not yet born; when Poland was 181 years old King Casmir was just putting together its primitive government. At that age England had not yet been swallowed up by the Empire of Julius Caesar. The Germans at that stage of growth were just coming out of the northern forests; Horatius was still at the bridge in Italy; Saint Patrick was just driving the last snakes out of Ireland.

As a young nation we have vigor, stamina, imagination; we have pride, alert thinking, volatile emotions. Like adolescents we neither love very deeply, nor hate very deeply. With one hand we can drop an atom bomb; with the other deluge the same nation with Marshall Plan wealth. And like youngsters, too, as a nation we are somewhat indifferent at times.

The successful American will not be indifferent. He will let his enthusiasms sweep into his patriotism and be an *individual* cog in the wheels that lead to a better world. President Eisenhower has truly said: "We are not helpless prisoners of history. We are free men." But only so long as the individual desires it! And works for it!

Pray Consistently and Confidently: The place was the South Pacific. The time—June, 1945. Virginia Company was lost. The brush was so thick they could not see ten feet in front of them. There had been a path but they had lost it miles back. The woods in front of them was alive with the enemy and the snarl of bullets whipped through the trees. Suddenly the bullets increased; the aim began to get better; men began to fall.

"Call headquarters," shouted the leader, "and find out if we can get some help!"

A few minutes later reserves were on their way to support the company. If Napoleon had been around, he never would have been able to understand. It would have been a mystery to Caesar and to Bismarck, even to General Foch. But every youngster in America today could have told them that it was a "walkie-talkie" that got them out of trouble.

Walkie-talkie is as old as Adam and Eve. We have all had one since the day we were able to talk. We did not have to wait for the improvements brought on by years of research in the world of radio communications. What I mean is that we have always had prayer. We have always been able to talk to general headquarters any time we wished. And we never had to worry that our Commanding Officer might think our call unimportant, or that we were lacking courage for consulting Him too frequently, or asking advice too often.

What I like about prayer is that it is a means of communication with God. You can speak to Him any time, night or day, and you can know with certainty that He is listening to you.

What I like about prayer is that there is no set formula for calling general headquarters on our private walkie-talkie. There are no call letters. You are free to send any message you want. You can just say "hello"; you can ask for something. You can tell Him that things are going rough and you need reinforcements—as those boys in the jungle did. You can call to thank Him for the things He has done for you. You can tell Him you are baffled, bewildered, discouraged or that you are the happiest person in the world.

For me, in personal living, in fulfilling our place in the world, in faithful use of our talents, each of these is a spoke in the circle of successful living. Prayer is the hub that holds the wheel together. Without our contact with God we are nothing. With it we are "a little lower than the angels, crowned with glory and honor."

We are successes in the Art of Living.